Grassroots Grants

An Activist's Guide

to

Proposal Writing

D1402162

Grassroots Grants

An Activist's Guide
to
Proposal Writing

Andy Robinson

Foreword by Kim Klein

Chardon Press
Oakland, California

"General Characteristics of Four Types of Foundations" and Foundation Center Cooperating Collections list reprinted by permission of the publisher from *The Foundation Directory, 1995 Edition*. Copyright 1995 by the Foundation Center, 79 Fifth Avenue, New York, NY 10003.

Excerpts from the essay "Foundation Leadership" by Jon M. Jensen, published in *Environmental Leadership*, edited by Joyce K. Berry and John C. Gordon, reprinted by permission of the publisher. Copyright 1993 by Island Press, Washington, D.C. and Covelo, California.

Excerpts from *Managing for Change: A Common Sense Guide to Evaluating Financial Management Health for Grassroots Organizations* by Terry Miller, reprinted by permission of the author. Copyright 1992 by Terry Miller.

Excerpts from *Evaluation Guide: What is Good Grantmaking for Social Justice?*, edited by Carol Mollner, Ellen Furnari, and Terry Odendahl, reprinted by permission of the publisher. Copyright 1995 by National Network of Grantmakers.

Excerpts from the *Religious Funding Resource Guide*, edited by Mary Eileen Paul and Andrea Flores, reprinted by permission of the publisher. Copyright 1995 by ResourceWomen, 4527 South Dakota Avenue, NE, Washington, DC 20017.

Excerpts from "Leveraging God's Resources from her Representatives on Earth" by Gary Delgado, reprinted by permission of the author. Copyright 1988 by Gary Delgado.

All grant proposals reproduced in this book are used with permission.

Copyright 1996, Andy Robinson

All rights reserved.

Chardon Press
3781 Broadway
Oakland CA 94611
www.chardonpress.com

Printed in the United States of America
Library of Congress Catalog Card Number: 96-83387
ISBN 0-9620222-5-X

Editing: Nancy Adess
Cover and Book Design: Bonnie Fisk-Hayden
Proofreading: Christopher D. Smith
Indexing: Ann Patrick Ware

Printed on recycled, chlorine-free paper with soy ink

CONTENTS

Foreword

by Kim Klein

If someone had told me a year ago that I would be publishing a book about grantwriting I would have said they were crazy. That was before I met Andy Robinson. Andy wrote to say he wanted my press, Chardon Press, to publish a book he proposed to write on how grassroots activists could write better grants. I put the letter away, thinking, "Why would I, who have spent the best part of 20 years teaching social change organizations how to develop reliable sources of funding (i.e. not grants), and have harangued thousands of groups on the pitfalls of relying on grant funding, now publish a book on proposal writing?"

When I next saw Deb Ross, a mutual friend, I asked her about Andy. She said he was a good person, had a long history of activism, and was also a very good trainer. She thought such a book was important and needed. I decided to talk to Andy, and I liked him right away. He overcame my ambivalence about publishing such a book when he said, "Grassroots groups look for grant funding, and they get it sometimes. They will not stop seeking grant money, and grants have helped many of them do good work. They could get funding more often if they knew more about how to look and what to write."

I was ambivalent about helping people be more effective in getting grants because I see how much time organizations put into grantwriting while little time goes into building a base of individual donors, even though individuals give away almost 90% of the money available to nonprofits and foundations only 7%. Many of the groups I have worked with have only gotten serious about expanding their individual donor base after being summarily dropped by a foundation, or after they have papered their walls with rejection letters, or after they have been told by a foundation to seek individual donor funding.

However, foundations are important to groups working for social change. The 7% of private-sector funding available from foundations is not an insignificant amount (about $10 billion in 1994). Further, there are increasing numbers of progressive foundations, and increasing numbers of activists getting jobs in foundations of all kinds, moving some grantmaking to an agenda more sympathetic to social change work. Foundations will sometimes fund start-up costs of unproved and untried ideas. They give large amounts of money at once, so that a successful proposal can raise money in far less time than can an individual donor strategy. Funding from one foundation will often lead to funding from another, and foundation funding helps with individual donor fundraising, as a kind of "seal of approval." One of the most important things foundations do is help organizations get their act together. If a group has a good idea and decides to "get a grant," the proposal-writing process will help them think through their idea. What is the budget? How will they evaluate the project? The discipline of being asked to describe a project in a short paragraph is invaluable for people who often need ten minutes just to state the problem and another hour to describe the solutions.

I am glad I made the decision to publish this book. As you will see, it is well written, helpful, concise, full of useful tips, and easy to read. Andy shows what grants are for, and what they are not for, what funders like, and what they don't. It is written for people working for social justice, which few fundraising books are. Of course I really like that the book emphasizes the need to develop an individual donor program in addition to whatever grantwriting you decide to do.

I am proud of this book, proud to advertise it along with my book, *Fundraising for Social Change,* and my magazine, the *Grassroots Fundraising Journal,* and to name it as a "must read."

I hope this book helps good groups find the funding they deserve.

Preface

In 1980, a few weeks after Ronald Reagan was elected President, I answered a classified advertisement in the Portland *Oregonian*. The first word was ACTIVIST. I can't remember the rest of the ad, but the main idea was that I would get paid to work for social justice. I was adrift and anxious about the future, and this seemed to me a small, tangible miracle.

The next day I was sitting on a cracked vinyl sofa, waiting for my interview. The linoleum was streaked with dirt and a pile of dead office machines (remember mimeographs?) rusted quietly in the corner, but the atmosphere was electric. Phones rang, people ran in and out with picket signs, a typewriter (remember typewriters?) chattered in the back room, and I overheard an argument in which the word "tactics" played a big role. I didn't know what was going on, but I wanted *in*.

That night I started knocking on doors, asking strangers for money to fight the utility company. I was — surprise! — a fundraiser. By the time I left Oregon Fair Share in 1983, I had visited thousands of homes and given my pitch ten thousand times. I received lots of training in community organizing and tactical research, but my door-to-door experience — talking with people about a better world and asking them to help pay for it — was the most compelling, frustrating, and empowering part of the job. My fundraising skills, coupled with an abiding desire for justice, have kept me in the movement for social change ever since.

Few of us set out to be fundraisers, but we see the need and we go to it with courage and persistence. We lead with our hearts, which is how it should be. Even today, when I sit down to write a grant proposal, I often picture a foundation officer opening her front door, dinner interrupted, napkin in hand, a quizzical look on her face.

"Good evening," I say. "We're going to change the world. Would you like to help?"

Who can resist an offer like that?

Andy Robinson
Tucson, Arizona
March 1996

Acknowledgments

It's taken me sixteen years to learn what's in this book. During that time, I've worked with hundreds of outstanding activists, community organizers, fundraisers, trainers, and troublemakers. If I were to thank them all, I would probably sell more books — since everyone loves to see their name in print — but there are simply too many names to include.

A few people, however, must be singled out. My father, Rocky Robinson, taught me at an early age that fundraising and sales are essentially the same thing, though neither of us knew it at the time. Somewhat later, my colleagues at Oregon Fair Share showed me the connections between fundraising and community organizing. More recently, my friends and co-workers at Native Seeds/SEARCH gave me the freedom to experiment as I worked to combine all three — fundraising, organizing, and sales — in the real world. For the gift of gentle supervision, my thanks to Mahina Drees and Angelo Joaquin, Jr.

Over the course of my career, several people have provided encouragement and insight when I didn't know what I was doing. These folks include Ed Abbey, Jeff Anderson, Chuck Bell, Kim Clerc, Felice and Jack Cohen-Joppa, Kevin Dahl, Mary Peace Douglas, Charles Geoffrion, Alan Gussow, Ginger Harmon, Bob Houston, Martha Moutray, Gary Nabhan, Mary O'Kief, Dyan Oldenburg, Cary Schayes, Donna Slepack and Karen Stinson Saró. I thank you all.

Many foundation staff and trustees took the time to fill out my survey for this book and talk with me over the phone. You'll find their names and comments throughout. By sharing their inside knowledge of grantsmanship, they added substance and wisdom to the book.

Several social change organizations allowed me to publish and critique their proposals. For their graciousness and exemplary work, my thanks to:

Richard Reed, Community Alliance with Family Farmers Foundation; Davis, CA

Charles "Punch" Woods, Community Food Bank; Tucson, AZ

Mark Schneider and Jeanne Elliott, Denver Community Reinvestment Alliance; Denver, CO

Andy Mahler and Phil Berck, Heartwood; Paoli, IN

Janet Groat and Bill Roath, Jobs with Peace; Minneapolis, MN

Deeda Seed, Justice, Economic Dignity and Independence for Women; Salt Lake City, UT

Alan Magree and Martha Davis, Mono Lake Committee; Pasadena, CA

Nina Morais, Penn Center and South Carolina Coastal Conservation League; St. Helena, SC, and Charleston, SC

Larry Kleinman, Pineros y Campesinos Unidos del Noroeste; Woodburn, OR

Joan Pearson, St. Paul Tenants Union; St. Paul, MN

Dana Beach, South Carolina Coastal Conservation League; Charleston, SC

Louis Head, SouthWest Organizing Project; Albuquerque, NM

Clayton Brascoupé, Traditional Native American Farmers Association; Tesuque, NM

Susan McLain and Jan Glick, Washington Citizens for Recycling; Seattle, WA

and everyone at Native Seeds/SEARCH; Tucson, AZ

The Foundation for Deep Ecology provided a crucial grant to underwrite some of my time at the keyboard. Tom and Margot Beeston at the Triangle L Ranch provided a quiet place to work. Jean Lewis of the Tucson-Pima Public Library and the staff of the Foundation Center in San Francisco (Nadya Disend, Susan Sheinfeld-Smith, Shawn Phillips, and Janet Camarena) assisted with the research. Terry Miller, accountant extraordinaire, reviewed my comments on planning and budgeting and made many helpful suggestions. For their encouragement, my thanks to Terry Odendahl and her staff at the National Network of Grantmakers, who set high standards for social change grantmaking.

A bow to my publishers, Kim Klein and Stephanie Roth, and my editor, Nancy Adess, for their good humor, professionalism, and flexibility with deadlines. This book began as a letter from one stranger to another — in effect, a grant proposal — so I am especially indebted to Kim for her positive (if initially ambivalent) response. Nancy's precision, intelligence, and hard work have made this a better book, and me a better writer.

Last and most, I gratefully acknowledge the love and support of Jan and Rosie Waterman (and Taja T. Bean), who give me lots of slack to do the work I was born to do.

In the words of Gandhi, "If the cause is right, the means will come." There are resources out there — in every community, however small and however poor. We need to begin to feel empowered to gain access to those resources for our causes.

> — Anne Firth Murray,
> Global Fund for Women

Before You Begin

This book is about two things: money and power. If you didn't need money for your organization, you wouldn't be reading these words. If you weren't trying to change the world, which involves challenging and changing the relations of power, you wouldn't be so concerned about raising money.

In our society, money is loaded with taboos, so the idea of fundraising makes most people nervous. To paraphrase Joan Flanagan, author of *The Grass Roots Fundraising Book*, money is like sex: everyone thinks about it, but most of us are uncomfortable talking about it. It's considered bad manners to ask other people, even trusted friends, about their income, because money is cloaked in privacy. We're not supposed to want money — even though we need it to survive — because we've heard that "money is the root of all evil." (This, of course, is a misquote. The Bible tells us, "The *love* of money is the root of all evil.") Earning money, we are taught, is good; asking for money without earning it is bad. These unspoken cultural assumptions about money, and our relationship to it, are endless.

The fact that money is both hard to discuss and hard to get can cause us to lose perspective. We tend to forget our other organizational assets, things that have no relation to the bank balance — for example, the skill and commitment of staff, board, and volunteers, and the good will our work creates in the community. We often get obsessive about the subject, which limits our capacity for good, hard-headed planning.

So before you begin writing grant proposals, or doing any kind of fundraising, I encourage you to step back, take a deep breath, and consider the following points.

MONEY IS JUST A TOOL. Money is important only because of what it can buy your organization. There are also other tools available. What you lack in money, you can often make up for with the talent, enthusiasm and track record of your members, supporters, board, and staff. While these assets won't pay the phone bill, they can help you through financially tough times and actually improve your capacity to raise funds.

FIND WAYS TO GET WHAT YOU NEED WITHOUT SPENDING MONEY. Consider in-kind donations, barter, free advertising, trading mailing lists with other organizations, and additional non-cash strategies. For example, used office equipment is often donated to nonprofits by large companies (in exchange for a tax write-off) or government agencies. Many professionals — lawyers, accountants, graphic artists, entertainers — will contribute their services or work for a reduced fee. As a rule, the less cash you need, the better off you'll be. In-kind donations will also improve your chances of getting grants, since they demonstrate community support for your work.

FUNDRAISING IS SELLING. While the word *sales* conjures up images of used car dealers and Madison Avenue hype, it really means developing a systematic way of analyzing your situation and playing to your strengths. Since a grant request is essentially a business plan, says John Powers of the Educational Foundation of America, "a nonprofit should be just as business-like as a for-profit company, just as fiscally responsible, and just as capable of operating 'in the black.'"

When you develop and write a proposal, you must use the same kind of analysis and answer many of the same questions a business person would address when seeking investors or customers. Who is your market, your audience? Why do they care about your organization/issue/service/product? How can you reach them most effectively and efficiently? How can you expand your market? Is it possible or necessary or even ethical for you to adapt your product (organization) to reach a larger market?

Forgive the business analogy, but if we want professional results, we need to borrow techniques from the professionals. To work best, your fundraising efforts — including your grants program — must be systematic and business-like.

FUNDRAISING IS ORGANIZING. Ideally, in the process of raising funds, you'll also be building your organization, developing leadership, and increasing community awareness of what you do. The best fundraising strategies succeed at both bringing in donations and furthering your program goals.

For many groups, the process of developing and writing a grant proposal is similar to the process of creating a community organizing plan. An effective proposal can serve as a road map to lead you where you want to go. On the other hand, if you can't organize your project on paper — if you can't draw the map — you'll have a hard time organizing it in the real world.

FUNDRAISING IS HARD WORK. Never underestimate the time and energy required to raise money. I have yet to find an easy way. You may think that grantwriting is a short cut to big contributions, but experience has taught me otherwise. (See Chapter 2 for a whole lot more on this subject.)

If you want to create effective proposals to help fund your good work, you need a clear, compelling mission, a thorough and reasonable plan of action, and talented people to carry out the plan. Most of all, you need common sense. Don't let your fears and frustrations about fundraising paralyze you or cause you to behave impulsively. If you take the time to analyze, evaluate, and plan, you'll raise lots of money, make lots of friends for your organization, and feel good about your efforts. When in doubt, think.

Own your organization. The slippery slope provided by some funders is not always easy to see ahead of time. Owning your organization means having a mix of funding types, and a mix of funders. It means having an understanding with your members and your board that you can turn down any money that transfers power away from your grassroots base to some outside interest, however well intentioned.

— Martin Teitel, CS Fund

Grants: What They'll Get You... And What They Won't

Many groups consider fundraising the most unpleasant subject possible, so they tend to avoid it. Here's a typical meeting: after fighting your way through a discussion about the latest staffing crisis, what the recent election means for your work, and why nobody washes the dirty dishes, you finally get around to the hole in your bank account. Everyone is tired and cranky. You talk of fundraisers past and future, but without much enthusiasm. Finally a voice is raised in hope: "I know! We'll get a grant!"

Watch out.

While the purpose of this book is to help you write better proposals and win more grants, you should understand that grant money comes with a variety of strings attached. Some of these strings are visible and beneficial, like the final report in which you describe, in detail, how you spent the money. Others are less obvious and potentially dangerous — as Martin Teitel points out, grants can sometimes disempower your organization.

Before evaluating the pros and cons of grant funding, let's take a quick look at the universe of charitable giving and see how grants figure in the mix.

Willie Sutton, the old-time gangster, was once asked why he robbed banks. "Because that's where the money is," he replied. If someone questioned you about submitting grant applications, you might give the same answer — and you'd be wrong.

WHO'S GOT THE MONEY?

In 1994, U.S. nonprofits received $129.9 billion from the private sector: foundations, corporations, and individuals. You might be surprised to learn that *88% of charitable money came from individuals, while only 12% was given by foundations and corporations* (the people who read grant proposals). These percentages change very little over time. In fact, dead people — through their estates — give away more money, year after year, than all U.S. corporations combined.

Here's another surprise: the vast majority of these donors aren't rich. Of the total funds provided by individuals (about $114 billion), *80% came from families earning less than $50,000 per year.*

This book is designed to help you raise money from the 12% of the private-sector pie that gives grants: corporations and foundations. However, many organizations are too small, too marginal, or too radical to receive corporate grants — indeed, hundreds of groups are directly challenging corporate power — which further reduces the field to the 7.6% of charitable funds provided by private foundations. Nonetheless, we're talking about $9.9 billion — a significant sum of money and certainly worth some effort.

If you're sensible, however, you'll understand that the time you put into grantwriting should be proportional to the potential return on your effort. If you rely too much on grant applications, you limit yourself to a small piece of a very large pie. Over the long run, you risk starving your organization to death.

THE PROS AND CONS OF CHASING GRANTS

Let's first consider the problems that accompany grant money.

1. **LOUSY ODDS.** Roughly 10-15% of all grant proposals are funded. There's a lot of competition for foundation grants. Many "successful" proposals are only partially funded, which leaves the grantee scrambling to run its project on a reduced budget or find additional money from other sources. If you want better odds, you have to go where the money is: individual donors.

2. **LONG WAITS.** In most cases, it takes three to six months to get an answer. I've waited a year, which is not uncommon. Even if you get funded, paperwork can delay the check for another month. If you need money today, or next week — and most of us do — grants are not a good solution.

3. **"SOFT MONEY."** Grants are seldom renewable. A particular foundation may provide support for three or four years, but not forever. Stephen Viederman of the Jessie Smith Noyes Foundation puts it this way: "While we have no fixed limit on how long we will work with an organization, there isn't a level playing field between grantor and grantee. Both sides must always realize that eventually we are going to have to say no."

This problem is compounded by the fact that most foundations are interested in new, innovative projects, and are less likely to fund ongoing programs. Individual donors, on the other hand, have been known to support a particular nonprofit for fifty years or more.

4. **RESTRICTED MONEY.** The majority of foundation grants are directed toward specific projects, not general support, which greatly limits your flexibility. A grant is a contract, and you are legally bound to use the money as described in your proposal. Any significant changes in the program or budget must be negotiated with the funder.

5. **GRANTS DON'T EMPOWER YOUR GROUP.** Grantwriting does not empower people or organizations the way that community-based fundraising does. When you write a proposal, you transfer a critical decision — whether you will have a portion of the money you need to operate — to someone outside your constituency. The more money you raise from your own community, the stronger your group will be.

6. **TOO FEW PEOPLE ARE INVOLVED IN THE PROCESS.** Grantwriting concentrates organizational power in the hands of a few people. Most proposals are developed by one or two staff members (and, in some cases, approved by a board of directors). When you rely too much on grants, you miss out on the leadership development opportunities that come with campaign planning, one-on-one solicitation, house meetings, benefit events, and other fundraising strategies involving lots of people.

7. **YOUR WORK CAN GET DISTORTED IN THE PURSUIT OF MONEY.** If you're not careful, grants can shift power over your programs to someone outside the organization.

   The process is usually subtle. Let's say your group sees a funding opportunity and develops a new project specifically to meet the guidelines, even though the project doesn't fit your mission very well. Much to your surprise, the proposal gets funded. Since this project pulls you in a new direction, it takes a lot of staff time trying to figure out how to manage it. Your core programs suffer from neglect. The tail — money — ends up wagging the dog, which is your mission. I've seen this happen with several nonprofits.

   In the worst case, you become more accountable to foundation supporters than to your own membership. You risk the charge of being under the influence of "outside interests" that don't live in the community and, according to the critics, don't have the community's benefit in mind.

8. **THE "DIRTY MONEY" SYNDROME.** Some organizations refuse to submit proposals to certain funders because they disagree with how the money was raised in the first place. For example, a number of environmental groups won't accept grants from oil companies or their corporate foundations — even when courted by those companies.

   While I understand this position, I urge a broader view. Virtually all foundation and corporate money comes from wealthy people. Wealth is generally acquired by exploiting natural resources or other human beings. All of us are culpable to some degree, depending on where we shop, what products we buy, and where we bank, so I'm not sure we can simply blame the rich and absolve everyone else. Most environmentalists I know (including me) continue to drive cars and consume gasoline, even as we organize against "big oil."

If you choose to claim the moral high ground on this issue (assuming you can find any), screen your prospective grantmakers carefully, as any socially responsible investor would. Foundations generally invest their assets and distribute the interest in the form of grants. Try to find out where the money came from — who or what was exploited along the way — to see if it meets your test of cleanliness. Even better, stick with grassroots fundraising and skip the grant proposals altogether.

Okay, that's the frustrating part. Now let's talk about why grants are attractive, useful, and worth the trouble.

1. **GRANT PROPOSALS ARE GUILT-FREE.** Most charitable foundations exist to give away money. That's their goal. They publish guidelines on how to apply, so there's no guesswork. (Of course, you should always, always, *always* follow the guidelines.) Since they advertise "FREE MONEY — LINE UP HERE," we don't feel like we're begging.

2. **LOTS OF OPTIONS.** With nearly 40,000 foundations in the U.S. (7,000 of which provide more than 90% of foundation support), you can probably find one or two that will help your group. When I worked at Native Seeds/SEARCH, a regional conservation group in Tucson, I maintained files on 250 foundation and corporate prospects. Forty of them provided funding at one time or another. Of course, grants research was an ongoing process, and it took five years to fill that file cabinet. You won't find 250 legitimate prospects in one trip to the library.

3. **YOU HAVE TO BE ORGANIZED.** A grant proposal is an organizing plan, and by putting the details down on paper — goals, objectives, deadlines, etc. — most of us become better organizers. The process of developing a proposal can help us do our work more effectively, even if we don't get funded.

4. **GRANTS COME IN LARGE AMOUNTS.** Most grassroots groups don't have major donors they can approach for gifts of $5,000 or $10,000. On the other hand, these are fairly modest grant amounts. Sometimes you need a big infusion of cash to create a new program or redefine and invigorate an old one.

5. **PREPARATION FOR A MAJOR DONOR CAMPAIGN.** The process of developing relationships with foundation officers and board members is a lot like courting major donors. It can help staff, board members, and volunteers develop the cultivation skills needed to approach individuals for big gifts.

6. **CREDIBILITY.** A foundation grant signals that someone outside the organization is impressed with your work and willing to invest in your success. This can improve your credibility with the news media, local

businesses, prospective major donors, and other foundations. Your opposition might even take you more seriously.

7. **LEVERAGE.** Some grants, specifically challenge grants, are designed to help you raise more money. For example, a foundation may provide a grant on the condition that you match it, dollar for dollar, with donations from your members. Challenge grants are very helpful in encouraging individual gifts. (For more information on grants leverage, see Chapter 8.)

8. **IT'S FUN.** I enjoy the detective work that goes into discovering new foundations and figuring out how best to approach them. I hope you will, too.

By now, you should have a clear idea of both the problems and opportunities associated with grants. Keep writing your proposals, but find other ways to raise money, too. Anne Firth Murray of the Global Fund for Women sums up the challenge:

> Diversity is essential in all aspects of the work of an organization; it is through diversity that one learns and is able to gain access to different groups of people and therefore different funding sources. It is essential that in a fundraising plan there be built-in goals for obtaining funding from several different sources.

If you raise most of your own money from grassroots sources, you will find it easier to get grants. This sounds like a paradox, but the idea is simple. Most foundations prefer to back solid organizations that aren't desperate for money, because these groups tend to be more effective. If your community helps to pay for your work, it shows that they care about your work. Drummond Pike of the Tides Foundation, in "How Foundations Decide Who Gets Their Money" (*Whole Earth Review*, Summer 1988), calls this "The 33% Self-Support Test." I would urge a more rigorous standard and encourage you to raise at least half of your budget from individuals, major donors, benefits, and earned income.

- ◆ **INDIVIDUAL GIFTS** include membership fees, annual donations, and any other contributions you receive from individuals. These gifts can be solicited by mail, over the phone, via computer network, or in person. You can even set up a monthly or quarterly pledge system and deduct the money directly from the donor's bank account (assuming they give you permission!).

- ◆ **MAJOR DONORS** are a special group of individuals who give relatively large gifts. For some groups, a major donor is anyone who contributes $100 per year; for other groups, the threshold is $10,000 per year. Wherever you draw the line, you need to solicit these folks differently and, once you receive the donation, give them special treatment.

- ◆ **BENEFIT EVENTS.** Benefits range from bake sales to walk-a-thons to black-tie balls. Despite the excellent public relations value of these events, it is far less efficient to organize fundraising benefits than to simply

HOW GRANTS FIT INTO A COMPLETE FUNDRAISING STRATEGY

approach potential donors and ask for gifts. Nevertheless, most successful groups still incorporate benefits into their fundraising program as a way to deepen their relationships with current donors, identify new prospects, and increase community awareness of their work.

◆ **EARNED INCOME.** Investigate ways to earn money from your programs. If you're working to preserve a wild and scenic area, why not charge for guided hikes or canoe tours? If you conduct public interest research, why not publish and sell your reports? Earned income, also called fee-for-service, is a great way to expand your budget while expanding your programs — assuming you can identify the right product to sell.

If you want to learn more about grassroots fundraising, the best books are *The Grass Roots Fundraising Book* by Joan Flanagan and *Fundraising for Social Change* by Kim Klein. Both are listed in the Bibliography.

AN EXAMPLE OF FUNDING DIVERSITY: NATIVE SEEDS/SEARCH

At Native Seeds/SEARCH, where I ran the fundraising program from 1990-1995, we developed a broad mix of funding to meet our $500,000 annual budget.

EARNED INCOME. Roughly 40% of our budget came from distribution of crop seeds, gardening and cook books, packaged native foods, and traditional Native American crafts purchased directly from farmers and crafters. All these items directly supported our mission of conserving endangered native crops and promoting cultural diversity, so the more items we distributed, the more successful our programs were. With catalog income increasing by 10-20% each year, we sold a lot of mission-related products. Our 3,000 customers were also excellent prospects for membership. Indeed, many customers started out as members, which means they wrote multiple checks to the organization each year.

INDIVIDUAL GIFTS, MAJOR DONORS, AND BENEFIT EVENTS. Another 25% of the budget was donated by individuals in the form of memberships, major gifts, and tickets to benefit events. By December 1995, we had 4,200 members from across the country. The major donor program was based on a series of private dinner parties featuring traditional desert foods prepared gourmet-style. Our annual Chile Fiesta, co-sponsored with the Tucson Botanical Gardens, drew almost 10,000 visitors each year, and we held benefit literary readings in Arizona and New Mexico.

GRANTS. The balance of the budget, roughly 35%, was raised from foundation and corporate grants; 15–25 funders participated each year. Grants ranged from $500 to $90,000, with most between $5,000 to $10,000. Nearly all of these grants paid for special projects, with only a few funding general operating costs.

Native Seeds/SEARCH was founded in 1983, so it has taken more than a decade of experimentation and hard work to develop such a broad-based fundraising program. Now this well-planned diversity guarantees the long-term survival of the organization and provides lots of opportunities for growth. Indeed, the group just completed a $250,000 capital campaign to purchase and restore an historic property for its expanded seed bank, library, and garden area. More than half the money was provided by one thousand members, while the balance was raised from foundations.

Even if Native Seeds/SEARCH suffers a big drop in grant income, it's unlikely to go out of business, since two-thirds of the budget is raised from other sources. The strategic plan calls for reducing grants to one-quarter of the budget over the next five years to assure the group's independence and good health.

One of our board members likes to say that grant-making is about saying no, not saying yes. I have mixed feelings about this. Over the years, I've gone the other way. When I'm screening grants, I'm looking for proposals to say yes to: Which are the best ones in here? What can I get excited about? What can I take to the board that best meets our priorities?

— Dan Petegorsky, formerly of the
Peace Development Fund

I have the great advantage of each day reading other people's dreams. When you say it that way it may sound sappy, but it carries a heavy responsibility.

— Stephen Viederman,
Jessie Smith Noyes Foundation

Why People (and Foundations) Give Away Their Money

A great deal of unnecessary mystery surrounds the process of philanthropy, which is a fancy word for "giving away money." Dozens of books, articles, and sociological studies have analyzed the typical donor, trying to understand the philanthropic impulse. Professional fundraisers study these documents like sacred texts. Because the task of raising money makes so many people so uncomfortable, much foolishness has been written — and sold — to help people deal with their discomfort.

I'm going to boil down the research and save you a bunch of reading. The number one reason people give away their money is simple: *somebody asked*. If it's someone they know and trust — their sister-in-law, parish priest, or car mechanic — so much the better. All fundraising, including grantwriting, begins with the simple act of one person asking another for money.

YOU, THE PHILANTHROPIST

People ask you for money every day. They send you mail, call you on the phone, ring your doorbell. Your neighbor collects for her daughter's softball team. Your son wants an increase in his allowance. Even the panhandler at your bus stop is a fundraiser. (By studying your reaction to panhandlers, you'll learn a lot about your attitudes regarding philanthropy.)

Mail is the most common way to approach a prospect. One-half of all Americans now purchase goods and services through the mail. Nearly every time you join an organization, make a contribution, or buy from a catalog, your name gets sold or traded to other direct mailers. In fact, the Mail Preference Service *removed* 875 million names from mailing lists in 1993 at the request of consumers. On average, every woman, man, and child in the U.S. had his or her name deleted from more than three lists apiece — but remained on dozens of other mailing lists.

I haven't seen the statistics for phone solicitation, but I'd guess the average big-city donor gets called several times per month. Unless you're very wealthy or incapable of saying no, you have to be selective in your giving — which summarizes the job of a foundation officer.

Before you research potential grantmakers and write proposals, it's useful to consider the criteria that foundations and other funding programs use when giving away their money. As you read through the list, think about how it relates to your own personal "giving behavior." How do you evaluate requests for donations? The staff and board members of foundations are human beings, too, and their criteria are similar to yours and mine.

In other words, *pretend it's your money*. You wouldn't give it to just anybody, would you? Your job as an organizer and grantwriter, then, is to set your group apart. Be creative, be thoughtful, be thorough.

WHO GETS THE MONEY? CRITERIA FOR GIVING

ISSUE. Do you care about what the organization does? Are the group's concerns also your concerns? Is the issue timely? If, in your heart of hearts, you don't care about whales, then a "Save the Whales" appeal from Greenpeace will end up in your trash can. On the other hand, you might respond to a Greenpeace appeal focusing on reduction of toxic garbage. In that case, the issue (and not necessarily the organization) is your primary motivation to give.

LEGITIMACY. Have you heard of the group? Do they strike you as being well-organized, competent, legitimate? Do they get things done, or do they just talk? Have you seen them on television or in the newspaper? News media coverage is helpful for most groups because it lends instant legitimacy. (Of course, there are many legitimate organizations that haven't made the news — yet.)

REFERRAL. Do you know about this group because a friend or family member has been involved? Do you check the letterhead to see if you know the board members? When we lack direct experience, most of us will take the recommendation of somebody we know and trust, or a least somebody we trust. This is why so many appeals — for commercial products as well as charities — carry the names of celebrities. This, in turn, has a lot to do with legitimacy.

Diane Ives of the Beldon Fund stresses these relationships when she reviews proposals. "I look for names and groups that I recognize," she says. "Someone from the community or movement whose work I know and respect. That sense of comaraderie and connection is important."

ENTHUSIASM. Do these people *really* care about their work? Can you sense their excitement?

When asked what grabs her attention in a grant proposal, Libby Ellis, former grants director for Patagonia, Inc., answers, "Passion." Marjorie Fine of the Unitarian Universalist Veatch Program at Shelter Rock emphasizes the same theme. "We start by looking to see if people are energized by their work," she says. "We look for strategic opportunities, where people are in motion — a movement is happening — not just issue areas."

ORGANIZATIONAL HISTORY. What have they done in the past? How do their accomplishments reflect on their ability to get things done in the future?

REALISTIC GOALS. If an organization asked me for money to abolish stupidity, I'd be pretty wary. If, on the other hand, they wanted to abolish illiteracy, and they had a reasonable plan to do it, I might write them a check. Goals can be difficult, but they must be perceived as attainable.

UNIQUENESS OF ORGANIZATION AND/OR PROJECT. Is the organization filling a unique niche? Are other nonprofits already doing what this group has set out to do? Do they have a new angle on an old problem? A new constituency? Or are they trying to solve a new problem? (AIDS researchers wouldn't have raised much money thirty years ago.) Beware of overlap with other groups.

SOURCES OF FUNDING. Grantmakers want to know who provided funding in the past, and which funders will be approached for new projects. Information about previous grants helps establish the group's credibility; a list of current prospects allows foundation staff to check with each other, discuss competing proposals, and avoid duplication of funding.

FINANCIAL SELF-SUFFICIENCY. Most grantors like to see organizations develop the capacity, over the long run, to raise their own funds — through membership development, major donors, program service fees, and benefit events. Organizations that can support themselves, rather than rely on outside sources such as foundations, are more likely to survive, grow, prosper, and get things done. We all like to back a winner. Most groups will do better with foundations if they can show a diversified funding base.

LEADERSHIP. Who's running this thing, anyway? Decisions are made by the organization's leadership, and grantmakers want to know who the decision-makers are: their experience, relevant training, etc.

*T*hink like a funder. Common sense is a great guide. Likely, each of us has been solicited for donations for some charitable purpose. Like a foundation, you and I go through a similar process of evaluation.

I evaluate a proposal applying five criteria:

1. Is the issue important to me?

2. Does this project have realistic and effective goals and approach?

3. Is the timing appropriate (urgent and important)?

4. Is this the best group to undertake this issue and project?

5. Given limited resources, does this group really need our money?

— John Powers, Educational Foundation of America

CONSTITUENCY. Who will benefit if the organization succeeds? Most foundations are trying to reach specific groups of people; grantseekers need to define theirs.

NETWORKING. Will there be any new collaborations, new combinations of constituencies or interest groups? On the principle of strength in numbers, a group that broadens its base and gets more people involved is more likely to succeed. Many foundations are particularly intrigued by joint projects involving new and/or existing organizations.

As Elaine Gross of the Unitarian Universalist Veatch Program puts it, "Seldom is any one group able to have a significant impact. I'm interested in the ways groups are working together to bring about change."

PROGRAM AND ORGANIZATIONAL DEVELOPMENT. What will be the long-term effect of the project, if successful? Will it build the organization? Will it significantly affect the lives of the constituents? Does it have the potential to develop into an ongoing program? Can it be replicated somewhere else? An organization is less likely to be funded if donors perceive it is heading for a dead end.

FINANCIAL MANAGEMENT. Can the grantee organization handle money in a professional way? Will they produce timely, accurate reports?

FOUNDATION CULTURE

First, let's get our terms straight. The chart on the facing page, reprinted courtesy of the Foundation Center, describes the differences among *independent, company-sponsored, operating,* and *community foundations.* Notice that not everything called a foundation gives out grants. For most activists, the first and last — independent and community foundations — provide the best opportunities for funding.

Most independent foundations are started with a large chunk of money. Foundation officers invest this money in stocks, bonds, business loans, or real estate, hoping to earn more money. A portion of the interest income is then used to pay for office costs, staff salaries, board travel, etc., with the balance distributed, by law, as grants. The assets (and in some cases the remainder of the interest income) are held aside and reinvested; only a small fraction of the foundation's net worth is given away at any one time.

As Mary Diamond of the Diamond Foundation stated in the *New York Times* (March 14, 1994), "Most foundations spend very little of their money. They're in the investment business." The Diamond Foundation recently chose to distribute all of its assets as grants and spend itself out of business — which created a lot of discussion in the foundation world.

A number of other granting sources, including service clubs, religious groups, and corporate giving programs, also accept proposals. They may look and act like foundations, but technically are not. For our purposes, these technicalities don't really matter, since they read proposals and give away money.

FIGURE A. GENERAL CHARACTERISTICS OF FOUR TYPES OF FOUNDATIONS

Foundation Type	Description	Source of Funds	Decision-Making Activity	Grantmaking Requirements	Reporting
Independent Foundation	An independent grant-making organization established to aid social, educational, religious, or other charitable activities.	Endowment generally derived from a single source such as an individual, a family, or a group of individuals. Contributions to endowment limited as to tax deductibility.	Decisions may be made by donor or members of the donor's family; by an independent board of directors or trustees; or by a bank or trust officer acting on the donor's behalf.	Broad discretionary giving allowed but may have specific guidelines and give only in a few specific fields. About 70% limit their giving to local area.	Annual information returns (990-PF) filed with IRS must be made available to public. A small percentage issue separately printed annual reports.
Company-Sponsored Foundation	Legally an independent grantmaking organization with close ties to the corporation providing funds.	Endowment and annual contributions from a profit-making corporation. May maintain small endowment and pay out most of contributions received annually in grants, or may maintain endowment to cover contributions in years when corporate profits are down.	Decisions made by board of directors often composed of corporate officials, but which may include individuals with no corporate affiliation. Decisions may also be made by local company officials.	Giving tends to be in fields related to corporate activities or in communities where corporation operates. Usually give more grants but in smaller dollar amounts than independent foundations.	Same as above.
Operating Foundation	An organization that uses its resources to conduct research or provide a direct service.	Endowment usually provided from a single source, but eligible for maximum deductible contributions from public.	Decisions generally made by independent board of directors.	Makes few, if any grants. Grants generally related directly to the foundation's program.	Same as above.
Community Foundation	A publicly sponsored organization that makes grants for social, educational, religious, or other charitable purposes in a specific community or region.	Contributions received from many donors. Usually eligible for maximum tax deductible contributions from public.	Decisions made by board of directors representing the diversity of the community.	Grants generally limited to charitable organizations in local community.	IRS 990 return available to public. Many publish full guidelines or annual reports.

THE FOUNDATION DIRECTORY, 1995 EDITION

The vast majority of foundations support religious charities, education, medicine, and mainstream social service agencies, such as the YMCA or the American Red Cross. Relatively few give grants for advocacy or social change organizing, despite the common rhetoric about promoting risk and innovation. The more controversial your efforts, or the greater the challenge to the status quo — in social relations, politics, art, whatever — the harder it will be to fund your work with grants. This makes perfect sense because the rich, who underwrite most foundations, *are* the status quo.

Happily, there are exceptions. In preparing this book, I surveyed 62 foundations and grants programs that fund groups working for social justice, human rights, and environmental conservation. Forty staff and board members responded to my questionnaire; you'll find their comments sprinkled throughout the book. Be aware that these folks are among the most progressive in the foundation world (which is not a terribly progressive community), so their views are not meant to represent "philanthropy in America."

You should also understand that, in the words of Stephen Viederman, "Any relationship between funder and prospective grantee is a power relationship; one has access to money, the other needs money." Since there are so many more applicants than grants, the people who make funding decisions have a lot of power over the health and success of applicant organizations. This is perhaps the best reason to develop an active grassroots fundraising program and reduce your reliance on grants.

Most foundations are structured like other nonprofits, with paid staff and volunteer boards. Some also use community review boards or consultants. The roles of these groups are described below.

THE STAFF. Pam Rogers, who works for the Haymarket People's Fund, teaches activists how to develop and write proposals. She describes, with tongue only slightly in cheek, the life of a foundation employee:

> When you write a grant, picture a person in a room with no windows, with proposals stacked everywhere. This person's entire job is to read proposals, day in and day out. Ask yourself: what can I do to make my organization's proposal stand out?

While very few foundation staff work in windowless rooms, they do deal with tons of paper. Even the smaller funding programs review hundreds of proposals each year, so the feeling of being crushed by words is very real. As Jon Jensen of the George Gund Foundation says, "The thing about this job is, you're under an avalanche of information, so it's easy for it to start to blur together after awhile."

In addition to digging out from beneath the paper, staff manage other day-to-day chores, including answering the phone, handling correspondence, and preparing materials for board review. Staff members also research new issue areas and even seek out new organizations to fund. While these employees seldom make final decisions about who gets the money, they advocate for applicants whose work they admire.

Foundation staff tend to come from academia, government, other foundations, or (if you're lucky) directly from the social change community. Jon Jensen, for example, went to graduate school, then ran a small conservation organization before going to work in the foundation world. He continues to serve as a volunteer board member for several conservation groups.

Some foundations make a point of hiring people with an activist background. As Stephen Viederman says,

> The more empathy you have for your grantees and the difficulties they face in raising a budget, the better. At the Noyes Foundation, both of our program officers are community organizers with fifteen or more years' experience. They've spent most of their professional lives on the other side of the table, asking for money and doing the organizing.

Marjorie Fine takes this point even further:

> Everyone in a foundation position should have at least two years' background in fundraising. They should be experienced in having to look for money and raise a budget. They should know what it's like to have people not answer your calls, turn down your proposals, etc. This is less of a problem in social change foundations, but it's still a problem. When I mentioned this idea at a "Meet the Grantmakers" symposium, the audience erupted in wild applause.

If you want to improve your odds, make friends with the staff. As John Tirman of the Winston Foundation for World Peace says, "We consider applicants and grantees to be peers, not subordinates, and we like being treated the same."

THE BOARD. The board of directors (sometimes called the board of trustees) defines the philanthropic goals of the foundation, reviews proposals screened by the staff, and selects which groups to fund. Both staff and board members sometimes conduct site visits with applicant organizations to get a better feel for their work. Thousands of smaller family foundations have no paid staff, so volunteer trustees handle all the chores — which explains why many won't accept unsolicited proposals.

In most cases, trustees are themselves donors to the foundation or heirs of the original donors. They are giving away their own money. You'll find a lot of relatives serving together on foundation boards. As in any organization, decision-making power can be concentrated in the hands of a few particularly active or persuasive board members.

Trustees are sometimes experts in issues such as economic development, reproductive rights, or cultural diversity. Others are chosen for their knowledge of investment strategy or tax law. Still others serve because of their corporate affiliations. Some are simply friends and neighbors of other board members.

With most foundations, it is considered taboo to contact trustees directly. When asked what really annoys him, John Tirman says, "Going around me to my board." However, other grantmakers designate board members to serve as "talent scouts" who evaluate organizations and seek out new grantees. If you can identify these people and interest them in your program, it will make your grant-seeking life a lot easier.

COMMUNITY REVIEW BOARDS. Several community-based foundations (including those affiliated with the Funding Exchange, a national consortium of social change grantmakers) add an additional layer of review: a community board, grants committee, or allocations committee. Proposals are reviewed by a group of peers — organizers and activists — to ensure that the community's wisdom and priorities are reflected in the grants. In some cases, these peer panels make final grant decisions; in other cases, they forward their recommendations to the board of directors for a vote.

Each time the Chicago Foundation for Women goes through a grants cycle, for example, more than fifty women are involved in screening proposals and visiting applicant organizations. This demystifies and democratizes the practice of grantmaking.

CONSULTANTS. Some foundations hire consultants to manage their grants programs. The consultant might be a local tax attorney specializing in the needs of small family foundations, or a former foundation officer providing grantmaking advice. Small foundations sometimes join together to create an umbrella organization and hire common staff to handle proposal review, bookkeeping, tax forms, and other tasks.

A consultant is, by definition, a walking catalog of ideas, names, and organizations. You should make it a point to find out which grants consultants cover your region and/or your issue, and introduce them to your work. If suitably impressed, they can open a lot of doors to potential funders.

A good proposal doesn't go on and on about the problem; it devotes time and intelligent discussion to strategies, plans, short- and long-term solutions.

— Marjorie Fine, Unitarian Universalist Veatch
Program at Shelter Rock

I am sometimes amazed by the confused and convoluted descriptions we get. Presumably, the applicants should be able to describe their work — but my experience has been otherwise!

— Katrin Verclas, Ottinger Foundation

Get Organized! The Grant Proposal as Organizing Plan

Grassroots groups tend to operate minute by minute and hand to mouth: dealing with crises, putting out "brush fires," worrying about the payroll. When the world is falling apart and your group is close behind, long-range planning is considered a luxury. For many of us, it's hard to justify taking time — our most precious resource, even more precious than money — to create a comprehensive plan to guide our strategy.

Under these conditions, improvisation becomes a way of life and, for many people, a badge of honor. After years of improvising their way from project to project, some organizers resist planning, fearing that it might limit their flexibility or autonomy. As activist and financial consultant Terry Miller writes in *Managing for Change*,

> Some will argue that they cannot plan because something unexpected may happen. There is no better way to ensure something unexpected happening than *not* to plan. If you have a plan and the situation changes, you will be working with a revised plan; otherwise, you will be working with revised instinct.

This is where the process of developing grant proposals can really help your work. For many groups, writing a proposal is the closest thing to creating a community organizing plan. If you take the time to design your project thoroughly and outline the plan in your proposal, you will benefit in at least three ways.

1. **The discipline of putting details on paper — goals, objectives, deadlines, expenses** — will focus your efforts in the field. Your project will be more successful and you'll have a bigger impact.

2. **THE PLANNING PROCESS PROVIDES AN OPPORTUNITY** to involve both your co-workers and your constituency in choosing the future of your organization. Peter Bahouth of the Turner Foundation puts it this way:

> We look for homegrown community involvement. The best projects come from communities most affected; solutions work best when they come from the community.

3. **YOU ARE MORE LIKELY TO WIN THE GRANT,** since you'll be so organized and professional. As Elaine Gross of the Unitarian Universalist Veatch Program says, "Don't submit a proposal before you have clear strategy for your work; a list of activities is not enough."

BUILDING THE CASE FOR SUPPORT

At an early stage in the planning process, you need to develop a set of background materials outlining why your organization exists — defining the problem you're trying to solve, describing your plan for solving it, and confirming your ability to do the work. The contents of this document, which is called a *case statement*, are nicely summarized in Kim Klein's *Fundraising for Social Change:*

1. **A STATEMENT OF MISSION** that tells the world why the group exists.

2. **A DESCRIPTION OF GOALS** that tells what the organization hopes to accomplish over the long term — in other words, what the organization intends to do about why it exists.

3. **A LIST OF OBJECTIVES** — specific, measurable, and time-limited — that tell how the goals will be met.

4. **A SUMMARY OF THE ORGANIZATION'S HISTORY** that shows that the organization is competent and can accomplish its goals.

5. **A DESCRIPTION OF THE STRUCTURE OF THE ORGANIZATION** including board and staff roles and what kind of people are involved in the group (such as clients, activists, business people, clergy).

6. **A FUNDRAISING PLAN.**

7. **A FINANCIAL STATEMENT** for the previous fiscal year and a budget for the current fiscal year.

Notice the sequence of the first three items. The mission statement tells *why* (the need); the goals statement tells *what* (your ambition); the objectives — along with a list of methods for reaching these objectives — tell *how* (your plan). Each one flows logically from the next. For this reason, you shouldn't try to develop a work plan (or a grant proposal) without reaching some sort of consensus within your group about how you define the need and your long-range goals for addressing the need. A more detailed discussion of goals, objectives, and methods appears on page 77.

A case statement is an internal document — it's too long and detailed for public consumption — but you can easily condense it for the public. Take a look at the Community Food Bank's case summary on page 24. In just one page, the authors outline:

◆ Their vision for the future

◆ The problem they are working to solve (including local statistics)

◆ The breadth of their programs and services

◆ Their niche — how their organization is unique and how they work with other groups

◆ What they want from the reader

This summary could easily serve as a "fact sheet" for inclusion with fundraising letters, news releases, and so forth. You might create something similar for your group.

You can also borrow entire paragraphs or pages from the case and insert them into your brochures, newsletters, membership recruitment letters, news releases, and even your grant proposals. In fact, the contents of a case statement look a lot like the sections of a proposal. If you take the time to carefully develop your case "boilerplate" — the standard language about who you are and what you do — your grantwriting chores will be much easier. Write it right, then use as needed.

It's heresy to mention this in a fundraising book, but your nonprofit can survive and even prosper without a formal case statement. The key word is *formal*. I've held development jobs with five organizations over fifteen years, yet only one group had a formal case statement (and I can't recall ever seeing it). But — and this is important — every one of those groups had the elements of the case written down and available. When needed, I would assemble the necessary pieces from the mission statement, articles of incorporation, previous grant proposals, newsletters, bylaws, and other fundraising and publicity materials. It would have been possible, without too much work, to gather everything into one notebook — which is not a bad idea. You don't need a shiny embossed folder with the words "Case Statement," but you'll be more effective if you have all the components at your fingertips.

PROGRAMS, PROJECTS, AND CAMPAIGNS

Your success in raising grant money will be based, in part, on your ability to plan your work strategically to make the most of available funds. What this usually means is breaking down your work into programs and/or projects, each with their own specific goals and deadlines, budgets and headaches.

Before going any further, let's get our terms straight. In describing their work, organizers and activists use words like programs, projects, and campaigns. Throughout this book, I have used *program* and *project* interchangeably (and limited the use of the word *campaign*, for reasons I will soon explain). Some grantmakers, however, encourage a more formal definition of these terms, as follows.

COMMUNITY FOOD BANK
SUMMARY OF CASE STATEMENT

THE VISION ... "The day that hunger is eradicated from the earth, there will be the greatest explosion that the world has ever known. Humanity cannot imagine the joy that will burst into the world on the day of that great revolution."

— *Federico Garcia Lorca, Spanish poet and dramatist, 1899-1936*

The Community Food Bank shares Garcia Lorca's vision to eradicate hunger. We do this by responding to the food needs of the people in Southeastern Arizona through education, advocacy and the acquisition and distribution of food.

THE NEED ... Hunger is involuntarily foregoing one or more meals during a month. A recent Michigan study found that those living in poverty miss 15 meals or more each month. In Tucson, that would mean that 90,000 people, 33,000 of whom are children, are missing at least 15 meals each month.

There are many programs that provide food assistance: food stamps, WIC (the special supplemental food program for Women, Infants, and Children), school meal programs, etc. However, all of these programs, in combination with personal buying power and private charitable food providers, do not meet the need.

COMMUNITY FOOD BANK SERVICES

1. *Food boxes* provide short term food assistance to families, infants and the elderly.

2. *Salvage food* saves good edible food from being thrown away and distributes it to agencies, thus reducing their food expenses.

3. *Gleaning* is the gathering of produce that has been left in the field or on the tree. It is also distributed to agencies.

4. *Surplus foods* are distributed to those in need under federal guidelines.

5. *Food Plus* provides food to children determined eligible by the Pima County Health Department.

6. *Hunger Awareness Resource Center* is the educational and advocacy arm of the Community Food Bank.

7. *FoodSHARE* is a food buying club done in cooperation with St. Mary's Food Bank in Phoenix and helps to stretch food dollars.

8. *Tucson's Table* collects perishable foods from local restaurants and distributes it to other nonprofit agencies.

9. *Coordination* of food bank services is done in Pima County, within Arizona and throughout the USA.

CFB is one of a kind ... No other organization in southern Arizona performs the food services, nor has the network of affiliations, nor serves so many people. CFB has multiple food services providing food to those in need while discouraging dependence on charity.

SUPPORT NEEDED ... Donations of cash, food, time, labor and talent are vital to the operation. Two-thirds of all labor is given by volunteers. Cash gifts pay for food boxes. Food donations complete the food boxes and/or are distributed to agencies for meal programs. All are needed to respond to the food needs in our community.

NO CHILD, MAN OR WOMAN SHOULD EVER BE HUNGRY

Programs are broad, ongoing areas of your work that are defined by the issues you address: health care reform, toxic waste reduction, abortion rights, and so on. *Projects* are more narrowly defined activities and typically focus on constituencies, geographic areas, or portions of the larger issue. A project can be a piece of your regular program, or it can be something new that moves your work in a different direction. Projects have specific, measurable outcomes; they begin and end on certain dates. Over time, some successful temporary projects become permanent programs, or spin off other projects. (See example on page 26.)

The word *campaign* has several meanings. In fundraising, the term is often used to describe a series of connected activities that move the organization toward a monetary goal — for example, a major donor campaign or a capital campaign to raise funds for buildings or equipment.

Campaign is also used to define a broad coalition effort to achieve a specific goal having little or nothing to do with fundraising or elections. The South Africa divestment campaign of the 1980s is a good example. Thousands of individuals and community groups from around the world pressured foundations, corporations, universities, and municipal governments to denounce apartheid by selling off their investments in companies doing business in racially segregated South Africa. The economic pressure from this "investment boycott" helped to end apartheid. Issue campaigns are an important and useful strategy for bringing groups together to create social change.

Among the general public, the word *campaign* is usually associated with elections, which is why I don't use it much in this book. Most grants are given to tax-exempt organizations recognized by the IRS under section 501(c)(3) of the tax code and qualifying as public charities. Donations to these groups are tax-deductible, a precondition for nearly all foundation gifts. The IRS prohibits all 501(c)(3) organizations from spending money to elect or defeat candidates for public office, and it sets limits on how much money public charities can spend on lobbying (which includes ballot initiatives). If your group focuses on traditional electoral campaigns or does substantial lobbying, you're probably registered as a 501(c)(4) or a political action committee, and won't be eligible for many grants.

Some organizations address this problem by splitting themselves in half and creating separate 501(c)(3) and 501(c)(4) entities with different names. One part handles research, education, and outreach; the other does lobbying and electoral work. This strategy requires a clear division of labor plus some fancy bookkeeping, so if you're thinking about it, seek advice from a good nonprofit accountant.

If you're confused about these terms, here's an illustration to help you sort things out. Let's say you work for a hypothetical citizen's group, Midwest Breadwinners, that organizes working-class people on economic issues. Your organization might be involved in three ongoing *programs* or *program areas*: public utility reform, fair lending, and tax equity. Each of these programs could incorporate multiple *projects*. For example, your public utility reform projects might include weatherization assistance for low-income families, plus an effort to change utility company policy on electric and gas shut-offs. Let's assume that Midwest Breadwinners is also involved in a coalition *campaign*, under your tax equity program, to repeal the state sales tax on food and medicine.

Graphically, your organization might look like this:

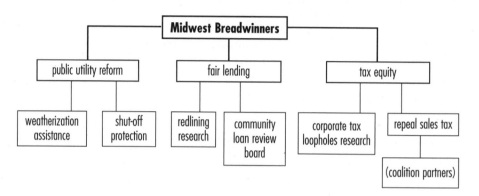

GENERAL SUPPORT GRANTS

It is much more difficult to win grants for general operational support than it is for specific projects. As Terry Miller says, "There is constant pressure from funders to get you to apply for funding only for 'special projects,' and yet your biggest need is general support money."

Some grants officers are aware of this dilemma and are working to correct it within their own foundations and among their peers. The National Network of Grantmakers, a consortium of progressive funders, makes the following point in its report, *What is Good Grantmaking for Social Justice?*:

> Social change is a long-term process which includes organizational, leadership, and issues development. There are no shortcuts to building strong organizations in which low income and other disenfranchised people are empowered.... Funders interested in supporting social change must commit to long-term support of this process in the form of general operating support, funds to build organizational and individual leadership capacity, and money for the development of policy alternatives.

Among the questions asked in this self-evaluation guide for grantmakers:

> To what extent are grants made for general support, to allow the grantee flexibility in using available resources to accomplish its mission and objectives?

> If project or program support grants are awarded, can the grant be spent on any/all reasonable costs of the program (including staffing, space, and "indirect" or "overhead" expenses necessary to carry out the project)?

Despite increased attention to the "general support gap," you'll have a hard time raising unrestricted funds through grants. This is one of the most important reasons to diversify your funding base with membership development and general donations, since these funds can be used for general expenses.

If you choose to seek general support grants, you'll have the best chance with a current or past funder who already knows and respects your work. Except for very small grants, it's rare to receive general support on your first approach to a grantmaker. To improve your odds, you might try to package your general proposal as program or project support. Ask yourself questions such as, "If we had more money to spend on developing the capacity of our organization — staff time, equipment, board development, fundraising, and so forth — how would we spend it?" Explore how these pieces might fit together, then write it up as a project proposal with a provocative title. Remember, the tighter the focus, the better your chances of getting funded.

We did this several years ago at Native Seeds/SEARCH under the boring but harmless title, "Systems Upgrade Program for 1989." After describing the growth of the organization and outlining our goals for the coming year, we listed six areas where we needed financial help to make our work more effective. These included an improved computer system, extra office space, better equipment for the seed bank, plus additional staff hours for seed collection, crop classification, and public education. The narrative emphasized how these areas would be linked together to improve our programs. The $30,000 request equalled 25% of the organization's budget at that time. It was fully funded.

As you gain more experience with fundraising and grantsmanship, you'll get a better feel for what is "grantable" and what isn't. The best way to learn is to bounce your ideas off other grantwriters, community organizers, nonprofit managers, and foundation staff. As you evaluate the fundability of your work, consider the following questions:

DESIGNING FUNDABLE PROJECTS: THE GRANTWRITER AS FEASIBILITY TESTER

1. **DOES YOUR PROJECT FILL A REAL NEED?** In other words, are you creating a problem and trying to solve it because you think there's money available, or did the problem exist before you discovered it?

2. **IS ANYONE ELSE WORKING ON A SIMILAR PROJECT?** Is the niche already filled? If so, can you build a coalition with other groups and share the wealth? Nonprofits are often competing for pieces of the same funding pie, so it benefits you to think up a new angle, a creative solution, or an unusual partnership. As Pam Rogers of the Haymarket People's Fund says, "I would invite you to collaborate with other organizations and expand your vision of the problem to include long-range solutions."

3. **HAVE FOUNDATIONS FUNDED SIMILAR PROJECTS?** If so, which foundations? Go to the library, talk with other nonprofits, call foundation offices. In

judging the feasibility and fundability of your program, try to see your work through the eyes of prospective grantmakers by studying their guidelines, reviewing their annual reports, and talking with foundation staff. Do your homework *before* you apply. You will only develop your sense of what's fundable and what isn't through ongoing research.

As you create a long-range plan, it's appropriate to take into account the fundability of your various programs, but be cautious about shifting your mission or direction just for the sake of bringing in additional funds.

For more information on grants research, see Chapter 5.

4. **HOW CONTROVERSIAL IS IT?** As the controversy factor increases, fundability decreases. When describing the characteristics of projects they prefer to support, foundations often use the words *risk* and *innovation*, and some actually put money behind these words. If you're trying something revolutionary, however, you'll be working from a smaller pool of prospects.

5. **WILL YOUR PROGRAM GRAB PEOPLE'S ATTENTION?** We return to rule number one: distinguish yourself. You don't have to use gimmicks, but if your project contains a unique "hook," use it. It will make a difference.

A hook can be something visual and compelling. My friend Alan Gussow created the Shadow Project in 1982 after viewing photos of atomic bomb victims at Hiroshima, whose "shadows" had been burned into sidewalks and buildings by the intense heat of the blast. Through this event, artists and activists painted their own silhouettes — thousands of them — in public places to commemorate the dead. After Alan's project in New York and a similar one in Portland, Oregon, coordinated by Donna Slepack, we joined together to organize the International Shadow Project on Hiroshima Day 1985. Nearly 10,000 people in 400 cities participated. In this case, the hook was the shadow image itself (see page 68) and the unusual collaboration between visual artists and peace activists.

Sometimes the threat or problem is the hook, rather than the solution. I once designed a fundraising mailing for a conservation group working in such a hostile community that they received death threats. A photo of the group's staff had even been tacked up in the local post office, with the crosshairs of a rifle drawn over their faces. So we used these death threats as the fundraising hook — the newest endangered species, we wrote, is your local environmental activist. This mailing, which more than doubled the group's membership, was their most successful ever. The same story could have been adapted for use in a grant proposal.

6. **DO YOU HAVE THE SKILLS TO RUN THE PROGRAM EFFECTIVELY?** Think big, but don't ask for more work or money than you can handle. To judge your capacity, consider how the proposed project will affect your staffing, budgeting, bookkeeping, management procedures, and other programs. As Betsy Taylor of the Merck Family Fund says, "Don't bullshit. Speak

the truth, both about your aspirations and your track record." Ellen Furnari — formerly of the Ben & Jerry's Foundation, now with the National Network of Grantmakers — encourages grantseekers to describe and build upon their previous success:

> People rarely talk about outcomes. If they don't tell me about the impact of their work, it looks like they're trying to hide the fact that they're not having an impact. With more than half the proposals I read, I have to ask, what was the impact?

Many nonprofits fail for lack of funding, but a surprising number die from accelerated growth. To live a long life, your group needs to grow in a rational, sustainable way. A giant infusion of cash can damage your organization by:

◆ Changing the culture of the organization — how it feels to participate in the work — which can lead to staff turnover

◆ Rapidly shifting power and accountability within the organization

◆ Reducing the need for community financial support, which reduces your accountability to the community you serve.

For an inside look at how one grantmaker might evaluate your project, consider the evaluation form on the next page. This sheet is used by the Unitarian Universalist Veatch Program to screen applications.

The first section, not surprisingly, weeds out groups that didn't do their homework. The second section addresses weaknesses within the issue area, and the third outlines concerns about the organization. This checklist provides a way for grant reviewers to measure their gut feelings against some objective criteria. I suspect that this form is also helpful in guiding staff debate, since every proposal must pass the same set of standards. How would your proposal measure up?

While I would never argue for grantwriting by committee, you have to find ways to involve and empower your co-workers. The proposal development process tends to concentrate power in the hands of the people who write the grant applications. In preparing proposals, they make choices — some subtle, others more visible — about how the organization will behave and how the project will be run. Stephen Viederman of the Jessie Smith Noyes Foundation addresses this issue when he says,

> We don't want a speech writer who's going to write for somebody else. We'd rather hear directly from the organizers and advocates, the people who will do the work. It's important that the people who are going to organize the process should write the proposal, or at a minimum be sure it actually reflects what they want to do.

To take this idea even further, the organizers should *control* the contents of the proposal.

To start the process at Native Seeds/SEARCH, we held a "grants brainstorm" at the beginning of each year. Our program managers would fanta-

*G*rantwriters should serve as both project developers and critics. You are engaged in a perpetual feasibility study and must ask yourself and your colleagues the same questions again and again:

1. **Will this project really meet the need or a significant portion of the need?**

2. **Is it realistic?**

3. **Do we have the capacity to manage it properly?**

4. **Will anybody pay for it?**

If the answer to any of these questions is no, you need to back off, reevaluate, redesign, or perhaps abandon the project.

INVOLVING YOUR CO-WORKERS

PINK SLIP -- NON DENOMINATIONAL PROPOSALS

FROM: **MF**   **AB**   **SB**   **JM**   **JF**

APPLICANT: _____

ISSUE/PROJECT: _____

DATE: Sent: _____   Rejected: _____

1. Outside GUIDELINES

100	[ ]	Direct service
101	[ ]	Individual
102	[ ]	Government
103	[ ]	Capital project
104	[ ]	Loan
105	[ ]	Endowment
106	[ ]	Conference
107	[ ]	Research
108	[ ]	Arts
109	[ ]	Historic preservation
110	[ ]	Overseas organization/work
111	[ ]	Media production
112	[ ]	Publication
113	[ ]	Other: _____

4. Current GRANTEE

400	[ ]	Grant in force
401	[ ]	Final grant made in _____
	[ ]	Renewal not recommended. See below.

500   [ ] **5. CLOSE OUT -- no letter**

_____
_____
_____
_____
_____

600   [ ] **6. OTHER** -- See Comments below

2. Not funding in this AREA because:

200	[ ]	No movement to speak of
210	[ ]	Insufficient strategic opportunity
220	[ ]	Insufficient justice orientation (race/politics/end of the day)
230	[ ]	Insufficient potential for structural impact (big picture)
240	[ ]	Lack of accountability throughout clump (elite dominated)
250	[ ]	Would require more investigation/analysis
260	[ ]	Other: _____

3. Problems with the ORGANIZATION/proposed work

300	[ ]	Not a social change strategy: _____
301	[ ]	Unconvincing strategy : _____
310	[ ]	Insufficient justice orientation
320	[ ]	Scope too local/no mitigating circumstances
330	[ ]	Not part of broader movement/operating in isolation
340	[ ]	Organizational difficulties: _____
341	[ ]	Governance problems: undemocratic/unaccountable
342	[ ]	Questionable "participation" by people
343	[ ]	Composition problems: no diverse/indigenous leadership/staff
344	[ ]	Inadequate experience/staff capacity
350	[ ]	Financial problems/ too reliant on Veatch: _____
360	[ ]	Work being done better by others: _____
370	[ ]	Other: _____

COMMENTS: _____
_____
_____
_____

© 1996 by the Unitarian Universalist Veatch Program at Shelter Rock

size out loud about what they could accomplish with more money, then we would begin to shape these fantasies into projects with specific goals and outcomes.

As the resident grantwriter, I tried to evaluate the fundability and feasibility of each idea. The process of brainstorming, by its very nature, generated more work than we could ever manage. Once all these projects were "on the table," we tried to ask tough questions about our management skills, staffing, and other financial needs. If the proposed project survived these concerns — and many did not — we roughed out a timeline and a budget.

As a next step, I would often prepare a brief outline based on my notes from the meeting, then circulate it to the appropriate staff members for review. (An example appears on the next page.) Members of the board or the relevant program committee were sometimes asked for their comments. I urge you to develop a similar summary for your next project, especially if you're new to proposal writing. Outlines can assist you in several ways:

1. **YOU MUST REDUCE THE PROJECT TO ITS MAIN POINTS,** which is another way of testing its feasibility. To quote Stephen Viederman, "One of my board members used to say, if you can't say it in two or three pages, you probably can't do it."

2. **THE STRENGTHS AND WEAKNESSES OF THE PROGRAM ARE EASIER TO SEE.** You can't mask potential problems with fancy words.

3. **ALMOST ANYONE CAN FIND THE TIME TO READ AND RESPOND TO A 2-PAGE DOCUMENT.** Hand your colleagues an 8-page proposal, however, and you might wait a long time for a reaction.

4. **OUTLINES CAN SAVE YOU A LOT OF WORK.** Nothing is more discouraging than writing a long, detailed proposal, passing it to your supervisor, and hearing her say, "I thought we agreed to drop this project." It works better to get everyone's input and approval at the outline stage.

Once the outline has been passed around, edited, and approved, make sure to involve the project managers in designing a specific work plan. They will be responsible for carrying out the plan and are probably the best people to figure out the tasks and timing. This is also a good stage to involve your constituency, through your program committee or board members with relevant expertise.

Work plans sound boring, but they don't have to be. When preparing a proposal to increase the endangered crop collections at Native Seeds/SEARCH, I asked Brett Bakker, New Mexico field manager, to create a seed collection itinerary. He took out a map, a calculator, and his contact list and spent a few hours mapping his routes and dreaming about the journeys ahead. His enthusiasm for the project is reflected in the detailed itinerary on page 34, which undoubtedly impressed and intrigued foundation staff. I'd like to visit these places; wouldn't you?

New Mexico Field Office: proposal outline 6/12/91

Introduction/Problem Statement (WHY)

1. Loss of crop diversity in Northern New Mexico; important area for native crops.

2. Assimilation pressure on Native American and Hispanic communities has greatly reduced number of farmers, leading to loss of crop varieties and changes in local culture/agriculture. Non-farm jobs, changes in economics of family farming.

3. Other groups attempting to preserve genetic diversity in the region failed due to mismanagement, poorly-defined goals, too broad a mission, and commercial pressure (the need to make money). Brief review of problems/limitations of Talavaya, Ghost Ranch (High Desert Research Farm), SNAC, San Juan Pueblo Project. NS/S has not previously worked in area to avoid duplicating work of other groups.

4. Role of NS/S in addressing these problems; track record. NS/S started due to requests from Native Americans for seeds and information. List of tribal groups we've helped in Arizona. Opportunity to expand our program to Hispanic farmers. Appropriate expansion of our range, given the Native American population of the area and the threat to native farming practices.

5. Proposed field rep, Brett, has exceptional qualifications, farming skills, and contacts among NAs in New Mexico.

Program Goals (WHO, WHAT, WHERE)

1. Seed collection from New Mexico for NS/S seed bank and catalog. Create small back-up seed bank in office for NM collections.

2. Provide support and expertise for creation of tribal and local seed banks.

3. Distribute seeds to Native Americans, and provide follow-up information on gardening techniques, as needed. Seed sales to general public during regular hours.

4. Distribution of educational materials (literature, slide show, videos, diabetes info) to NAs in NM.

5. Coordination of seed grow-outs for NS/S from NAs.

6. Educational outreach to schools, churches, gardening clubs, seniors, etc. Could include gardening workshops stressing traditional techniques.

7. Local fundraising to support local programs.

8. Provide call-in or walk-in support for local gardeners and those interested in native crops. Staff office one day per week; have phone machine for message pick-up.

9. Provide articles on NM crops and farmers for NS/S newsletter and public media.

10. Coordination and networking of seed-saving groups and farmers in the area; for example, work on organizing next seed summit.

Methods (HOW, WHEN)

1. Set up office, phone, bank acct. Establish regular hours.

2. Send mailing to New Mexico members and those on mail list, announcing opening of NM office (hours, menu of services, etc.) and seeking donations.

3. Send announcement to local/regional press, including office hours, available services, etc. all around to media to arrange for feature stories on NS/S.

4. Schedule and hold grand opening event (Gary as speaker?).

5. Recruit volunteers to help staff office and provide support.

6. Make periodic seed collection and technical support trips to regional NA and Hispanic farmers; offer support services as necessary.

7. Bring collections to Tucson for storage (fall); pick up seeds for distribution in Tucson (spring). Restock supplies.

Specific Objectives/Evaluation (MEASURING SUCCESS)

1. Add 50 new accessions to NS/S seed bank.

2. Arrange for grow-out of 50 varieties for NS/S catalog distribution, preservation, and/or research.

3. Increase NS/S seed distribution by 25% in New Mexico, while improving the quality of follow-up support for our growers.

4. Provide 6 educational presentations to local groups.

5. Arrange for 5 articles and stories on NS/S, seed saving, genetic diversity, diabetes, etc. in local/regional media.

6. Attend/support 3 regional gardening/seed-saving events, to distribute NS/S information and seeds.

7. Raise $2,500 in local/regional support for program through increased membership, outreach, and seed sales in first year; $5,000 in second year.

Budget (HOW MUCH $ for one year)

Salary and fringe (1/2 time = $935/mo)	$11,220
Rent and utilities (Peace Center)	1,200
Phone service: Hook-up	85
Basic local	500
Long distance	500
Typing/word processing support	500
Furniture (desk, table, chairs, shelves, lamp, file cabinet; all used)	300
Equipment: Phone	45
Answering machine	100
Slide projector	150
Office supplies	250
Postage and shipping	1,000
Printing and photocopying	500
Travel	1,650
TOTAL	**$18,000**

Letters of support requested from: San Juan Pueblo; Ghost Ranch; Flowering Tree Permaculture

Proposed Itinerary, New Mexico & Colorado
(minimum goal: 6 trips)

1. **Rio Chama Valley & Tierra Amarilla.** Española, Ojo Caliente, La Madera, El Rito, Canijilon, Ensenada, Los Ojos, La Puente, Abiquiu. 450 miles, 3-4 days.

2. **Northwest New Mexico & Southwest Colorado.** Laguna Pueblo, Acoma Pueblo, Navajo, Ute, Cortez, Dove Creek, Farmington, Shiprock, Chuska Mountains. 750 miles, 4-5 days.

3. **Taos Region/East Slope, Sangre de Christo.** Ranchos de Taos, Penasco, Mora, Las Vegas, Ribera, Pecos. 450 miles, 3-4 days.

4. **South-Central Colorado/San Luis Valley.** Raton, Trinidad, Walsenberg, Alamosa, Mosca, San Luis, Conejos. 750 miles, 4-5 days.

5. **Alamo Navajo & Middle Rio Grande Valley.** Tome, Belen, Socorro, Magdalena, Alamo. 350 miles, 3-4 days.

6. **Mescalero Apache.** Socorro, Carrizozo, Mescalero, Tularosa. 500 miles, 3-4 days.

7. **Ramah Navajo. Ramah.** 250 miles, 2-3 days.

8. **Manzano Mountains.** Tijeras, Chilili, Torreon, Manzano, Mountainair, Belen. 200 miles, 2-3 days.

9. **Rio Arriba Valley/Chimayo.** San Juan Pueblo, Dixon, Picuris Pueblo, Penasco, Las Trampas, Chimayo, Nambe Pueblo, Santa Fe. 350 miles, 3 days.

Total miles: 4050

Total travel days: 30-35

(All mileage is round trip from the Native Seeds/SEARCH office in Albuquerque.)

Once the proposal is funded, it's important to keep your colleagues actively involved in documenting the program for the purpose of grant reporting. The project manager is generally in charge of spending the money, but it will probably fall to you, the grantwriter, to produce the interim and final reports for the grantmaker. Let the organizers know *in advance* what information you will require in order to prepare thorough and accurate reports. For more detail on grants administration, see Chapter 9.

Whenever I teach a grants workshop, someone always wants to know, "How much money should we ask for?" The simple and intuitively correct answer is, "Ask for as much as you need." Of course, this answer seldom makes anyone happy, so I will attempt a more thorough explanation by asking a few additional questions. This discussion covers general budgeting issues; when you're ready to learn about the nuts and bolts of preparing and formatting a project budget, see page 87.

HOW MUCH MONEY? DEVELOPING BUDGETS FOR GRANT-FUNDED PROJECTS

1. **HOW MUCH MONEY WILL YOU NEED TO DO THE JOB RIGHT?** Calculate *all* relevant expenses. Novice grantwriters remember the "hard costs," such as printing expenses for the new outreach brochure, but tend to forget the staff time needed to write, edit, design, and distribute the brochure. A standard checklist for most project budgets should contain:

   ◆ Salary (organizers, supervisor, support staff)

   ◆ Benefits (social security/payroll taxes and, if relevant, worker's compensation, health insurance, pension plan)

   ◆ Printing and photocopying

   ◆ Postage and shipping

   ◆ Long-distance telephone

   ◆ Materials and supplies

   ◆ Mileage and travel (air fare, rental car, hotel, meals)

   ◆ Outside services and non-staff support

   Not every project requires all these items, and many project budgets will include expenses not covered here — but this list is a good place to start. For examples of how this checklist has been adapted for the real world, take a look at the proposals featured in Chapter 7.

   As a first step, estimate staff time. Most staff are involved in a variety of activities; apportion their time accordingly. How many hours per week will each person be expected to work on the project? If a staff member is assigned to the project quarter-time, then one-quarter of her salary should be covered under the grant budget.

   For most other items, consult your past expense records and use these numbers to calculate future costs. For some items you'll need outside assistance. To estimate the cost of your new outreach brochure, don't guess—call your printer, give the specifications, and ask for a bid. To figure the price of a plane ticket, call the airlines or your local travel agent.

The following tips from Terry Miller are designed to help with your annual organizational budget, but can be applied to grant-funded projects as well:

◆ Use last year's records for developing your estimates.

◆ Save your calculations on work papers in the budget file.

◆ Involve other people — ask them to check your thinking.

◆ Break larger estimates into smaller sub-estimates.

2. **HOW MUCH OF YOUR OVERHEAD CAN YOU INCLUDE IN THE BUDGET?** All organizations have certain fixed expenses: rent, utilities, basic phone service, and perhaps office staff. It also takes money to manage grants, since you pay for bookkeeping, bank fees, supervisory staff, etc. Your group can't survive without paying these bills, but relatively few foundations provide general support to underwrite the basic costs of doing business.

The traditional way to solve this problem is to divide up your overhead and include a fraction in each of your project proposals. This line item is usually called *administration and overhead* or *indirect costs*. Some funders refuse to pay indirect costs, but others will consider it if the percentage is reasonable. While big institutions such as universities have been known to double their grant requests just to cover overhead, I suggest that you limit indirect costs in your project budgets to 15% or less.

As an alternative, develop specific budget lines for all items listed above — rent, office staff, etc. — and include them in the project budget. If you anticipate that 10% of the bookkeeper's time will be spent administering the grant, then bill 10% of her hours to the project. You can do the same with secretarial time, local phone charges, rent, and so forth. Funders are wary about paying indirect costs, in part, because they want a specific record of where the money goes. If you can show them — in advance, in detail, on paper — it will increase their comfort level.

3. **WHO IS LIKELY TO FUND YOUR PROJECT, AND HOW MUCH ARE THEY LIKELY TO GIVE?** As you conduct your grants research, pay attention to both the interests of prospective foundations *and* the typical range of their grants. If your project will cost $25,000 and your best prospects give grants in the $5,000 - $15,000 range, you should try to raise the total budget from several smaller grants. This is a common and effective strategy.

When approaching a grantmaker who has not previously funded your organization, it's wise to ask for a small grant — less than their median amount. In other words, if the foundation gives grants of $5000 – $15,000, don't ask for more than $10,000 on your first approach. If you receive the grant and demonstrate credibility by doing a good job with the project, you will then be in a position to ask for more money, since the largest grants generally go to grantees who have a proven track record.

The amount of your request should also be measured against your overall budget. Start small. If you try to double your organizational budget with one grant, you are likely to be turned down.

Your project budget should include not just anticipated expenses, but also an accounting of revenue in-hand, pledged, and sought. In other words, don't just describe how you're going to spend the money — demonstrate how you plan to raise it, including how much you've already raised. The first grant is always the hardest, so once you've secured partial funding, trumpet your success. When foundation officers see a commitment from one of their peers, they are more likely to provide additional grants. For an example of how to format the revenue section of your budget, see page 89.

4. **HOW WILL YOU MANAGE THE DIFFERENCE BETWEEN THE AMOUNT YOU NEED AND THE AMOUNT YOU THINK YOU CAN RAISE?** At some point in this process — preferably before you start writing the proposal — your fantasy must be measured against reality. If you need $50,000 for your program and think you can raise only $25,000 in grant money, reevaluate and plan accordingly. Here are your choices:

   ◆ Scale back the work and reduce the budget. Organize in fewer neighborhoods, print fewer brochures, be less ambitious.

   ◆ Use a "special appeal" to try to raise the balance from your members or donors. To help motivate these donors, you might encourage foundation supporters to make challenge grants. (For more information on leveraging money, see Chapter 8.)

   ◆ If you can afford it, underwrite some of the costs from your general budget. These contributions should be itemized and included in the revenue portion of your project budget. (For an example, see the Pineros y Campesinos Unidos del Noroeste proposal on page 149.) Be very cautious with this strategy — you can easily overextend your staff and budget by trying to pay for line items you can't afford.

   ◆ Intensify your research. Identify additional foundation prospects and submit more proposals. Be prepared to do less work, and spend less money, if the grants don't come through. To protect yourself, develop a contingency budget based on a lower level of funding.

Partial funding, in my experience, is the rule rather than the exception. "Grassroots" means learning to make do with less. This doesn't mean that you should set your sights low, but be prepared to scale back if you don't receive all the money you want.

5. **HOW MUCH UNCERTAINTY CAN YOU HANDLE?** This is a critical question, because budgets are prospective documents. When you write a budget you're trying to predict the future, so you estimate. You guess. You make up the numbers. When you invent these numbers and put them on paper, you begin to shape an uncertain future, because these figures determine your goals for both fundraising and spending.

Don't be afraid. Make your most realistic guess, then plunge forward into the mist. As time goes by, you'll keep raising the money and paying it out, and the mist will clear. If the proposed budget turns out to be significantly different from your actual income and expenses, you can always contact the funders and negotiate changes.

Try to figure out where your potential funding source is coming from: how do they see the world? Now, think about your programs — which most closely fit the foundation's interests? Can you describe your program in their words and feel that your integrity is intact?

— Pam Rogers, Haymarket People's Fund

We get dozens of proposals from organizations that clearly never did a lick of homework, and waste our time and the precious funds of their members sending out hopeless proposals to the wrong funders. I often wonder if these same people try to buy their groceries in hardware stores.

— Martin Teitel, CS Fund

Grants Research and Grantmaker Relations

I once had a student who wanted to paper the world with grant proposals. When I described the odds of raising funds through grants — on average, perhaps 10-15% of all proposals get funded, and many "successful" ones receive only partial funding — she responded, "It's a numbers game, right? If we submit enough applications, eventually we'll get all the money we need."

Her response touched a raw nerve and I reacted. I had spent the afternoon in the library, reading through the foundation directories, and had discovered more than a dozen promising entries marked with the words, *preselected organizations only — unsolicited applications not accepted.* "Don't do it," I told her. "You'll bury the funders under piles of useless paper. Eventually they will stop accepting applications. If you choose to be lazy or greedy by sending out your proposals at random, you mess things up for everyone."

Rather than launch into my standard lecture about proposal abuse, allow me to quote Ellen Furnari, speaking of her experience directing the grants program at Ben & Jerry's Foundation:

DO YOUR HOMEWORK!

> 60-70% of the proposals we receive don't match our guidelines; 50% miss by a wide margin. We need to respond respectfully, and it costs staff time to respond to all these people. We try to limit our administrative costs to 10% of our budget, and lot of our time is absorbed saying "no."

Stephen Viederman of the Jessie Smith Noyes Foundation echoes this theme:

> Do your homework. It's a simple thing. We all believe our idea is the most important idea, which is how it should be — but if you don't do your homework you just clog up my desk and waste your own time.

Faced with increasing volumes of paper, more and more foundations are pulling in their welcome mats. Can you blame them?

That's the bad news. The good news is this: if you do your homework, build solid relationships with foundation officers, and carefully target your proposals, you can raise a lot of money. During the last two years I worked at Native Seeds/SEARCH, 40-50% of our proposals were funded. We submitted applications to about 60 well-chosen funders annually and received between 25 and 30 grants per year. We had a unique program with lots of fundraising handles, but the main reason for our success was the quality of our *research*. Before we submitted a proposal, we did a lot of investigative work.

Careful grants research should be the norm, but it's not. The more thoroughly you conduct your research, ask good questions, and cultivate foundation contacts, the more your organization will stand out from the crowd. As Robert Musser of the General Service Foundation says,

> I find that I am most receptive to grantseekers who have done their homework, whose proposals are clear, concise, and devoid of "grantese."

FOLLOW THE GUIDELINES

Before we dive into the research process, I must emphasize the most obvious point, which is also the most important point: *follow directions*. Most grantmakers — especially those who are bold enough to accept unsolicited applications — publish *guidelines* to help you, the grantwriter, decide if you meet their criteria. Not only that, but they even tell you how to format your proposal, when to submit it, how many copies to send, and what to attach. Unfortunately, many grantseekers are too desperate or lazy or blindly optimistic to follow (or even request) the guidelines.

When asked what really annoys her in a grant proposal, Judy Claude of the Bread and Roses Community Fund says, "Trying to convince staff a proposal fits social change guidelines when we all know it does not." As you can see from the following comments, many of her colleagues agree.

Steve Starkey, Wisconsin Community Fund:

> Don't try to change the foundation to make it fit your mission or project.

Diane Ives, Beldon Fund:

> If you don't fit the guidelines, don't submit the proposal.

Molly Connaghan, formerly of the Chinook Fund:

> Does your organization fall within the guidelines or are you pushing to make it fit?

Joy Palmer, Headwaters Fund:

> Grantseekers could save everyone time by reading the guidelines. We recently had a Youth Hunting Club apply for a grant. The purpose was to expose inner city youth to nature by teaching them how to hunt. Because social change is clearly defined as a priority in our mission and our grant guidelines, this was not an appropriate request for funding.

Before submitting your proposal, *study the guidelines* to determine if your project is appropriate. If you're uncertain, pick up the telephone and ask. By doing your homework, you will use your time more efficiently, submit fewer proposals, win more grants, and reduce the amount of frivolous paper in the world.

Fundraising, like any other task, becomes second nature if you do it long enough. After sixteen years of doing this work, I never stop tracking the scent of money. When I pick up a nonprofit newsletter I automatically flip to the donor acknowledgment page. When I go to the theater, the usher hands me a program; everyone else reads about the actors, I read about the benefactors. When the word "foundation" appears in a newspaper, I study the article with a little more care.

You can, and should, reserve time for grants research. In the next few pages I'll tell you what I know about the subject. But before we begin, remember this: your research never ends.

THINKING LIKE A DETECTIVE

◆ If you stop thinking about prospecting when you leave the library

◆ If you collect data on a dozen foundations and forget about grants research for the rest of the year

◆ If you have ten conversations with ten colleagues and the word *fundraising* is never mentioned — then you're not doing your job properly.

A good detective is always sniffing around for clues, asking questions, drawing conclusions, and testing those conclusions against the evidence. For fundraisers, clues are everywhere. The following questions will help to hone your detective skills.

1. **WHO FUNDS YOUR PEERS?** How are similar organizations raising money? Keep an eye on local nonprofits, regardless of their issues or programs, plus groups in other geographic areas with programs that resemble yours. The local connection is important, since most foundations restrict their giving to certain communities or states. The program connection is just as important, because regional and national grantmakers tend to focus their funding on certain subjects and constituencies.

   To learn about other organizations, read their newsletters. Many nonprofits also publish annual reports with lists of contributors, including foundations. Contact all the groups you can think of — national, regional, and local — who work with similar issues and population groups, and request their annual reports. Even better, make a donation and have your name added to their mailing lists. If you can't afford to contribute, suggest a free publication exchange between your groups. More and more organizations have home pages on the Internet and distribute this information electronically.

Contact staff members of other nonprofits for ideas and recommendations. If appropriate, discuss the potential for joint projects and proposals. Join the local chapter of the National Society of Fund Raising Executives (NSFRE) or other professional associations that focus on fundraising. By brainstorming with your peers, you'll pick up lots of useful suggestions.

2. **How can you present or "package" your work to interest the widest range of potential funders?** As mentioned in the previous chapter, your success at getting grants will be based, in part, on your ability to divide your work into separate programs and projects. If you haven't done so by now, start to think about your work in terms of categories and constituencies. What's your issue or subject? Who are you trying to reach, to serve? Do you work with a variety of population groups? Do you have a variety of projects? Do you operate in more than one city or state? In other words, how many fundraising "handles" can you create?

3. **What relationships can you call upon to help raise money?** Who do you know in the philanthropic world? Funding decisions are often based on the relationship between grantseeker and grantmaker. Everyone in your organization should be involved in identifying and cultivating prospective donors, including foundation officers.

As a first step, compile lists of board members of foundations that fund in your geographic area and are interested in your issues (see library research below), then circulate these lists to your board, staff, and key volunteers. Anyone with a "live" relationship should be involved in the grant application by signing the cover letter, making a phone call, and/or participating in a site visit.

You should also make an appointment to meet the staff of your local and state community foundations. These people serve as professional matchmakers and, if impressed with your programs, can recommend you to prospective donors. For more information on how to work with community foundations, see the section on donor-directed grants on page 58.

Remember to ask your current foundation supporters for suggestions. Because they work in the funding world, they often have the most up-to-date information and the strongest relationships with their peers. They might be willing to recommend your organization to other grantmakers or write letters of support.

As you answer these questions, you will start to gather leads, names, and ideas. I encourage you to create a file marked "Grant leads — to be checked." When you find a list of foundation supporters in an annual report, tear it out (or photocopy it) and put it in the file. If you see a story about a local foundation in the daily newspaper, clip it. When a colleague says, "You should investigate the Easy Money Fund," write a note and file it. Take the file with you when you go to the library. The more leads you bring, the more productive your research will be.

The Foundation Center is an independent national service organization established by foundations to provide an authoritative source of information on foundation and corporate giving. The Foundation Center operates reference collections in New York, Washington, D.C., Atlanta, Cleveland, and San Francisco. It also helps libraries, community foundations, and other nonprofit agencies create Cooperating Collections that include materials on grants research and proposal writing. Currently, there are more than 200 cooperating collections spread throughout all fifty U.S. states and Puerto Rico (see Appendix A).

USING THE FOUNDATION CENTER LIBRARY COLLECTIONS

Each Cooperating Collection includes certain reference books specified by the Foundation Center. In many locations, you'll also find copies of tax returns filed by local foundations; these tax forms (called 990-PF) contain information about the foundation's giving history, including a list of grant recipients.

Some grants research collections serve a broader function as local nonprofit resource centers, with books and magazines on general fundraising techniques, direct mail solicitation, benefit events, board development, publicity, strategic planning, incorporation and tax issues, philanthropic trends, and nonprofit management. The grants collection at the Tucson-Pima Public Library, for example, contains 250 books, plus lots of magazines, news clippings, and foundation annual reports, but only half the materials focus on grants research.

The following grants research system can and should be adapted to meet your own needs. If you'd like assistance or other ideas, talk with your local librarian. Some libraries offer a hands-on orientation session to get you started. If your computer has CD-ROM capability or is connected to the Internet, you can begin your foundation search from your home or office; see the next section on computers and grants research.

1. **WHEN YOU GO TO THE LIBRARY,** bring a pen or pencil, blank paper to write on, scrap paper (to tear into strips for bookmarks) and coins for the photocopy machine. Don't forget your "Grant leads - to be checked" file, with leads gleaned from reading newsletters, talking with foundation staff, and so forth. (Even without a folder full of leads, you can still benefit from a trip to the library — read on.)

2. **COLLECT SEVERAL GRANTS DIRECTORIES** from the shelves and carry them to your work table. The most useful resources are *The Foundation Directory, The Foundation Directory Part 2, The Foundation 1000, The Foundation Grants Index* (all published by the Foundation Center) and

the *Foundation Reporter* (published by Taft). There are also many subject-specific directories. If you're looking for grants from major corporations or corporate foundations, start with Taft's *Corporate Giving Directory* and the Foundation Center's *National Directory of Corporate Giving*. (For a listing of additional resources, see the bibliography.)

3. **WORK THROUGH THE NAMES IN YOUR FILE.** The *Foundation 1000* and the *Foundation Reporter* have the most in-depth information, so look up your prospects in these directories first. If you can't locate a particular prospect, try *The Foundation Directory, Parts 1 and 2*. These books cover a lot more grantmakers, but in much less detail. As you read through the entries, be aware of:

   A. **GEOGRAPHIC RESTRICTIONS.** Most funders limit their donations to groups working in certain cities, states, or regions. Does your group fit within their geographic boundaries?

   B. **FIELDS OF INTERESTS.** These define the issues, subjects, and types of organizations grantors prefer to support. Broadly speaking, are they interested in the kind of work you do?

   C. **GRANT SIZE.** Do they offer an appropriate amount of money for your project? Too small is fine, since you can piece together multiple grants — unless you're trying to raise $25,000 from funders who give $1,000 grants. On the other hand, you're unlikely to raise $2,000 from a foundation whose normal grants range from $25,000 to $200,000.

   D. **A LIST OF RECENT GRANTS.** Review the list, if one is available. Are any current grantees doing work that relates to, or overlaps with, the work of your organization?

If the answer to these questions is yes, you've identified a prospect. Write the appropriate information on a piece of paper or use a book mark to hold the page so you can photocopy it later. (Make sure to follow all applicable copyright laws.) When you get back to your office, send query letters to your new prospects, requesting guidelines and annual reports (see below).

Even if you go to the library without a list of leads, you can still identify lots of prospects, though the process will take a little longer. Grants directories are generally indexed by the name of the foundation, the names of their officers and trustees, the geographic areas in which they contribute, and the subjects/issues/constituencies they fund. Review the subject index and find your program area(s). If, for example, your group provides job counseling services to Hispanic women, look for headings such as "women's issues," "minorities - Hispanic" and "employment counseling." Beyond that, it's simply a matter of reading the entries of each foundation listed in your subject and geographic areas, and matching your programs with the interests of potential grantmakers.

The Foundation Grants Index is another useful research tool. The 1996 edition lists more than 74,000 grants of $10,000 or more, indexed by grantmaker, recipient, geographic region, and subject area. You can use this directory in at least three ways:

1. **IF YOU IDENTIFY A PROSPECTIVE FUNDER** but can't locate a list of grant recipients, this is the first place to look. (If your prospect isn't included, the librarian can help you find the foundation's IRS 990-PF tax report, which should identify grant recipients.)

2. **YOU CAN LEARN WHICH FOUNDATIONS ARE FUNDING COMPARABLE ORGANIZATIONS.** When I worked at Planned Parenthood of Southern Arizona, for example, I used this book to identify grants received by groups concerned with family planning and reproductive rights, then opened the other directories to learn more about the grantmakers.

3. **USING THE SUBJECT INDEX, YOU CAN TRACK GRANTS MADE IN YOUR PROGRAM AREA.** Because this index covers thousands of key words, spend some time looking through it and noting all words that apply to your organization and its work. This is a time-consuming strategy, so prepare accordingly. (This directory is also available through the KR Information on-line service and the FC Search CD-ROM product; see the section on computer resources below.)

By the way, *The Foundation Grants Index* — a huge book with tiny type — is a partial listing. Many smaller foundations and grants are not included.

A list of state and local foundation directories is included in the *Guide to U.S. Foundations, Their Trustees, Officers, and Donors*; the appropriate guides should be available in your public library. For example, Arizona guides are published by the Junior League of Phoenix and Arizona Human Services Magazine; the University of New Mexico produces a grants directory for their state. With local directories, the best strategy is to simply browse through the book and see what you can find.

If you choose to solicit help from your board and staff in developing relationships with foundation officers, the best resource is the *Guide to U.S. Foundations* mentioned above, which is published by the Foundation Center. This massive directory lists the board members of nearly 40,000 foundations, and includes an alphabetical index of trustees by name.

Another terrific resource is the periodical *The Chronicle of Philanthropy*, which is published 24 times per year. Each issue contains a listing of "New Grants," which you can use to identify new prospects and update your older foundation files. The publication also includes a regular "Deadlines" feature that describes current Requests for Proposals (RFPs) from a variety of foundation, corporate, and government grants programs. Check your local library for the *Chronicle of Philanthropy*; subscription information is included in the Bibliography on page 189.

I urge you to spend some time at your nearest funding information library. Even if you go without a research plan, you'll learn something useful just looking through the stacks. Try to spend three or four days throughout the year in your local grants collection. If you need to travel from out of town to get there, budget the time and money for at least one trip per year, and plan to stay at least one full day (two is better).

COMPUTERS AND GRANTS RESEARCH

The information age is upon us, we are told, and everything we want to know will appear with a few keystrokes and the click of a mouse. Given today's costs for computer-accessible grants information, however, we haven't yet reached the promised land. Grassroots groups are usually a few years behind the technology curve, and most small community organizations can barely afford a good computer, let alone the cost of a CD-ROM database or a subscription data service.

Nevertheless, for those who have computer capability and would like to conduct their research on-line or with CD-ROM and diskette products, here is a brief overview of the resources available in early 1996.

1. **SUBSCRIPTION DATABASES.** The Knight-Ridder Information on-line service (formerly DIALOG Information Services) includes electronic versions of *The Foundation Directory* and *The Foundation Grants Index* created by the Foundation Center, plus the grants database derived from the Oryx Press directories. The first two databases are limited to foundation activity; the third includes foundation, government, corporate, and service association grants and is geared to the needs of academics (see CD-ROM information below).

   KR Information charges a one-time subscription fee of $295. According to Knight-Ridder, the average on-line search costs an additional $50; depending upon the scope of your programs and funding needs, you might initiate several database searches per year. It takes considerable practice to master the search protocols, so if you're planning to subscribe, budget money for on-line practice time and a good manual.

   As an alternative, some libraries subscribe to the KR Information service, and your local librarian might be willing to do a free or low-cost search. The Foundation Center Associates Program ($495 per year) also provides on-call research support, including access to their comprehensive fundraising library. If you want them to do an on-line search, however, plan to spend an extra $95 for up to 75 grantmaker records.

2. **DIRECTORIES ON CD-ROM AND DISKETTE.** Five grant research products are currently available in CD-ROM and/or diskette formats, with a sixth to be released in 1996. Having tried out four of them, I offer informal assessments on the next page.

   For many grassroots groups, it's still most cost-effective to go to the library and use the books. If you have free access to these computer products — some of the Foundation Center Cooperating Collections are equipped with computers and CD-ROMs — use them to start your research, then glean additional information from the directories and the foundations themselves (see query letters below).

CHRONICLE OF PHILANTHROPY GUIDE TO GRANTS

FORMAT: CD-ROM or diskette

COVERAGE: 12,000 private, corporate, and community foundation grants of $10,000 or more awarded during recent years (more on CD-ROM).

UPDATED: bimonthly

PRICE: $395 per year for CD-ROM, $295 for diskette

STRENGTHS:
◆ easy to use
◆ search by key word (including trustees and staff) allows for a focused search
◆ current information; drawn from recent grants

WEAKNESSES:
◆ incomplete; limited to the largest foundations
◆ describes the grants, but includes little descriptive information about the grantmaker

KR INFORMATION ONDISC GRANTS DATABASE

FORMAT: CD-ROM

COVERAGE: 8,900 grants available from governments, commercial organizations, associations, and foundations

UPDATED: bimonthly

PRICE: $850 per year

STRENGTHS:
◆ very easy to use
◆ search by key word
◆ broadest range of grant sources; only product of the four to include government grants

WEAKNESSES:
◆ drawn from directories of research, health care, and humanities grants; with its academic focus, few grant opportunities for social activism

ORCA SOURCES OF FOUNDATIONS

FORMAT: CD-ROM or diskette

COVERAGE: 14,000 private, corporate, and community foundations

UPDATED: annually

PRICE: national version $399; updates $145 (with directors and trustees $125 extra; updates $75)
state and regional versions $129-$249; updates $50-$105

STRENGTHS:
◆ search by key word
◆ shows grants by state; easy regional search
◆ includes funding guidelines and range of grants

WEAKNESSES:
◆ limited information on grants and recipient groups

TAFT PROSPECTOR'S CHOICE

FORMAT:	CD-ROM or diskette
COVERAGE:	12,000 corporate and private foundations
UPDATED:	annually
PRICE:	$849 single-user; $1,045 multi-user
STRENGTHS:	◆ broad range of sources
	◆ most information for each foundation, including a list of grants and trustee information
WEAKNESSES:	◆ no search by key word; search parameters too broad
	◆ awkward to use; information is spread over 8 screens
	◆ not current; information is drawn from IRS records, which are often 3-5 years old.

Taft recently released another product, Grants on Disk, which lists 160,000 recently-awarded grants, plus an additional 30,000 grants with each quarterly update. This product allows for searches by key word. The cost is $695 per year for the single-user version or $895 for the multi-user version.

The Foundation Center is preparing a new CD-ROM product, *FC Search*, to be released in 1996. It is based on data from *The Foundation Directory, Foundation Grants Index, Guide to U.S. Foundations,* and the *National Guide to Corporate Giving* — nearly 40,000 foundations are included. On first review, this looks to be the one of the most thorough and powerful CD-ROM products available. It will cost $995 for the single-user version; check with the Foundation Center for the multi-user price.

3. **RESOURCES ON THE INTERNET.** As of June 1999, about 750 U.S. foundations (out of nearly 45,000) had established home pages on the Internet. These sites typically include guidelines, annual reports, and grants lists, plus any additional publications or reports sponsored by the foundation.

A number of other organizations and businesses also have Internet sites with information on grant research, fundraising, and resources for nonprofits. Here's a sampling to get you started. (Beware the U.S. Grant Network home page — it sounds like a great resource for grantseekers, but it features Ulysses S. Grant, 18th president of the United States.)

http://fdncenter.org   The Foundation Center
Contains links to foundation resources, plus a weekly news service for grantseekers, instructional materials on proposal writing, excerpts from Foundation Center publications, and a directory of Cooperating Collections (see Appendix A).

http://www.cof.org   The Council on Foundations
An overview of the foundation world, including lists of grantmaker affinity groups and regional associations of grantmakers — some of which publish funding directories.

http://www.foundations.org   Foundations On-Line
A directory of foundation home pages, plus links to other fundraising resources. This site is maintained by the Northern California Community Foundation.

http://www.nsfre.org   National Society of Fund Raising Executives
NSFRE is the professional association for fundraisers. Their site includes information about the organization, plus links to other philanthropy and fundraising sites.

http://www.nptimes.com   The NonProfit Times
An electronic version of the monthly magazine, which includes features on fundraising and other nonprofit management issues.

http://www.clark.net/pub/pwalker/
Nonprofit Resources Catalogue
A resource directory for nonprofits, including links to information about funders. This site is updated regularly by Philip A. Walker, information systems specialist with the United Way of America.

http://www.igc.org   Institute for Global Communication
IGC maintains a series of networks for social change activists, including PeaceNet, EcoNet, ConflictNet, WomensNet and LaborNet.

http://www.webactive.com   Web Active
Contains information for, and about, activist groups.

http://www.nonprofits.org   Internet NonProfit Center
This site, which includes home pages for dozens of nonprofits, is designed primarily for donors seeking information about charitable groups.

4. **GRANTSEEKERS DATABASE.** The National Network of Grantmakers manages a database, called "Pocket Docket," that includes more than 3,500 organizations that work for social, political, economic, and environmental justice. Participating funders use this service to find out about prospective grantees and learn which groups receive funding from other progressive foundations. If you would like your organization to be listed (at no cost), contact the National Network of Grantmakers, (619) 231-1348.

Once you've completed your work in the library (or on-line), don't assume that the research phase is over. As Quincey Tompkins Imhoff of the Foundation for Deep Ecology says, "I would advise against simply relying on a directory." Foundation directories are incredibly helpful, but they have two significant drawbacks.

QUERY LETTERS, TELEPHONE CALLS, AND SITE VISITS

1. **THE INFORMATION IS INCOMPLETE.** There's a lot to learn about each prospective funder and the necessary data can't be adequately covered in a few paragraphs or even a few pages.

2. **THE INFORMATION IS DATED.** Most directories are drawn from IRS records that are typically three to five years old. Foundation programs and guidelines change, and you need to know what the grantmakers are funding now — not three years ago.

To complete your research, go straight to the source: the grantmakers themselves. As a first step, write a *query letter*. This is a request for information, not money, and can be sent via the postal service or e-mail, if available. You can also request guidelines by phone (though I've always had better luck through the mail).

The query letter is your first contact with the funder and might spark the interest of foundation staff, so be sure to include background information on your work. Briefly outline your mission, programs, budget, and sources of revenue, including other foundation supporters. *Request the grantmaker's guidelines and annual report, including a list of recent grantees.* You'll find a sample query from Native Seeds/SEARCH on the opposite page. Notice that this letter has been formatted for mail-merge. We often sent ten or twenty of these letters at a time, depending upon how many prospects we found at the library.

In my experience, about 80% of grantmakers will respond, although some require a reminder letter. Their responses range from polite, one-paragraph notes ("Sorry, we do not publish our guidelines") to glossy, full-color annual reports. Occasionally you will be turned down on the basis of your query letter, even though you have not explicitly asked for money. This is one of the benefits of including information about your organization in the query: if you're going to face rejection anyway, be grateful you didn't go to the trouble of preparing a full proposal.

Read these materials carefully. Get out your highlighter or red pen and mark them up. Compare the foundation-produced materials with whatever data you've gathered from the library directories, and note any important discrepancies, such as changes in deadlines, program focus, or grant amounts. Once you've read and digested the guidelines and reviewed the list of grantees, write down any questions that aren't answered in the written materials. This is a good time to create prospect files for all promising grantmakers — include their guidelines, annual reports, and any relevant research data gathered from the library.

Now try to match your programs and projects with the funder's interests. Pam Rogers' comment, which opens this chapter, offers a wonderful insight into the matching process. If you think you've got a viable match, or if you want your questions answered, *pick up the phone.* As Dan Petegorsky, formerly of the Peace Development Fund, now with the Western States Center, says,

Native Seeds • SEARCH

2509 N. Campbell Ave. #325
Tucson, AZ 85719
520/327-9123
FAX: 520/327-5821

«date»

«nametitle»
«foundation»
«street»
«citystatezip»

RE: Request for current proposal guidelines and annual report

Dear «salutation»,

Native Seeds/SEARCH is a nonprofit conservation organization based in Tucson, Arizona, with a field office in Albuquerque, New Mexico. Founded in 1983, NS/S seeks to conserve traditional Native American crop varieties of the southwestern U.S. and northern Mexico, as well as their wild relatives. We also work to preserve and revive what remains of the ancient traditions of southwestern agriculture by distributing seeds to gardeners, family farmers, researchers, and especially Native Americans.

Our seed bank now contains more than 1300 varieties, many of them rare or endangered. These crops have adapted to the most difficult growing conditions and are often resistant to pests, disease and drought. They provide an irreplaceable "genetic library" to help ensure sustainable, environmentally safe agriculture in the future.

Roughly 40% of our budget comes from distribution of seeds, native crafts, and books. An additional 25% is raised through membership dues, donations, and events. Past grant support has been provided by the CS Fund, Educational Foundation of America, Wallace Genetic Foundation, Tucson and Albuquerque Community Foundations, and other sources. One of our founders (and current board president), Gary Paul Nabhan, has received fellowships from the MacArthur Foundation and the Pew Environmental Scholars Program.

We are now updating our files and would like current information on your giving program. *Please send us guidelines for proposals and a copy of your most recent annual report, including a grants list.* Thank you.

Sincerely,

Andy Robinson
Development Director

A non-profit organization working to conserve traditional crops, seeds, and farming methods that have sustained native peoples throughout the Greater Southwest.

Don't send a cold proposal. Call and have a conversation first; it's an invaluable way to start the process. Nothing substitutes for verbal communication. Establishing a person-to-person relationship before submitting a proposal is very important.

Dan's colleague Rose Sackey-Milligan, who works at the Peace Development Fund's east coast office, says simply, "Please call to speak to a program officer before submitting a proposal." Jon Jensen of the George Gund Foundation agrees:

> Call foundation staff and tell them what you're doing. Give them a quick, simple description of your project — no more than 90 seconds — then ask your questions. I can think of a number of proposals I would have declined to support without first having had a phone conversation and forming a positive opinion about the person on the other end of the line.

If you're like me, sometimes you're afflicted with phone phobia. "I don't want to pester them," I'll say to myself, feeling meek. "I'll just ask a lot of stupid questions. Besides, my proposal is really marginal." To be honest, I often gave in to this urge — perhaps one-quarter of the successful proposals I've written were submitted without any prior phone calls or personal contact. But I can also testify that the personal touch makes a big difference. Conquer your phone phobia and make that call. Listen to Dan Petegorsky:

> Do not be deterred or embarrassed about calling up and asking for advice. I'm not doing anybody any favors by telling them how to get money from us — that's my job.

Foundation staff are terrific sources of information. They can help you interpret their guidelines, tell you how best to pitch your project and, if it's a poor fit, they might recommend other sources of funding. Best of all, they can guide you through the peculiarities of the grants process, as described by Jon Jensen:

> If you get me on the phone you get five times as much information as we list in our guidelines. This is by design; we want to be responsive, not prescriptive. My job is to demystify the process — I tell you everything I can at every stage of the game. I can also help you identify the strengths and weaknesses of your proposal and the obstacles you'll need to overcome if you want to get funded.

Once you get into the habit of making these calls, you will send out fewer long-shot proposals and your success rate will improve. Jon Jensen expands upon this theme in his essay, "Foundation Leadership," which appears in *Environmental Leadership* (Island Press, 1993):

> Foundation-wise applicants know how to time the asking of the key question: "What are our chances of getting a grant?" It is often an unasked question because the applicant doesn't want to hear the answer. If asked at the appropriate time, however, this question can save the grantseeker a great deal of time, labor, and anxiety.

Now that you're eager to pick up the telephone, *be aware that some funders discourage phone calls.* If you're not sure whether to call, read their written materials and re-check the information you've gleaned from the grants directories. If you don't see the words, "no phone calls, please," make the call.

Once you've mastered the telephone, the next step is the *site visit.* The term "site visit" generally refers to a meeting with foundation officers at your facility; in most cases, this happens after you submit a proposal. Here, however, allow me to broaden the term to include any kind of face-to-face contact between funder and grantseeker.

The value of these contacts should not be underestimated. In their evaluation guide, *What is Good Grantmaking for Social Justice?*, the National Network of Grantmakers Philanthropic Reform Committee acknowledges the importance of face-to-face interaction. "Personal meetings with foundation staff (or trustees, if acting as staff) are critical," they write. "Grantseekers who get to present their case personally have a far better chance of obtaining funds than those who do not."

When asked for the most important piece of advice she could give grantseekers, Charlotte Talberth of the Max and Anna Levinson Foundation responds, "Try to meet the funder in person." John Tirman of the Winston Foundation for World Peace takes this advice a step further:

> Get an interview with the funder. Making the call in person is infinitely better than sending in a proposal. Budget in trips to New York City and other funding centers.

So how can you personally introduce yourself, and your organization, to grantmakers? Here are a few suggestions.

1. **MEET THEM AT THE FOUNDATION OFFICE.** The simplest solution is to call and, after you've described your project and gauged their interest, request a meeting. Prior to your call, however, you should read the guidelines and assess your likelihood of getting a grant. No grants officer will choose to meet with you if your work is completely outside the foundation's area of interest, so do your homework first.

2. **ATTEND "MEET THE GRANTMAKER" EVENTS.** A number of community foundations and nonprofit resource centers host "meet the grantmakers" workshops, which include panel discussions, questions from the audience, and opportunities for grantseekers to meet foundation and corporate philanthropy staff. Check with your local community foundation, United Way, Foundation Center library collection, volunteer center, or other community service centers to learn if something similar is offered in your area.

3. **ATTEND GRANTMAKER-SPONSORED EVENTS.** Some foundations designate a special day to meet the grantseekers. One of these events is described by Linda Reymers of the McKenzie River Gathering:

We have a Presentation Day which caps each grant-making cycle. We believe that the opportunity for groups that have been screened in as finalists to address all of the decision makers is fundamental to the process.... The ability to make their case in person often expresses the compelling nature of their work better than their written words.

If you're invited to participate in such an event, make it a priority to attend.

4. **GO TO CONFERENCES.** Hang out where the funders meet and shake as many hands as you can. For example, the National Network of Grantmakers (NNG) and the Environmental Grantmakers Association (EGA) both hold annual conferences for member foundations. NNG invites a limited number of social change organizations in the host region to participate in their conference. EGA, on the other hand, restricts attendance to grants officers.

If you can get in, events like these provide good opportunities to meet foundation staff. Unfortunately, most conferees go home with a bad case of information overload, and names and faces tend to blur together. A one-on-one meeting, without all the distractions of a conference, is probably more effective.

5. **INVITE GRANTS OFFICERS TO VISIT YOUR FACILITY.** This is the traditional "site visit," which typically occurs after you have submitted a proposal. These meetings are often initiated by foundation staff: "Your group has been chosen as a finalist for our next grant round, and we would like to come out to meet with you to discuss the project." However, there is no reason why you can't initiate contact and invite the grantmaker to tour your facility. Nearly all the cover letters I've ever written end with the phrase, "If you need more information, or would like to arrange a site visit, please contact me." Sometimes I would follow the letter with a phone call to personally repeat the invitation.

If your group is selected for a site visit, consider the following points of etiquette:

◆ **ENERGIZE YOUR WORKPLACE.** Nobody wants to give money to a comatose organization. Drummond Pike, in his article "How Foundations Decide Who Gets Their Money" (*Whole Earth Review*, Summer 1988), calls this, "The Smelling-and-Listening-and-Looking Test." He writes,

> Try to go see the people in their place of business. Find out if the phones ring, if people talk and smile at one another, and if the place smells busy. See if they talk TO you or AT you. And find out if they can make you a cup of coffee or tea; if not, you might wonder how much time people really spend there.

While you're warming up the coffee pot, you might get out the broom and mop and clean the office.

◆ **GIVE YOUR BEST SHOW AND TELL.** At Native Seeds/SEARCH, we always joked that if we could just get foundation staff into our seed bank, they would fund our proposals. Why? The seed bank is a stimulating place, filled with beautiful crops, pungent smells, and lots of interesting textures. Spend a few minutes among the jars of beans, ears of multi-colored corn, chiles tied into *ristras*, and dried gourds hanging from the ceiling, and the connections between genetic and cultural diversity become abundantly clear. For people besieged with paper, direct sensory experience is a treat. It helps them understand your mission on an instinctive, emotional level.

Think about how you can best present the emotional side of your organization. If you run a clinic, a pre-school, or a shelter, give funders a chance to tour the facility and talk with the clients. If you sponsor a community garden, don't meet in the office — go to the garden. If you're launching a capital campaign for a new building, go out to the site, unroll the blueprints, and walk around — "The front door will be here with a view of the mountains to the north, the nursery will be over here..." In other words, take your ideas — which have been thoughtfully laid out in your proposal — and make them tangible.

◆ **INVITE FUNDERS TO OBSERVE YOUR GROUP IN ACTION.** Encourage grantmakers to attend your next public event — rally, performance, news conference, voter education workshop. You can also (if you dare) invite funders to attend internal meetings or strategy sessions. Here's an anecdote from Charlotte Talberth:

> My most useful experience of the year was going uninvited to a meeting, which turned out to be for members only, of the Southwest Network for Environmental and Economic Justice. Because I'd come a long way, they let me stay. There were about 150 activists present and I learned a tremendous amount. Including funders at activist meetings can be a good idea.

The advantage of this arrangement is that it helps to break down the "we" and "they" barriers between grantee and grantor. On the other hand, the presence of funders will change the dynamic of the meeting and may dampen some people's desire to be fully honest or outspoken. It's also possible that grantmakers will try to change the agenda or participate in other inappropriate ways.

◆ **IF YOU NEED TO RESCHEDULE THE MEETING, GIVE YOUR VISITORS PLENTY OF WARNING.** Lynn Gisi, formerly of the Needmor Fund, tells this instructive story:

> We site visit each organization before awarding a grant. Once, we flew several thousand miles and drove several hundred more to visit an organization which, when we arrived, announced they were withdrawing their proposal. Agghh! A simple phone call would have been appreciated.

DEVELOPING RELATIONSHIPS WITH FOUNDATION OFFICERS

If you want to raise money through grant proposals, one of the most important things you can do is develop strong, peer-to-peer relationships with the decision makers. The value of relationships is stressed in the National Network of Grantmaker's booklet, *What is Good Grantmaking for Social Justice?:*

> While it is less of a "good old boys" network, grantmaking is still conducted primarily within a "closed" community to which few grantseekers have access.... "Who knows whom" is still the operative question in determining likely success in raising money for an organization or project.... If we are genuinely interested in redistribution of resources and systemic change, we must examine how accessible our institutions are.

The old fundraiser's cliche, "People give money to people, not organizations," is also relevant to the grantmaking world. One of the proposals featured in Chapter 7, the Sea Islands Land Retention Project, was funded, in part, because of the mutual respect between grantmaker and grantee. Judy Austermiller of the Boehm Foundation tells the story this way:

> Nina Morais, the author and project developer, convinced me to meet with her, having been recommended by a colleague. We made a $5,000 seed grant. The key was Nina Morais herself — an impressive woman. In the end, we fund not just good plans or ideas, but people who we "bet" have the skill and drive and commitment to carry the plans off.

Here are a few guidelines for creating healthy, productive relationships with the funding world.

1. **ALL GRANTMAKERS ARE UNIQUE.** As Jon Jensen says, "Every foundation is different. Treat them like different people. It's not a standard process." Indeed, most foundations are guided by several individuals, each with their own interests, priorities, peculiarities, and relative degrees of power over grantmaking decisions.

2. **TREAT FOUNDATION OFFICERS AS PEERS.** This can be difficult to do, given the basic power inequities in the relationship. However, I've found that most funders want to be addressed as equals. Gayle Rothrock of the Northwest Fund for the Environment warns against "written fawning or overt flattery." When asked what annoys him, Martin Teitel says,

> People who use drippy, obsequious, beseeching language as if they are Mozart and I am the Duke of Salzburg. A little dignity looks good in a proposal!

Marjorie Fine of the Unitarian Universalist Veatch Program at Shelter Rock says point-blank, "Don't suck up to grantmakers. On the other hand, don't be impolite. Grantmakers each have their own points of view — don't treat them like blank slates."

3. **YOU'RE HUMAN, SO ADMIT IT.** Treating foundation officers as peers means acknowledging your discomfort and mistakes. You should present your organization in the best possible light, but it's also important to tell the truth about your errors and the obstacles you face. Diane Ives offers an anecdote:

We got a proposal from someone I had met informally a couple of times, and she sent the package to "Susan Ives." Her handwritten note said, "Susan, I will call to discuss this." She never called. After six weeks of waiting, I finally phoned her to discuss the proposal. She said, "I was so mortified that we had gotten the wrong name that I was too embarrassed to call." Instead of following through on her note, and admitting that she used the wrong name — which is no big deal — she froze.

4. **BE PROFESSIONAL.** Professionalism begins with homework; do the most thorough and accurate job you can. At a basic level, this means proofreading your letters and proposals, spelling names correctly, keeping track of who works at which foundation, and so forth. For an example of how *not* to be professional, listen to Quincey Tompkins Imhoff:

Our foundation used to be named Ira-Hiti (a Native American word). It was changed two years ago, yet we still get mail addressed to Mr. Ira Hiti: "Dear Mr. Hiti...."

Professionalism also means treating everyone with courtesy, regardless of their job title or status. As Marjorie Fine says,

Be very respectful to administrative staff — they're not just secretarial cardboard. I understand the frustration with the concept of gatekeepers, but if you get to know the administrative people well, a lot of doors will open for you.

Professionals accept defeat gracefully and move on to the next funder or the next proposal. In researching this book, I was amazed to learn that, upon receiving a rejection letter, some people actually dump their frustration on foundation staff. Ellen Furnari tells this story:

I welcome people calling to ask about their proposals, but sometimes they're angry and nasty. And I wonder, do they think this will help? You don't want a grantmaker to think you're desperate.

Complaining is a big strategic mistake, since you might want to approach the same funder in the future. There's no advantage to burning your bridges behind you. As John Tirman says, "Whining about not getting a grant almost ensures you won't be considered seriously the next time."

Assuming you can maintain your composure, it's acceptable to call the foundation and ask why your proposal wasn't approved. (Unless, of course, they don't have a listed phone number or they specifically discourage phone calls.) It's much easier to do this, and maintain a friendly tone of voice, if you've had previous contact with the foundation officer. You might even receive some encouragement. As Cinthia Schuman of the Rockefeller Family Fund says,

Our foundation has funded organizations we previously rejected. While I don't recommend coming back on a regular basis, if you feel it was a close call, it can be useful to check in every year or so.

Foundation officers can also suggest other prospects. Jon Jensen recommends:

Ask foundation staff about other potential funders. Many will give you names, especially if they've said no to your proposal. They might feel guilty and want to do something to help you.

THE PRE-PROPOSAL LETTER (LETTER OF INTENT)

More and more funders now insist that you send a brief letter — usually a page or two — before you submit a proposal. This "letter of intent" gives them an opportunity to screen applicants without handling large volumes of paper. If the letter grabs their attention, they can request a full proposal or even a site visit.

Edith Eddy of the Compton Foundation suggests that you send a letter first, even if it's not required.

> Something that more people should do, and almost no one does, is to write a two or three pager outlining your project. Then follow up a week or two later with a phone call and find out how well you fit.

Your job, when writing a pre-proposal letter, is to condense your proposal to the required length. Describe the problem, your qualifications for dealing with it, and your plan of action. This may seem difficult, but it's a terrific exercise in organizing. If you can't effectively outline your project in a page or two (see Chapter 4), you need to rethink the project.

Some funders, like the Turner Foundation, now request a three-page proposal — period. According to Peter Bahouth, they do this, in part, "because it indicates your ability to get your issue across to the general public." Given our universal need for community support, and the intense competition for public attention, this seems to me a very sensible approach.

Here's an example of a pre-proposal letter for the Traditional Native American Farmers Association (TNAFA), which began as a Native Seeds/SEARCH project and is now sponsored by the Seventh Generation Fund.

Details make this an effective letter. In just a few pages the reader knows why this group was formed, what problems they are working to address, their goals, how many people are involved, and what they've accomplished so far.

Unfortunately, the letter doesn't include much of a work plan. How — specifically — does TNAFA propose to spend the money? The reader can only guess. Because of space limits, we chose to highlight the past and present, hint at the future, and hope that the grantmaker would be interested enough to ask for more information. In this case, the strategy worked — the foundation requested a full proposal, which contained a detailed work plan and budget for the coming year.

DONOR-DIRECTED GRANTS

A number of foundations, especially community foundations, manage "donor-directed funds." These are separate accounts set up by individuals who channel their money through the foundation to charities of their choice. Foundation staff sort through incoming proposals and serve as

Native Seeds • SEARCH

2509 N. Campbell Ave. #325
Tucson, AZ 85719
520/327-9123
FAX: 520/327-5821

July 26, 1995

Michele Lord
Norman Foundation
147 East 48th Street
New York, NY 10017

Dear Ms. Lord:

Native Seeds/SEARCH (NS/S) works to conserve the traditional crops, seeds, and farming methods that have sustained native peoples through the southwestern U.S. and northern Mexico. We promote the use of these ancient crops and their wild relatives by gathering, safeguarding, and distributing their seeds, while sharing benefits with traditional communities. Through research, training, and community education, NS/S works to protect biodiversity and celebrate cultural diversity.

NS/S was founded in 1983 as a result of requests from Native Americans on the Tohono O'odham reservation near Tucson, who wished to grow traditional crops but could not locate seeds. Since that time, we have grown to become a regional seed bank with offices in Tucson and Albuquerque.

We seek $10,000 from the Norman Foundation in support of the Traditional Native American Farmers Association. Farmers are a stabilizing force in many Native American communities. They conserve historic seeds adapted to local conditions, keep alive traditional agricultural and land stewardship practices, provide corn and other crops for ceremonies, and feed extended families from their fields. Unfortunately, it's becoming more and more difficult to make a living as a farmer.

In 1991, Native Seeds/SEARCH conducted a survey of 62 Native American farm families in Arizona and New Mexico. Native farmers face the usual problems of water quality, erosion, pest and weed control, but also face a lack of community support. In 1992, NS/S organized a conference for survey participants in Gallup, New Mexico. Everyone present was enthusiastic about the prospect of working together to solve common problems. By unanimous consent, they agreed to form the Traditional Native American Farmers Association (TNAFA). The participants asked NS/S to assist with grantwriting and financial management. The plan calls for TNAFA to separate from NS/S in 1996 and become an independent organization.

TNAFA has an active seven member board of directors, two half-time staff persons, and has held subsequent annual conferences at Camp Verde (1993) and Santa Fe (1994). TNAFA now includes 50 farming families from 18 tribes in New Mexico and Arizona.

A non-profit organization working to conserve traditional crops, seeds, and farming methods that have sustained native peoples throughout the Greater Southwest.

At the 1994 conference, participants defined goals for eleven program areas, including planting, pest control, equipment, harvesting, water, idle land, outside resources, education, youth awareness, family, and community. In the past year staff:

◆ developed an information packet to recruit new members and spoke with more than 50 families;

◆ located technical advisors to provide hands-on training in organic farming and certification, natural pest equipment maintenance, land preparation, greenhouses, and other topics;

◆ identified potential markets for crops — specific restaurants and grocery stores — and talked with buyers;

◆ networked with other farm organizations;

◆ received TV coverage on the nationally-syndicated PBS program, "The New Garden."

A new feature of TNAFA is the Tesuque Land Reclamation Project at Tesuque Pueblo, New Mexico. Through this demonstration project, TNAFA staff and volunteers are reclaiming and planting an acre of vacant tribal land, using a combination of techniques from permaculture and traditional agriculture. Permaculture is a garden and landscape design system that stresses water harvesting, erosion control, use of beneficial insects, local crop varieties, and the sustainable harvest of fruits and vegetables throughout the year. Permaculture promotes a healthy, diverse environment and economic self-sufficiency, and complements traditional agricultural practices.

This project serves as a training ground for local youth and farmers, provides a site for regional workshops, and offers opportunities for adapting traditional agricultural techniques to modern technology and life.

With your help, more Native American farmers and gardeners, both young and old, will get the technical assistance needed to maintain their traditions and earn a living by farming their land. TNAFA is also the perfect vehicle for disseminating the information and techniques learned at Tesuque to Native Americans across the southwest.

If you'd like to review a full proposal or have any questions, please contact me at 520/327-9123 or Clayton Brascoupé, TNAFA agricultural advisor, at PO Box 170, Tesuque NM 87574, 505/983-4047. Thanks!

Sincerely,

Angelo Joaquin, Jr.
Executive Director

matchmakers between community organizations and philanthropists by presenting proposals they think will interest specific donors. The foundation also administers the grants and, in some cases, provides a degree of anonymity to the donors.

In general, it's best to stay out of the way and let foundation staff do their jobs. If you know the donor personally or have a good letter of reference, however, you can involve yourself in a more active way. This process is similar to cultivating a major donor, except that you are unlikely to have any direct contact with the prospect. Here's how to proceed.

1. **REVIEW THE ANNUAL REPORTS OF THE COMMUNITY-BASED FOUNDATIONS OPERATING IN YOUR AREA.** These reports should include lists of all (non-anonymous) donor-directed funds, and may also indicate their areas of interest. Share these names with your board members, major donors, and other foundation supporters, and ask them to identify any people they know.

2. **ADD THESE PROSPECTS TO YOUR MAILING LIST.** If you can't locate a home address, use the community foundation address. Send a brief letter — if possible, signed by the person who knows the prospect — introducing the organization.

3. **MAKE AN APPOINTMENT TO TALK WITH COMMUNITY FOUNDATION STAFF** long before the grant deadline. Describe your work, request their opinions about its fundability, and ask them to try to make a match once the proposal is submitted. It's appropriate to mention any relationship or contact you have with a specific donor, but *do not* ask for donor names or addresses at this time.

4. **WHEN THE DEADLINE NEARS, SEND THE PROPOSAL TO THE FOUNDATION.**

5. **IF YOU RECEIVE THE GRANT, SEND THANK YOU LETTERS TO BOTH THE FOUNDATION AND THE DONOR.** This is the time to ask foundation staff for the contributor's name, address, and phone. If they won't release this information, send your correspondence care of the foundation. In either case, make sure that the donor receives your newsletter and is invited to any special events you host.

Be succinct and to the point. 99.9% of the pro-posals we receive are good and valuable. We want to know — quickly — why your work meets our criteria in a concrete and specific way.

— Kelly Brown, Vanguard Public Foundation

When I'm going through a stack of proposals, I naturally gravitate to the ones that look like they won't give me a headache.

— Dan Petegorsky, formerly of the
Peace Development Fund

Building Your Proposal, Piece by Piece

My friend Charles Geoffrion has served for several years as a grants panelist for a regional foundation. Every grants cycle — about twice each year — he comes home with a twenty-pound box of proposals. He clears off his dining room table, grabs a cup of coffee (or maybe a beer, depending upon his mood), and makes a first pass through the stack, spending a minute or two with each application. In the process, he sorts them into three piles.

1. **THE "LIKELY" PILE.** These grant proposals are, at a glance, well organized and cleanly laid out, with wide margins and lots of white space. Something on the first page — the project title, the group, the name of a board member, a sentence or two in the executive summary — grabs his attention. The main goal is clearly and effectively stated.

   Most of these projects will eventually get funded because a) a positive first impression naturally leads to a more generous and careful reading of the proposal, and b) Charles will read this stack first, before he gets tired and irritable. Your goal as a grantwriter: steer your proposal into this pile.

2. **THE "MAYBE" PILE.** These evoke mixed reactions. Perhaps Charles knows and admires the work of the group, but finds the proposal to be poorly organized. Maybe the idea presented has merit, but there's no work plan showing how the idea will be implemented. Perhaps the budget is out of proportion with the proposed activities. A few of these proposals will be moved to the likely pile after a more thorough reading, but most will be turned down despite their strengths. The simple reason: when there are lots of worthy projects and not enough money to go around, grant reviewers start looking for reasons to say no.

3. The "forget it" pile. These proposals may be printed in tiny type on crinkled paper and accented with coffee stains. Or the pages aren't numbered, so the sequence isn't clear. Or the authors have disregarded all instructions about format and page limits, and included scrapbooks filled with old news articles, love letters, and multiple revisions of the organizational bylaws.

If you think I'm exaggerating, listen to Charles:

> I'll never forget the kindergarten school that submitted a five-page proposal on day-glo colored paper from the children's art supply. Each page radiated a different color as if it glowed from radioactivity. It was impossible to read the type against the bright, almost repulsive colors.... I'm sure the teacher who prepared this proposal thought it was "cute"!

After spending a few minutes fighting his way through these applications, he can't figure out what these groups do all day. He will give this stack of proposals a second look later on, but without much enthusiasm. If your proposal ends up in this pile, you can forget your hopes for funding.

I tell this story to illustrate several points. Number one, first impressions count. Number two, the way a grant proposal looks is nearly as important as what it says. Number three, grant reviewers face the usual human limits of stamina and concentration; do what you can to help them out.

Before we review the components of a successful proposal, let's consider the basic building blocks: words and layout.

WRESTLING WITH WORDS

When it's time to put words on paper, or type them onto the computer screen, most of us freeze up. Somewhere back in grammar school we learned that the written language is supposed to be formal and proper, and consequently we can't, or won't, write the way we speak. We haul out the big words and try to impress the reader with our vocabulary. We use lots of jargon and technical terms. We create elaborate sentences that are hard to read and even harder to understand.

I once asked a student of mine to describe her group's mission. She said, "Intervention for case management."

"Excuse me?"

"We work with disabled children and teach them how to use their bodies."

Can you see the difference? The first sentence sounds impressive but means nothing. The second sentence paints a picture using simple, clear words. After enduring my criticism with a smile, she wrote a marvelous mission statement describing what it was like to watch a 2-year-old pick up a ball and hold it in her hands for the first time. The class was practically in tears. We were all reaching for our checkbooks.

The voices of your constituents — the people who benefit from your work

— can make your grant application more informal and increase its emotional appeal. Nothing involves the reader like a good story or a compelling quote (but make sure to get permission before you use other people's words; most folks are flattered to be asked). As Pam Rogers of the Haymarket People's Fund says,

> Let your constituents speak. They speak from the heart. Their stories are moving.... You can do this in a way that does not exploit people's pain or their situation.

For an example of how to use quotations, take a look at the Mono Lake Committee proposal that begins on page 125.

Among foundation officers, there are two distinct schools of thought about the importance of good writing. One group stresses the need to do things right; their perspective is best summed up by John Powers of the Educational Foundation of America:

> Every contact you have with a foundation is a window through which your work will be seen. It is important to be accurate, thorough, and prompt. Sloppiness in spelling, grammar, typos, style, and jargon will lead the reader (funder) to infer that the organization is sloppy and possibly ineffective in its work.

If my survey is any indication, foundation staff are besieged with unfocused, overly long proposals. It's no surprise, as Katrin Verclas of the Ottinger Foundation says, that they appreciate "brevity and clarity." The Compton Foundation's Edith Eddy says,

> What really annoys me is people who send us volumes of materials when, as an environmental funder, we ourselves are doing everything we can to conserve paper. Keep it simple, keep it short.

Some, like Nanette Silva of the Chicago Foundation for Women, address this same problem from the positive side. When asked what grabs her attention in a proposal, she says, "Succinct, organized writing style. We want to be able to look at a proposal and figure out very quickly what you are asking for."

Other grantmakers, however, are less interested in your writing skills. Diane Ives of the Beldon Fund admits, "Quite frankly, the proposal is the least important part.... It's the whole relationship process, building a relationship with the foundation."

Barbara Meyer of the Bert and Mary Meyer Foundation takes this idea even further.

> For us, the proposal is only a small piece. Sometimes we get really unclear or unfocused proposals, because people are so busy carrying out their program that they don't stop long enough to think through the process of articulating what it is they do. When we visit, we discover the group and their work is outstanding. So we take the proposal lightly.... [What really annoys me is] a very polished presentation from a paid grants writer with a lot of statistics and quotes from books, instead of the real experience of the people who are having the problem.

I once travelled all the way to New York to present a proposal I had written, only to run into this obstacle. The grants officer was extremely interested — she talked with me for an hour and asked several perceptive questions — but felt that the proposal was too well-written. She needed to get past the mouthpiece (me) and deal directly with the people who were running the project. Several months later she went to New Mexico to meet the leadership, a group of Native American farmers, and eventually funded the organization.

Martin Teitel of the CS Fund offers the following words of hope to proposal novices and people who just don't like to write:

> The philanthropist Irwin Sweeney Miller once admonished his fellow funders not to become "connoisseurs of proposals." If we do our job well, we can see through the deathless prose and find the hard work and community behind it. Some great folks doing wonderful work may not be as articulate as some slick people with no special project who went to proposal writing school. While proposals are indeed our medium of communication, the important thing is the good work, and letting the passion and commitment shine through. We'll take care of the rest.

Enjoy these words of encouragement, but don't use them as an excuse to slap something together at the last minute. A thoughtful, well-written proposal will improve your odds of getting funded. In a crowded field, you want your organization to stand out, and the written word is one of the best tools available. Use it. Without getting too fancy, write the cleanest, sharpest prose that you can. Whack the reader on the nose with clear, direct language.

LAYOUT: EASY ON THE EYEBALLS

The basic principles of layout can be summed up with the cliche, "less is more." In general:

◆ The less type on the page, the easier it is to read.

◆ The less clutter on the page, the easier it is to understand.

Dan Petegorsky sums up the most common layout problems: "Bad copies, faint typewriter ribbons, proposals with tiny type, words running to the edge of the paper. If you can't read it, you can't get it."

You don't need to be a graphic artist to create an attractive proposal. Just keep in mind the following points:

1. **FOLLOW THE GUIDELINES.** Forgive me for repeating myself, but you need to request, read, understand, and follow the application guidelines, which vary from grantmaker to grantmaker. Many foundations publish specific instructions, including the length and format of proposals. Some foundations and corporations — and virtually all government agencies — require you to fill out forms, or request that you use their outline in presenting your proposal.

Honor their rules; *do not* submit your standard proposal and assume they will adapt. Steve Starkey of the Wisconsin Community Fund tells a typical story: "Many groups have sent in applications without a budget, without a narrative, sent only one copy when 15 are requested, etc." Amazing as it seems, you'll get lots of credit for simply following directions.

My experience has been that most foundation staff are very helpful and will try to accommodate you *within their guidelines.* A number of foundations, especially those affiliated with the National Network of Grantmakers, are moving toward acceptance of a common application form, which will make life easier for all of us grantseekers. (About 30 foundations now accept the NNG application — for a directory, see Grantmaker Affinity Groups in the Bibliography.) Unfortunately, the era of "prepare-one-application-and-submit-it-to-everyone" is still a long way off, so please do your homework.

2. **LEAVE LOTS OF WHITE SPACE.** Leave margins of at least one inch on all sides of the page; a bit more is helpful. It's okay to make the text single spaced, but if you do, add an extra space between paragraphs. All the proposals featured in the next chapter use this format.

3. **USE 12-POINT (OR LARGER) TYPE.** Twelve-point type is the standard size for most computer fonts. Do not switch to smaller type face to squeeze more words onto the page — figure out a way to tell your story with fewer words.

4. **USE RUNNING HEADS, NOT JUST PAGE NUMBERS.** A running head is a word or phrase that appears on the top of each page; it can include the page number and an identifying phrase. (Look at the top of this page.) This is a courtesy to the reader and a big help to the photocopy staff at the foundation office. All word processing programs can create running heads for you.

5. **BREAK UP THE PAGE.** Nothing tires the eyes more than repetition. If your pages all look the same, the reader's eyes start to wander, and his or her mind won't be far behind.

Use *bold text, underlining, italic text, bullets, lists, and indented paragraphs* to build some visual variety into your pages. These techniques, used judiciously, also guide the reader through your grant application, highlighting the most important points. For a fine example, see the Heartwood proposal that begins on page 113.

As you use these techniques, be selective. Dan Petegorsky warns us about "bullet abuse":

> Some people don't make enough use of bold face and underlining to prioritize, or else they overuse these tools. When the whole proposal is presented in bullets, I don't know what's important. I can't understand the flow of strategy.

6. **DON'T JUSTIFY THE TEXT.** "Justification" means that the words line up on both sides of the page. This works fine in narrow columns, like a news-

---

*W*hen you write your proposal:

- ◆ It's okay to use an informal, we're-all-in-this-together tone. Think of the reader as an interested friend.

- ◆ Avoid jargon and fancy language. Keep it simple.

- ◆ Write the way you speak. If you're having trouble, try talking into a tape recorder, then transcribe and edit your words. If tape recorders make you uncomfortable, ask a friend to write down your spoken words. If you can talk, you can write.

- ◆ Ask a co-worker or friend who writes well to read your proposal and make sure that it's clear and concise.

THE INTERNATIONAL

SHADOW PROJECT

1985

Community
Alliance *with*
Family
Farmers
foundation

page 4

paper, but it's harder to read across the width of a standard page. Leave the right side of your text "ragged."

7. USE GRAPHICS WHERE APPROPRIATE. Some information just can't be reduced to words, or is better presented in other ways. In these situations, graphs, charts, maps and even artwork can be incorporated directly into the proposal.

In 1985, I helped organize the International Shadow Project to commemorate the 40th anniversary of the bombing of Hiroshima. Artists and activists painted their silhouettes on sidewalks and streets around the world in memory of atomic bomb victims who had been vaporized, leaving only their "shadows" behind. Our logo was based on one of these painted shadows: a ghostly silhouette running up a stairway, arms outstretched. As you can imagine, we worked this image into everything we created, including our grant proposals.

There are dozens of computer programs available to help you create graphics, and the most popular operating systems allow you to "paste" these design elements right into your proposal. In the example below, the Community Alliance with Family Farmers Foundation (CAFF) uses a map to show the scope of their farm outreach program. Note the unique design of their running head. Because this proposal looks both professional and a little different, it should catch the eye of a grant reviewer.

These monthly Lighthouse meetings provide a support network for over 500 farmers and other agricultural professionals. Activities of the Network include farm tours and field days, an annual state-wide meeting, technical presentations and focused discussion about specific production problems faced by practitioners of ecological farming. These activities are coordinated by five field organizers (one full-time and four part-time) with the active support of volunteer regional steering committees. There is substantial participation in every area by local University extension agents.

LFN's one page, monthly *Foghorn* (Attachment 1) recaps the events and discussions within the eleven chapters and is mailed free to all participants. In addition to sharing technical information, *Foghorn* gives Lighthouse members the feeling of participating in a significant and growing movement.

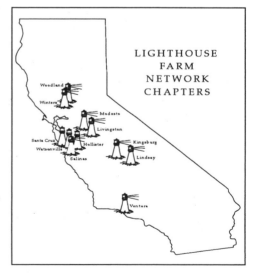

The Lighthouse Farm Network provides policymakers, the media, researchers and conventional farmers with highly visible examples of both the process and the benefits of biologically based farming. The LFN has hosted tours for top California and U.S. public agency officials, and environmental organizations use Lighthouse Farms as living proof that pesticide reduction is practical and economically viable. CNN, Frontline, the *LA Times*, Canadian Broadcasting Service, Irish Public Television and many agricultural industry magazines have featured Lighthouse farmers (Attachment 2).

8. **PRINT YOUR PROPOSAL ON STANDARD 8-1/2 BY 11 INCH PAPER.** Stick with white or off-white paper; several funders now ask you to use recycled stock. Laser or ink jet printers are best because they produce the cleanest, darkest type. If you don't have access to a high-quality printer, many photocopy shops will rent you time on theirs; they generally charge by the page.

9. **SINGLE OR DOUBLE-SIDED?** It's becoming more acceptable to print your proposals on both sides of the page to save paper. In fact, some funders now specify that you do so. Read the guidelines carefully and if you're still not certain, call and ask. When in doubt, do it the old-fashioned, wasteful way: print on one side of the page.

10. **CLIP, DON'T STAPLE.** Once your proposal lands in the foundation office, it will likely be photocopied for distribution to board members or other grant reviewers. Unless given other instructions, *use a paper clip* to hold the pages together. *Do not* use staples, folders, or fancy plastic covers.

The remainder of this chapter describes the basic components of a grant proposal. The requirements for format and content will vary according to the grantmaker, so use this section as a general guide. If your prospective funder doesn't suggest a specific format, it's acceptable to combine and rearrange these sections, but make sure all this material is contained somewhere in the proposal.

> **The basic components of a grant proposal are:**
>
> Cover page and executive summary
> Organizational history
> Problem statement
> Program goals and objectives
> Strategy and implementation (methods)
> Timeline
> Evaluation
> Personnel
> Budgets
> Attachments
> Cover letter

COVER PAGE AND EXECUTIVE SUMMARY

Put this on letterhead and address the funder directly: "A proposal from the Peace and Justice League to The John Q. Public Foundation." *Do not exceed one page.* You should include:

◆ Title of the project

◆ Submission date

◆ Beginning and ending dates for the project

◆ Total project budget

◆ Amount requested

◆ Contact persons and phone numbers for your organization

◆ A brief summary, sometimes called an *executive summary*, describing the need and your proposed activities to address the need. This should not exceed two paragraphs.

Many foundations require an executive summary. As Quincey Tompkins Imhoff of the Foundation for Deep Ecology says, "This is useful whether it is requested or not. You have a *much* better chance if you can get your message across quickly. We get 700 proposals a year!"

For a fine example of a cover page and executive summary, see the Sea Islands Land Retention Project proposal on page 97. This proposal was submitted jointly by the South Carolina Coastal Conservation League, Penn Center, and the Neighborhood Legal Assistance Program.

ORGANIZATIONAL HISTORY

Describe your mission, your constituency, your goals, your accomplishments. Why do you deserve support? This is your opportunity to brag. Emphasize aspects of your work that have a direct bearing on your ability to develop and manage the proposed project. As Drummond Pike of the Tides Foundation says, "What an organization has done defines it more than what they promise to do."

In outlining the history of your group, beware of what Jon Jensen of the George Gund Foundation calls "the Dawn of Time approach, which includes five pages about the group and very little information about what they're going to do with the grant." If you can't do justice to your accomplishments in a page or two, he suggests that you include your best *brief* description in this section of the proposal, then attach an appendix outlining your track record in more detail.

As you read the following example from Washington Citizens for Recycling, notice the tone of the writing. This is one "can-do" organization. While the grant writers occasionally slip in jargon ("the public and private sector," "postconsumer content"), the writing inspires confidence.

The key here is brevity. The authors squeeze a lot of information onto one page without burying us under an avalanche of facts. We know:

◆ When the group was formed and how long they've been working on the issue.

◆ The size of their membership.

◆ Where they fit within the larger environmental movement — their niche.

◆ What they've accomplished in specific, measurable terms (note the impressive statistic about recycled oil).

◆ The breadth of their programs.

If you can cover this much ground in such a small space, you're sure to impress foundation staff and improve your odds for success.

If you're working with a new organization, you will probably have a less impressive track record to brag about. To solve this problem, you might combine your organizational history with the personnel section of the proposal and discuss the relevant experience of your leadership and project organizers. Some of their personal know-how and commitment to the cause will transfer to the group as a whole. (Of course, if the guidelines require separate sections on personnel and organizational history, follow instructions.)

Finally, a word about sequence: with some proposals, it makes more sense to go straight from the cover page into the problem statement and save the organizational history for later. The document should flow. Use your best judgment as to order.

[Washington Citizens for Recycling — *Organizational History*]

Washington is nationally recognized as one of the country's most beautiful states. Replete with lush forests and cascading mountains, Washington is filled with natural resources and rich biodiversity.

Washington Citizens for Recycling (WCFR), founded in 1972 and incorporated in 1982, was developed with the goal of preserving those resources by encouraging environmentally sustainable practices at the corporate, consumer, and government levels. WCFR is unique to the state — the only Washington nonprofit dedicated solely to the issues of resource conservation, recycling, and waste reduction. With an active membership base of 2,800 Washington citizens, WCFR has truly established itself as one of the state's premier grassroots environmental organizations.

Over the past twenty years, WCFR has helped to make Washington the nation's leading recycling state by working toward "bottle bill" initiatives promoting increased recycling collection, developing markets for recyclables, and building partnerships with local governments and other recycling organizations. Highlights of WCFR's major achievements follow:

◆ **The Waste Not Washington Act** — Passed into law in 1989, Washington Citizens for Recycling was the sponsor of this legislation to establish a statewide curbside recycling system.

◆ **Closed Loop Oil Recycling** — This campaign was initiated to increase recycling of do-it-yourself used motor oil to 65% by the year 2000. Since its inception in 1990, the program has been instrumental in establishing used motor oil collection sites and developing markets for re-refined oil products. Since the program's implementation, one million gallons of waste oil have been collected statewide that would otherwise have contaminated Washington's lakes, streams, and groundwater.

◆ **Packaging Source Reductions** — By working directly with manufacturers, WCFR is developing strategies to reduce, reuse, and eliminate excessive packaging in manufacturing and distribution. Among the companies WCFR has worked with are Derby Cycle and Sears Roebuck.

◆ **Buy Recycled Campaign** — The WCFR campaign is a grassroots effort to increase public awareness and procurement of high quality recycled products made with postconsumer content. Currently, the campaign is producing a guide to recycled product availability throughout King County, which will apply to most of Washington's urban areas.

Washington Citizens for Recycling is garnering increased support and visibility in the public and private sector with sustained project development and legislative advocacy. WCFR will continue to enjoy recognition and increased support with the next phase of the Reach for Unbleached Campaign.

PROBLEM STATEMENT (BACKGROUND OR NEEDS STATEMENT)

What's the current situation? How did it get that way? On the assumption that you are trying to solve a problem, you have to define it first. What's the relevant background on the issue, the constituency, the local scene? Why is your proposed action necessary?

It's not enough, for example, to say that your neighborhood copper miners are out of work. Give specific figures and perhaps a typical case history. Then, and only then, will your program to retrain the miners for new employment seem necessary.

Ellen Furnari, formerly of the Ben and Jerry's Foundation (in Vermont), expands upon this idea:

> Don't assume I know anything, especially when you're talking about the history of a community. We received a proposal from a group work-ing in a land grant community in New Mexico; well, we don't know about land grants here in the Northeast. I had to call and find out — which is my job — but it would be helpful if you could provide some details in your proposal.

Even if your grant isn't approved, you'll be educating foundation staff and board, and you might be laying the groundwork for future funding.

Don't wear out your welcome with too much background information. Your grant application must find a balance between describing the problem and defining the solution. Dan Petegorsky tells a typical story:

> I just reviewed 122 proposals from our youth docket, and nearly every one started with a litany of what's wrong with our society. Far fewer devoted the same amount of space to what they were doing to address these problems.

Elaine Gross of the Unitarian Universalist Veatch Program echoes the same sentiments. What really annoys her in a grant proposal? "Endless pages describing the problems of society and very little discussion of the solu-tions, and *how this particular group is important to those solutions.*"

I've emphasized part of her comment because she hints at an important idea. When writing your proposal, try to define the problem in such a way that it's clear that your group can actually do something to solve it. Shape problems into community organizing issues, then show how you will orga-nize to address them. This links your background statement to the strategy section, where you'll lay out your organizing plan.

The following example from the SouthWest Organizing Project (SWOP), based in Albuquerque, does a nice job of defining the issues. I've excerpted a portion of the problem statement, subtitled "Development, Environment, Race and Class in New Mexico."

This analysis pulls no punches. The tone is tough but factual, hard-hitting without being self-righteous. While the people who wrote this see them-selves as victims of injustice (which they document with lots of specific examples), they also project a sense of power. Things are about to change. The tone of the writing inspires confidence.

[SouthWest Organizing Project — *Problem Statement*]

New Mexico's path of development has led to economic structures and environmental degradation which most acutely affect people of color in the state.

◆ New Mexico has been a free trade zone for years. Industries come here in search of weak regulations and government enforcement capacity, to obtain enormous public subsidy, to avoid stringent regulations and enforcement, and to take advantage of an unorganized labor force. Mining and wood processing industries have historically endangered workers and communities. Modern "high tech" manufacturers — despite the "clean industry" label — pollute our groundwater and air and expose workers to the most dangerous chemicals. Hundreds of GTE/Lenkurt workers in Albuquerque were poisoned by solvents. Over 20 have died, most of them women. The plant moved to Mexico to "solve" the problem. GTE's successor company obtained a $70 million industrial revenue bond from the city of Albuquerque and then skipped town for Florida, leaving behind a major soil and groundwater contamination problem.

◆ Military facilities, such as Kirtland Air Force Base and Sandia and Los Alamos National Weapons Laboratories, pollute local environments and communities, and employ people of color in the most dangerous jobs. Uranium mining has poisoned thousands of workers and devastated Native American communities. New Mexico is now being targeted as a disposal site for the nation's nuclear waste.

◆ Infrastructure financed by taxpayers is provided at bargain rates for outside industry and the military, while the needs of working class communities are not addressed. While industries and developers in southern New Mexico obtain roads, bridges, and ports of entry to Mexico, Mesilla Valley workers live without water and sewer services. The Albuquerque South Valley is home to the City of Albuquerque sewage plant. South Valley residents who have lived here for many generations go without sewers and potable water, while Intel Corporation, twenty-five miles away in another county, has access to the plant through a "sweetheart deal" with the City.

◆ Pesticides are a constant danger to farmworkers in southern New Mexico. While the State Agriculture Department turns a blind eye, agribusinesses routinely use organo-phosphates and other chemicals which poison farmworkers and groundwater supplies of local communities, causing cancer and other preventable illnesses among many people.

◆ "Gentrification" has a long history in New Mexico. While federal agencies and private interests such as real estate developers continue the rural land grab to this day, urban Chicano communities are being displaced as well. Santa Fe has become unaffordable for Chicanos. The Las Vegas area, 60 miles northeast, is now being targeted by the same developers responsible for the gentrification of Santa Fe. Such displacement destroys communities and social and religious institutions, and amounts to cultural genocide.

◆ Pollution knows no boundaries, especially in this era of "free trade." In the Mexico-Texas-New Mexico border community of Sunland Park, New Mexico, a regional landfill adjacent to Chicano/Mexicano residential areas and elementary schools is suspected of polluting water supplies and endangering residents. Residents cite the instance of dumping at the facility of industrial wastes from Mexico.

[continued]

This is the same pattern of environmental racism and economic injustice which occurs in communities throughout the country. The human costs are high, with the greatest impacts on communities and workers of color, particularly on women, youth, and children. When affected communities organize to address such issues they are subjected to economic extortion or "jobmail." Workers in Las Vegas, New Mexico, who went on strike in 1990 for safe working conditions and higher pay at a fiberboard plant were permanently replaced — the company threatened to leave town. In exchange for a vague, non-binding commitment of 1,000 jobs, Intel Corporation has extracted hundreds of millions of dollars in tax abatements, rights to huge quantities of water, and streamlined environmental permitting from the state. Economically depressed communities and tribal and municipal governments are increasingly being offered landfills, incinerators, and nuclear waste dumps in the name of economic development.

New Mexico's path of development has remained fundamentally unchanged for 150 years. This path is not sustainable for indigenous and working people who have a long term vested interest here, nor for the fragile desert ecosystem. The challenge today is for people of color and working class people to define for ourselves, in practice and through our actions, what is in fact sustainable for us.

SWOP has chosen to itemize these particular problems because they most strongly affect the group's constituency: New Mexico's working-class Chicanos and Native Americans. In the remainder of the proposal, SWOP leadership describes, in great detail, how they plan to organize their communities around these issues. Their organizing plan — the proposed strategies, tactics, and solutions — starts with this analysis of the problem and its uncompromising tone.

The problem statement is also a good place to build some emotion into your appeal. I once heard the aphorism, "Statistics raise eyebrows but emotions raise money." Far too many grant applications are dry and intellectual. The best proposals, on the other hand, hit the reader in the head, heart, and gut at the same time. That's what I admire about the following problem statement submitted by the St. Paul Tenants Union (SPTU) to the Headwaters Fund.

When I first read this proposal I grew angry at the abuses it describes. I've read it four times and I'm *still* angry. If you can generate this much emotion in your readers, you'll make an impact.

Let's consider what makes this problem statement work.

1. **THE PROBLEM IS CLEARLY DEFINED.** Most Americans feel strongly about the presumption of innocence and equal protection under the law, at least in the abstract. By giving specific examples, this proposal develops a strong indictment of how these principles are being ignored and abused in the poorer communities of St. Paul. When a landlord can call up the police station and request criminal records on a prospective client, somebody's rights are being violated. If the police can bust down your door and then evict you because your apartment is no longer secure, something is wrong.

[St. Paul Tenants Union — *Problem Statement*]

The St. Paul Tenants Union (SPTU) has seen an increase in "hotline" calls over the past year from tenants who have been denied housing based on negative rental history reports given to prospective landlords by community based tenant screening companies. In a climate of fear and anti-crime frenzy, alliances of landlords, homeowners and the police have been forming across the Twin Cities to "keep out the undesirables" by sharing information on "problem tenants."

These reports are often based on anecdotal, incomplete, or incorrect information, and in many cases are clearly the result of racial discrimination or retaliation. Several SPTU members have found that their names appear on a database of "problem tenants" for reasons ranging from having an Unlawful Detainer (U.D., or eviction) on their records, to organizing for repairs. Many landlords, including most nonprofit housing developments, refuse to rent to a tenant who has even one U.D. on his or her record, even if the tenant prevailed in court or the case was dismissed. Mistaken identities are commonplace, since U.D.'s are filed by the tenant's name only. One tenant by the name of Fred Brown had five U.D.'s listed on his rental history report, only one of which was legitimately his...

One particular tenant screening group [is] the St. Paul Crime Prevention Coalition (SPCPC), whose sole approach to fighting crime is keeping out "problem tenants." The police provide landlords with *free* criminal history checks (by phone) on the prospective tenants. Authorization forms bearing the City's logo were being used in rental applications, asking tenants questions like, "Do you or have you ever had a case worker from a public housing agency or county human services agency?" and "Have the police ever come to your residence?" The implications of these questions are clear. Tenants who refuse to answer, or those who answer "yes", are frequently denied housing. One single parent who was trying to move to escape an abusive boyfriend was repeatedly turned down by prospective landlords because the SPCPC had reported that she had "loud children" and repeated police calls.

In a related issue, low income tenants living in substandard properties in areas with a high concentration of drug activity are increasingly at risk of being forced out of their homes through condemnation, resulting from a new City program called FORCE. This program provides for City housing inspectors to "accompany police on drug raids and *conduct code compliance inspections on the suspected drug house, and where appropriate condemn and placard the dwelling.*" (City Council Resolution) If an apartment door is broken down by police during a drug raid, *even if no drugs are found*, that unit can be condemned through FORCE because the apartment is no longer secure. Tenants are vacated, most likely losing both that month's rent and their security deposit.

SPTU has received several calls from tenants who have had to vacate on 24 hours notice, even though no evidence of illegal activity was found... [A] tenant was made homeless and subsequently hospitalized when her apartment was condemned by FORCE for alleged code violations. Gladys, the leaseholder, had called the police herself when her roommate brought home a boyfriend who was involved with drugs. She certainly had not anticipated that this call would result in losing her home.

[continued]

SPTU believes that city-sponsored programs such as FORCE deny people's civil rights, and are simply poor public policy. The police department, through FORCE and SPCPC, contributes to problems of displacement and homelessness. The Housing Information Office estimates that there are three to four hundred condemnations in St. Paul each year; at least 15% of these are estimated to be through FORCE...

SPTU has concerns that these city-sponsored programs are essentially racist. Preliminary research shows that the majority of FORCE raids have been conducted on households of color. We also suspect that a disproportionate number of free criminal history checks are being conducted on people of color, primarily black males...

Low income renters, of course, share homeowners' concerns about security and neighborhood stability. The current use of tenant screening and condemnations as "quick fix" solutions to crime, however, appears to be based on the prejudice that tenants are second class citizens, and results in further division and hostilities between rich and poor, homeowner and tenant, people of color and whites. Unless tenants are "at the table" when public policies or community based solutions to urban problems are being developed, the interests of low income people are not likely to be protected.

2. **THE ISSUES COME ALIVE THROUGH THE USE OF STORIES.** When we read about the fellow who can't rent an apartment because of mistaken identity, or the woman who calls the cops for help with a drug situation and finds herself evicted and homeless, we feel empathy for these people and want to help them. It's much more difficult to create empathy with statistics.

3. **THE PROBLEM IS BROKEN DOWN INTO ISSUES, EACH OF WHICH SUGGESTS A RANGE OF STRATEGIES AND POSSIBLE TARGETS.** These "next steps" are based upon specific information provided in the problem statement, and could include:

   ◆ Additional research to confirm the inequities associated with FORCE raids on households of color, and to measure how this program affects and increases the homeless population.

   ◆ Educating tenants about their rights, using SPTU's knowledge of the law and their research on how the law is being inequitably applied.

   ◆ Involving the news media by inviting them to cover one of the FORCE raids described above.

   ◆ Organizing against the police and city hall by protesting unfair laws and police policies addressed in the problem statement.

   ◆ Organizing against unfair landlords, using data that SPTU has collected to identify and target the worst landlords.

   ◆ Creating alternative ways to screen prospective tenants that involve low income renters, as suggested in the last paragraph of the problem statement.

Each of these strategies is discussed in greater detail later in the proposal, but the seeds are planted in the problem statement section.

What do you hope to achieve with your project? Without clear goals and definite, measurable objectives, you will have a much harder time winning grants (and knowing when your organization has achieved success).

PROGRAM GOALS AND OBJECTIVES

Goals restate the need your group seeks to address. Here's an example for the fictional Metropolis Food Bank: "We aim to end hunger in Metropolis by the year 2000." Depending on the nature of the project, your goals may be covered in your organizational history portion, but it's helpful to restate them in this section of the proposal.

Objectives are outcomes; the most clearly stated objectives can be measured: "We plan to provide food service to 5000 families this year." These should not be confused with *methods* (see the next section), which describe *how* you will meet these objectives. In the food bank example, methods could include distributing government surplus foods, gleaning crops from local farms, giving out holiday food baskets, and organizing a meals-on-wheels program.

Some grantsmanship trainers emphasize the need to describe your goals, objectives, and methods separately in your proposal, and they've created exercises and workbooks to help you sort things out. While I support this impulse in the interest of clarity, it makes me a bit nervous. I'm reminded of kids who don't want their peas and mashed potatoes to touch each other on the dinner plate. I've seen people waste a lot of time fretting about these categories.

As we discussed in Chapter 4, the best proposals serve as road maps to help you get from here (your problem) to there (your solution). The *goal* is your destination, *objectives* serve as mileage signs you pass along the way to help measure your progress, and *methods* are your modes of travel. You're the driver, so the map should be drawn in your own handwriting. Many fine proposals describe the applicant's goals, objectives, and methods (see next section) in one discussion. If it works — if the reader understands where you're going and how you plan to get there — then you've done your job.

Here's a wonderfully brief, clear statement of goals and objectives from the Denver Community Reinvestment Alliance (DCRA), which works to ensure fair-lending practices for people of color and people with disabilities. Banks in many communities, including Denver, have historically made it harder for people of color to get loans, compared to whites with similar incomes, assets, and credit histories. DCRA is working to end lending discrimination by abolishing "redlining," the practice of identifying specific neighborhoods where loans are limited or excluded.

[Denver Community Reinvestment Alliance — *Goals and Objectives*]

DCRA's goal is to build a strong grassroots coalition that will use a combination of research, community education and direct action protest to change both banking and government policies that allow discrimination in lending and banking services to continue.

Beginning last September, DCRA members have been busy creating a strategic plan to guide them for the next five years. Members have also drafted three realistic goals for 1995:

1) Building the organization in terms of numbers of active members, leaders and overall power.

   Objectives: For 1995, DCRA expects to 1) double the number of active members from 25 to 50 and the total membership from 100 to 200; 2) develop five new key leaders; and 3) become a model for other organizations in the Southwest.

2) Creating an infrastructure for the organization to sustain itself over the long term.

   Objectives: DCRA expects to have by January, 1996: 1) one full-time staff and one half-time staff intern; 2) a permanent home for its office and general meetings; 3) a $50,000 annual budget; and 4) be incorporated as a nonprofit 501(c)(3).

3) Continue to forge strong agreements with local banks and hold them accountable.

   Objectives: During 1995, DCRA expects to 1) create agreements with local lenders to make at least $50,000,000 worth of new affordable loans to people of color, people with disabilities, and low income people; 2) get a commitment from at least one bank to achieve lending parity between Anglos and people of color; 3) have one seat on a local bank Board of Directors; 4) help draft and introduce a local Community Reinvestment law in the state legislature; 5) get an agreement with one bank to create a community review board composed of DCRA members; and 6) form a small business lending committee to address discrimination issues in commercial lending.

They've taken their long-term goal — to end lending discrimination — and created three short-term goals for the coming year. Notice how two of the three goals focus on building the organization. Many newer, smaller groups put all their effort into fighting the opposition, while ignoring basic chores like finding new members and developing leaders. By explicitly setting internal goals — and listing them before their issue goals — DCRA shows a lot of savvy. Any organization can take on a bank, but only a strong, self-sufficient group can take on a bank and win. The Denver Community Reinvestment Alliance is designing itself for the long haul.

They've also done a nice job of setting measurable objectives, which will make it easy to evaluate their progress and adjust their course one year later. Twelve of the thirteen objectives listed can be easily checked. There's only one subjective item: "Become a model for other organizations in the Southwest." If DCRA can form a working coalition, or present a workshop at a community reinvestment conference, or even answer (and log) phone calls from other grassroots groups considering fairness-in-lending campaigns, they can probably claim success on that objective, too.

Now that you've defined *what* you're going to do, *how* are you going to do it? This is the nuts-and-bolts portion of the proposal where you explain your detailed plan for creating change. Show the funder that you've thought through all possible action scenarios, and you're prepared to control the project and not be controlled by it. Specifics are always helpful, but don't overdo it. As Dan Petegorsky says,

> Focus on benefits, not features. The fact that you have six subcommittees will not make or break the grant; we want to know what you're going to do. Don't bog down your proposal with details we don't need to know.

As mentioned earlier, it's acceptable to combine your goals, objectives, and work plan into one section. The examples discussed below do this to some degree.

Here's an excerpt from the SouthWest Organizing Project (SWOP), describing their voter registration and education program. Notice how they list their goals at the beginning, briefly restate their successes to date, then combine their objectives and methods in each of the numbered paragraphs.

Obviously, these folks have given a lot of thought to this project. A weaker proposal might simply say, "We're going to organize a voter registration drive," and list a few outreach strategies. SWOP, in contrast, has created a 2-page manual on *how* to do voter outreach. If anything, this proposal provides too much detail for the reader, but that's a minor problem because of the clear way the information is organized. It's easy for readers to skim through the list of objectives and pick out whatever interests them.

STRATEGY AND IMPLEMENTATION (METHODS)

The SWOP "Take Back New Mexico Campaign" will:

◆ increase informed electoral participation of people of color in targeted areas of New Mexico during 1994

◆ educate voters on key justice issues in the targeted areas

◆ work for increased levels of accountability of elected officials toward New Mexico communities

◆ lay a foundation for first-time grassroots legislative initiatives during the "long" (eight week) 1995 legislative session

◆ begin a long-term (but applied) process of monitoring the financial contributions to candidates for office by major corporations

◆ strengthen SWOP through the recruitment and training of new members from throughout the state

The Campaign has already had some success. In Santa Fe, over 30 volunteers knocked on more than 2,000 doors on the City's west side, and registered over 400 new voters. The drive made a significant contribution to the 18% increase in voter turnout there. Other drives took place in Albuquerque and also in Las Vegas, where 140 residents were surveyed door-to-door on quality of life issues.

The Take Back New Mexico Campaign is targeting San Miguel and Mora Counties (Las Vegas area), Santa Fe County, Sandoval and Bernalillo Counties (Albuquerque metro area), and Doña Ana County (Las Cruces, Mesilla Valley) in southern New Mexico during the Summer and Fall of 1994. SWOP has seven main objectives, as outlined below.

1. **Register 2,000 new voters** in Bernalillo, Santa Fe, San Miguel, and Doña Ana Counties during the Summer and Fall of 1994 through non-partisan door-to-door and site registration activities in targeted precincts in each area. Door-to-door efforts will include four *Solidarity Saturdays* involving grassroots organizations, churches and individuals in each area. SWOP and other participating organizations will recruit a total of 200 volunteers for these special one-day drives.

2. **Conduct surveys in some of the targeted areas** to identify key local and state issues, as well as identify actual and potential community leaders.

3. **Educate voters,** both newly and previously registered, in each area on key issues.

   • Develop and distribute or present fact sheets and audio visual materials relevant to each geographic area which relate to both key issues and the nature of the Campaign.

   • Distribute *Voces Unidas* and other non-partisan materials raising Campaign issues to newly registered voters and others in each area.

   • Develop and distribute non-partisan TV and radio PSAs on issue and voter participation themes.

[continued]

4. **Obtain commitments from candidates** for local, state, and federal offices to take specific steps to address issues of importance.

   - Research positions of targeted candidates on key issues in each area.

   - Conduct candidate accountability forum activities with targeted candidates and their opponents where "yes" or "no" responses will be solicited regarding possible future actions on specific issues.

   - Publicize commitments by candidates in the media and through ongoing educational work in targeted communities.

5. **Increase voter turnout in targeted precincts and districts** for municipal, state, and federal elections.

   - Use the "three contact" method of follow-up with newly registered voters through door-to-door work, leafletting and phone banking.

   - Organize block leaders to remind residents of election dates and polling places.

   - Provide rides to polls on election days.

6. **Train 50 SWOP members and other volunteers** in non-partisan voter registration, education, and get-out-the-vote methods in the targeted areas.

   - Recruit Campaign volunteers from SWOP membership and target communities during the course of the Summer and Fall.

   - Conduct group training sessions in each area, timed to coincide with drives in each.

7. **Recruit 100 new SWOP members statewide.**

   - Develop new SWOP short video and new brochure to be used in Campaign to describe the organization, its work and membership.

   - Solicit membership during all activities.

   - Conduct new member orientations in each area during the year. Each of these objectives will be applied in the targeted areas listed below.

8. **Develop grassroots legislative agenda for 1995 legislature.** Conduct broad statewide meeting to define issue priorities during the late Summer of 1994.

   - Initiate dialogue with New Mexico Conference of Churches and other religious institutions to establish a legislative partnership.[1]

   - Monitor corporate campaign contributions during course of elections, and continue work with organizations pushing for campaign finance reform.

   - Call for Legislative Hearings on development issues for Summer of 1995.

---

[1] SWOP *will not* engage directly in lobbying. We are exploring ways to integrate issues defined through this campaign into the agendas of religious organizations and others with the flexibility to lobby the state legislature.

In Utah, Justice, Economic Dignity, and Independence for Women organizes low-income women around issues of housing, jobs, child care, and real welfare reform. Their acronym, JEDI Women, reminds us of the warriors in the Star Wars movies, but these women are fighting for economic justice here on Earth. Here's an excerpt from a recent proposal.

This piece works for several reasons.

1. **THE LANGUAGE IS CONCISE AND EASY TO UNDERSTAND.** Bureaucrats and politicians often use technical terms to muddy the truth or shift the focus away from the real issues. By keeping the language simple, the authors remind us what welfare really means: ensuring that poor children are housed, fed, and healthy.

2. **THE PROPOSAL IS WRITTEN IN THE FIRST PERSON FORM ("WE") AND AVOIDS THE THIRD PERSON FORM ("THE GROUP," "JEDI WOMEN").** This makes it more personal and accessible. Consider how the last sentence would change if written in the third person: "If welfare reform is passed at the state and/or national level, JEDI Women would involve itself..." Sounds a lot more formal and awkward, doesn't it? As long as you use the name of the group every now and then to remind the reader who "we" is — as is done twice in the excerpt above — it's appropriate to write your proposal from the perspective of "we."

3. **THEY GET POINTS FOR CHUTZPAH.** JEDI Women is a small, relatively young organization with a limited staff and budget, proposing to organize a simultaneous event in 30 cities. Some grants officers would look at this skeptically, and with good reason. While the group has had success on the local level, there's nothing in the proposal that makes the reader think they can successfully manage a national event — other than their air of confidence. In community organizing, attitude counts for a lot. If you're trying to raise money for an ambitious project, study the tone of this proposal.

[Justice, Economic Dignity, and Independence for Women — *Strategy*]

Goal 1. Welfare Reform Which Helps Low-Income Families Attain Economic Security: To ensure that the welfare reform debate results in real reform which gives low-income families the opportunity and tools to improve their economic circumstances.

For this to be accomplished, there must be recognition of the four main elements of family economic security (housing, health care, child care and jobs) and a willingness to incorporate these elements in welfare reform. Recently, JEDI members conducted an analysis of welfare benefits packages using average Utah rents and benefit levels for a family of three. We found that if our hypothetical family had housing assistance, child care assistance, health care assistance and monthly receipt of an advance on their Earned Income Tax Credit, a full-time $5 per hour job would bring the family just above the poverty line. What this says is that *housing, child care, and health care, along with jobs*, are what it takes to improve the economic security of single parent households.

1. National/Regional Organizing:

A.) We are organizing "Our Children's Hearts Are in Your Hands," a grassroots National Day of Action to call attention to the needs of low-income children and their parents. We hope to have at least 30 cities across the country involved (we may get more). As we organize the day of action, we will involve the groups we make connections with in an ongoing public education campaign to ensure that welfare reform does not harm low-income women and children, and we'll create a national network of grassroots activists.

B.) We'll publish a bimonthly newsletter which will be mailed to groups participating in the National Day of Action. The newsletter will focus on grassroots organizing on welfare issues taking place across the country, will profile what groups are doing, and will contain ideas and strategies used, as well as suggestions for future unified action.

C.) We will organize and hold a conference which brings together grassroots leaders and organizers from across the country — to share ideas and strategies for community action on social justice issues.

2. Local Organizing:

A.) We'll closely monitor the welfare reform debate to ensure that the facts (as opposed to myths) about welfare are considered and that the voices of low-income women are listened to. We will organize events as needed to help educate the public about the very vulnerable people whose lives are at stake in this debate.

B.) We'll conduct an "economic security" survey with 150 women, to involve them with JEDI in the debate on welfare, to get information we can use to demonstrate what is necessary for economic security, and will write a report based on our findings for use with policy makers.

C.) We will expand the coalition of groups working on welfare related issues.

D.) Our members are designing a welfare myth busting workshop designed to educate people with no welfare experience about what the system is like and positive ways to change it. We'll conduct 20 workshops with groups across the state.

E.) If welfare reform is passed at the state and/or national level, we'll involve ourselves in its implementation to ensure that it's as helpful as possible to families who'll receive services.

TIMELINE

It's useful to include a timeline indicating when your objectives will be met. As John Tirman of the Winston Foundation for World Peace says, "A work schedule is always impressive." A straightforward list of deadlines or benchmarks will also give you an easy way to measure your progress once you begin the project.

You can build deadlines into your strategy section or create a separate timeline that stands alone. Here's an effective example from the Community Alliance with Family Farmers Foundation (formerly the California Action Network) for the "Lighthouse Farm Organizing Campaign," which promotes sustainable, environmentally safe agriculture by developing a network of model farms (and farmers) across California.

A good timeline, like this one, shows forethought. CAFF has built its organizing calendar around the needs and availability of the group's constituents — farmers — and they're smart enough to kick off the media campaign in the spring, when the farms will be most photogenic. This is nothing more than common sense transferred to the page.

Many groups are uncomfortable including a work schedule because they fear it might restrict their freedom or they don't know how long each task will take. My advice: give it your best estimate. The advantages of developing a timeline far outweigh the disadvantages. If you fall behind or need to shift your focus a little, most foundations will accept these adjustments, as long as you keep them informed.

EVALUATION

How will you know if you succeed? How will you measure your success or failure? How will you use what you've learned? As Deborah Brouse of the Environmental Support Center says,

> Be very concrete in describing what the grant will make possible. If we give you the money you request, what will change as a result? What difference will it make?

Your evaluation section is the place where "the difference" is defined, counted, and weighed.

Your evaluation plan should be designed to measure the success of each of your objectives, so it's useful if they are stated in measurable terms. Design your project to generate some numbers when the grant period is over: number of people served, increase in membership, performances staged, neighborhood houses renovated, newsletters distributed, acres or species protected — whatever relates to your program goals. Find a way to quantify the results of your work.

The following evaluation piece was included in a Native Seeds/SEARCH proposal for collecting and preserving endangered native crop varieties. Seven of the nine evaluation points are numerical.

Timeline

Our timeline is designed around the cycle of farm schedules. Farmers have the most free time from November to February. Farms are the most beautiful to visit in mid to late spring. Farmers have only intermittent breaks in a heavy work schedule from June through October.

November: Send letters to friends within the farming community, asking for recommendations or new contacts within the four target regions. Prepare a packet of outreach materials outlining the mission of the Lighthouse Farm Campaign. Make phone contact with farmers and schedule visits.

December: Visit the Sacramento Valley area (two weeks). Meet with local Agricultural Extension Agent; identify and contact Lighthouse farms in each area and organize a meeting of those farmers. Formulate a regional plan.

January: Visit the Salinas Valley and the Oxnard Plain area near Los Angeles (two weeks each). Meet with local Agricultural Extension Agent; identify and contact Lighthouse farms in each area and organize a meeting of those farmers. Formulate a regional plan.

February: Visit the San Joaquin Valley near Fresno (two weeks). Meet with local Agricultural Extension Agent; identify and contact Lighthouse farms in each area and organize a meeting of those farmers. Formulate a regional plan. Plan statewide meeting of all Lighthouse farmers.

March: Convene a statewide meeting of Lighthouse farmers in the Fresno area to develop strategy, expand the FAAR (Farmers for Alternative Agricultural Research) Steering Committee, and coordinate regional plans. After the meeting we will initiate discussions with other organizations and with the media.

April-May: Each area will begin implementing their plan. This will involve meetings with extension agents, holding farm tours and networking with others in the community.

June through October: As farming schedules permit, continue outreach to additional growers, hold local presentations and forums on the benefits of alternative farming for the local community, and meet with the press.

The following staff activities are ongoing:

◆ monthly calls to each grower

◆ regular conference calls to prepare for upcoming activities, e.g., a visit to the local extension office, a farm tour, etc.
  * monthly mailing to all Lighthouse farmers describing the latest goings-on in the network

The following farmer activities are ongoing:

◆ monthly meetings to share information

◆ outreach to local extension agents

◆ presentations to local community groups

◆ farm tours and press work

---

1. **Organize** and carry out a minimum of six collection trips each in northern Mexico and New Mexico/Colorado.

2. **Collect** a minimum of 200 new accessions in Mexico and 50 new accessions in New Mexico and Colorado.

3. **Identify** 5-10 farmers interested in becoming contract growers or traditional food gatherers for NS/S.

4. **Identify** 5-10 farmers from whom we could purchase crafts, providing them with income to help them stay on their land.

5. **Recruit** 50 additional families for the Traditional Native American Farmers Association.

6. **Purchase** sufficient quantities of at least 20 "new" crops to offer in our seed catalog in 1995 and 1996, providing direct benefits to our members, customers, and Native American farmers and gardeners who use us as a seed source.

7. **Organize** at least one seed bank workshop for farmers.

8. **Work** to improve the quality and accessibility of local knowledge collected with each crop.

9. **Continue** to provide free seed to all Native Americans.

This is an effective evaluation plan, but it could be improved with even more attention to the numbers. For example, in item 6 above, how many seeds equal a "sufficient quantity?" For item 8, can the task of "improving the quality and accessibility of local knowledge" be broken down into measurable steps?

It's okay to include a few subjective items (see number 9), but if all your evaluation points are subjective — "We will work to make people feel more secure" — you'll have a difficult time judging your success. Of course, you can always survey your constituents about how they're feeling when the project is over; just make sure to set numerical goals for the number of questionnaires you distribute and collect.

PERSONNEL

Provide one-paragraph biographies of the main project organizers and staff. Some foundations request full resumes, in which case these biographical sketches are unnecessary.

An excellent personnel section can be found on page 109. It's part of the Sea Islands Land Retention Project proposal presented to the Boehm Foundation.

Unless you're submitting a request for general support, *you'll need two budgets: one for the featured project, plus an annual budget for the entire organization.* For some grant reviewers, the project budget is the most important page in the grant application. Many otherwise fine proposals don't get funded because their financial documents are unclear or unrealistic. (For a discussion of how to begin the budgeting process, see Chapter 4.)

The project budget should itemize expenses and show the status of your fundraising: how much project revenue is in-hand, pledged, and sought. It's acceptable to round your line items to the nearest $50 or $100, though you can also estimate costs to the nearest dollar. For most projects, ten to fifteen expense lines is plenty (see the Mono Lake Committee proposal on page 137). I've seen small budgets handled adequately with five or six line items.

You might have to piece together several grants to pay for the total cost of a project. Below your expense figures, list all funders you will be approaching as "income sought," along with the amount requested from each. Because some of your proposals will be turned down, it's acceptable to show that you've applied for more funding than you need; be sure to include a sentence at the bottom of the budget page stating that you don't expect to receive full funding from all sources. Rather than make you look greedy, this indicates you're serious about raising enough money to complete the project.

If you're applying for partial funding from a specific foundation — for example, you're seeking $10,000 toward a $25,000 project budget — foundation staff might want to know which line items they are being asked to underwrite. I discourage you from offering this information unless requested, because it complicates your bookkeeping. If you need to break your expenses down by funder, however, on the next page is an example from the Native Seeds/SEARCH diabetes project. This program promotes the consumption of traditional desert foods, such as prickly pear, mesquite flour and tepary beans, to combat diabetes in the Native American community.

(FTE, or Full Time Equivalent, is a way of measuring staff time. One FTE equals a full-time job, or 40+ hours per week.)

BUDGETS

1992 Budget, Diabetes Prevention Project

(Wallace Foundation request items shown in bold type.)

Primary Staff: (salary & fringe)

Nutritionist/Project Director (.5 FTE) $16,500
Education Director (.4 FTE) 8,800
  (Wallace Foundation share = $4,400)
Research Director (4 weeks/year) . . . . in-kind

Consulting and support staff

Outreach assistant (.25 FTE) **3,300**
Administrative Assistant (.5 FTE) 7,700
Nutritionist (4 weeks/year) 2,400
Recipe Tester (2.5 weeks) 1,500
Cultural Consultant (2.5 weeks/year) 1,500
                                                           Subtotal: $41,700

Supplies:

Office 600
Nutrition software 500
Display/materials for education **250**
Food purchases for recipe testing 200
Food purchases for demonstrations **1,000**
Books/publications for free distribution 250
Seeds for free distribution . . . . in-kind
                                                           Subtotal: $2,800

Services:

Video production $3,000
Library search: medical literature 200
Photocopying and printing 2,500
  (Wallace Foundation share = $1,500)
Mailing/shipping 1,000
  (Wallace Foundation share = $500)
Phone **500**
Publication of kitchen manual 600
                                                           Subtotal: $7,800

Travel:

Mileage/per diem, outreach to reservations $4,000
  (Wallace Foundation share = $1,500)
Conferences and professional presentations 3,000
                                                           Subtotal: $7,000
Administration and overhead (10%) $5,900
  (Wallace Foundation share = $1,300)
                                                           TOTAL: $65,200

Total request to the Wallace Foundation **$14,250**

After studying the grants directories at the library and calling the foundation, we decided that $14,250 was an appropriate request to this funder. Because of their expressed interest in community health — as opposed to nutritional research — we selected line items for their grant that supported our community outreach efforts.

This budget would have been improved with an income section, showing how we proposed to raise the remaining $50,000. If included, it might have looked something like this:

Projected Revenue

Pledged:	Stocker Foundation $7,500	
	Subtotal: $7,500	
Sought:	Wallace Foundation $14,250	
	other foundations* $40,000	
	major donors 3,450	
	Subtotal: $57,700	
	Total: $65,200	

*Proposal status:

ABC Foundation (pending) $20,000
XYZ Foundation (to be submitted) 10,000
Other foundations to be determined 10,000

As it turns out, we raised about $25,000 for the project in 1992, including $14,000 from the Wallace Foundation, and scaled back our plans accordingly. Several line items were reduced or eliminated — we didn't make a video or finish the cookbook — and the work went forward in a more modest fashion.

Notice that two line items are marked "in-kind." We chose to pay for these expenses out of the general budget to demonstrate our commitment to the project, and also to simplify our bookkeeping. In a sense, this is the opposite of including indirect costs in a grant request, because it shows that the group is willing to "match" the foundation's gift with resources of its own. This kind of grants leverage is discussed in greater detail in Chapter 8.

Many grantmakers are also interested in your *long-range fundraising plan*. What happens to the project at the end of the grant period? Is it designed to achieve a goal and shut down? If not, will you seek alternate funding, absorb the project costs into your general budget, or let it die? Grants are known as "soft money" because they are seldom renewable. Even if you don't submit a long-range funding plan with your proposal, it wouldn't hurt to develop one for internal use.

Next, let's talk about the big picture: your organizational budget.

◆ You should always submit an organizational budget for the current year, which is based on projected income and expenses. If appropriate, include a brief budget narrative describing any line items that might seem questionable to an outsider.

◆ Many funders also ask to review the previous year's financial statements, which are drawn from real numbers, not projections. Diane Ives of the Beldon Fund gets frustrated when she receives current budgets without past financial statements because, in her words, "I want to see the trends in your budget."

If your organization raises and spends more than $100,000 per year, you should consider getting an *audited financial statement*. You can hire a certified public accountant (CPA) to review your books and verify that you're handling the money in an appropriate way. Some CPAs specialize in the needs of nonprofits, and as part of the audit will give you advice about how to improve your bookkeeping. Your audited financial statement can then serve as "last year's budget" when you include it with your grant proposals.

Audits normally costs three to five thousand dollars, but you might be able to negotiate a discount if the accountant is supportive of your work. According to accountant and trainer Terry Miller, if you receive federal grants (or federal money passed through your state or local government), you should expect to pay *twice as much* for an audit, since government accounting standards are so rigorous. In fact, Miller suggests that you hire a CPA *before applying for federal grants* to review your accounting procedures and make sure you can handle the reporting requirements.

Here's a sample annual budget from Minnesota Jobs With Peace, which promotes the economic conversion of military facilities and industries to peaceful production.

This page provides lots of useful information in a simple, easy-to-understand format. While 73% of their budget — a dangerously high percentage — is raised from grants and government contracts, it's encouraging to note that Minnesota Jobs with Peace has an active membership and major donor program, and is also soliciting funds from religious organizations and unions. All of these areas show potential for growth.

To provide additional perspective on their funding history, the authors attach a "five-year income breakdown" listing the amounts and percentages raised from grants, memberships, events, major donors, speaker fees, and other sources between 1989 and 1993. Unfortunately, there's no way to compare projected expenses in the above budget to actual numbers from previous years. It would be helpful to include a 1994 financial statement produced *in the same format*. Grant reviewers could then lay the two pages side by side and compare each line item.

Minnesota Jobs with Peace 1995 Budget (proposed)

Income

Grants (net after fiscal agent fees)	$42,740
MN Extension Service (MES) - in-kind	24,389
Membership and small donations	9,160
Major donors	6,000
Events (gross)	6,400
Religious organizations	2,000
Unions	500
Speakers fees / honoraria	250
Other miscellaneous income	250

Total income: **$91,689**

Expenses

Personnel

Executive director (+ 3% raise)	$28,387
Membership & events coordinator (.25 FTE)	4,732
Taxes & benefits	5,175
Accounting	1,200
Contracted services/legal fees	885
MES-funded Community Education Coordinator (.5 FTE)	12,195
MES-funded research asst. (.5 FTE)	12,194

Subtotal personnel: **$64,768**

Operating Expenses

Rent	$ 4,248
Office equipment	400
Office supplies	1,200
Phone	1,440
Long distance	1,050
Printing & copying	2,200
Postage	2,296
Mileage & parking	1,567
Conferences & meetings	500
Travel	1,050
Dues	405
Publications & subscriptions	500
Jobs with Peace newsletter	2,800
Workshops & program events	2,000
Fundraising events	2,500
IRS & state filing fees	565
Miscellaneous	500

Subtotal operating expenses: **$25,221**

1994 payables: .... $ 1,700

Total expenses: **$91,689**

ATTACHMENTS

Funders sometimes require you to include extra materials with your grant proposal. The most commonly requested items are:

◆ A copy of your *Internal Revenue Service tax-exemption letter*. (If you don't have tax-exempt status and are using a *fiscal agent*, attach their IRS letter and a note, on their letterhead, explaining that they will be handling the money.)

◆ A list of your board members and/or brief biographical notes about your board.

◆ A current brochure or newsletter.

◆ Letters of support from your constituents or other organizations. As mentioned earlier in the chapter, you can use quotations from these letters in the body of your proposal.

The key phrase is "requested items." If you take one final message from this chapter, let it be this: include only what they ask for, because foundation officers hate to receive big piles of unsolicited stuff. When asked what really annoys her, Polly Lawrence of the Wallace Genetic Foundation says, "A proposal with pages, pages, pages ... and pages (!) of supporting material." Her concerns are echoed in the voices of her colleagues. Their comments should serve as a kind of Greek chorus, warning you about the dangers of excess.

John Powers, Educational Foundation of America:

> *Do not* do a filing cabinet dump (gee, let's send the last two year's newsletters, some publicity about us, our generic grant request, etc.) If the donor wants a two-page letter of inquiry, send exactly that.

Katrin Verclas, Ottinger Foundation:

> Worst proposal: 5-inch thick three-ring binder, *packed* ... letters of support flooding the office, phone calls, rude to the assistant — sure way to annoy.

Betsy Taylor, Merck Family Fund:

> Hold the packages jammed with videos, books and every report you've ever produced. Focus on quality, not quantity!

Steve Starkey, Wisconsin Community Fund:

> One group sent a video, a newspaper, and a book at the letter of intent stage. Another group brought 15 copies of a book that they had published to our office, and then were mad when we made them take the books home.

Let me repeat: do your homework and send only what's requested. Occasionally you will be given the option of enclosing whatever you think is most relevant. Be judicious. In my experience, the most effective attachments are:

◆ One or two recent press clippings. Select stories that have a direct bearing on your proposed project. Do not send your entire news file.

◆ Testimonials or letters of support from your clients or cooperating organizations. This material can also be excerpted for use in the main portion of your proposal.

◆ Photographs, where appropriate. Choose action pictures that demonstrate your work — volunteers cleaning up an abandoned house, protesters picketing the public utilities commission, children studying wildlife in the woods. Skip the boring snapshots of your annual awards dinner or board members sitting around a table. Betsy Taylor doesn't want your videos, but she encourages photos. They take a lot less time to view.

COVER LETTER

The cover letter is the first thing that emerges from the envelope, but the last thing you write. This letter serves as a friendly introduction and helps to establish rapport between you and your foundation contact. When you write it, make sure to:

1. **REMIND THE READER OF ANY PREVIOUS COMMUNICATION OR RELATIONSHIP** between your organization and the funder. Here are some typical opening sentences:

    "Thanks for taking the time to meet with me to discuss our community organizing programs."

    "Last year, your foundation provided a $____ grant to underwrite our successful community outreach efforts. With the enclosed proposal, we seek your renewed support."

    "We submit this proposal with the encouragement of Ms. Goodpeer, who thought you might be interested in our work."

2. **STATE HOW MUCH MONEY YOU'RE REQUESTING.**

3. **DESCRIBE — BRIEFLY — THE MISSION OF YOUR ORGANIZATION,** and why the featured project is essential to your work.

4. **IF YOU WISH, EXPLAIN HOW YOUR PROPOSAL MEETS THE FOUNDATION'S GUIDELINES AND INTERESTS.** If you've done your homework and carefully screened the funder, the fit should be self-evident. Nonetheless, some foundations want to hear you talk about why *you* chose *them*.

5. **OFFER TO PROVIDE ADDITIONAL INFORMATION,** if needed, and suggest a site visit at which foundation staff and board can see your work first-hand.

Never include any important information that is not covered elsewhere in the main proposal. Here's why: your proposal will likely be photocopied for distribution to the grant reviewers. Don't assume that the letter will be copied and passed along as part of the package.

Keep your cover letter short and to the point. One page is preferable, two pages is acceptable. The Mono Lake Committee proposal, which you'll find on page 125, includes an excellent cover letter.

There you have it: all the pieces of a successful grant proposal. In the next chapter we'll analyze four complete proposals and discuss what makes them work.

What grabs my attention in a grant proposal?
Brevity, frankness, clarity, honesty, innovation.

— Tia Oros, Seventh Generation Fund

Four Winners:
Proposals that Work

We all need role models. On the following pages you'll find four successful proposals. They're each different in tone, writing style, constituency, issue, and format — and they all work. The moral: there are many "right ways" to do this job.

These proposals are well written and well organized, but, just as important, the projects they describe are interesting and provide good fundraising handles. Therefore, my comments address both what makes the proposals effective and the programs compelling.

Ellen Furnari, who used to direct the Ben & Jerry's Foundation, says that the grants review process is sometimes "whimsical and subjective." I suspect this reality is more common than most professionals would admit. If grant reviewers are operating, to some degree, on instinct, then we grantwriters need to develop the same kinds of instincts. To truly serve as feasibility testers, we must have the skill to judge the fundability of the work *before* investing a lot of time writing the grant application. In other words, why create a technically superb proposal for a dull, seen-it-before program? More than likely, it won't get funded.

By analyzing these applications, you can begin to develop your own sense about what makes a proposal effective. I will walk you through each one, page by page, offering praise and suggestions for improvement. As you read, keep track of your reactions. What gets your attention? What makes you uncomfortable? Do you have questions about the group or the project that haven't been addressed? What can you borrow and adapt for your own work?

SEA ISLANDS

COVER PAGE. This is a collaborative project — the groups have identified it as such at the top of the first page, making it clear that the proposal has been submitted by all three organizations.

There's nothing fancy about this effective cover page — no unusual type faces or flashy graphics. It looks professional. The essential information is easy to find. The wide margins create lots of white space, which makes it easy to read.

One problem: who's the audience? Generally, the cover page begins, "Proposal submitted to..." When the authors prepared this proposal, they personalized it by inserting the foundation name (in the space above "Applicant"), with the "Amount Requested" changed as appropriate.

This is a great summary. In just nine sentences, the authors:

◆ define the problem

◆ identify their constituency by region, race, and class

◆ lay out their strategy

◆ describe their short- and long-term goals

◆ list the coalition members

Conciseness — saying a lot with a few words — will always improve your proposals and increase your chances of getting the grant. This is a fine example. If you have a hard time fitting big ideas into small spaces, keep practicing. Break your ideas into their component parts, then put one part in each sentence, as the authors have done here.

SEA ISLANDS LAND RETENTION PROJECT
South Carolina Coastal Conservation League
Penn Center
Neighborhood Legal Assistance Program

APPLICANT: South Carolina Coastal Conservation League
                        Box 1765
                        Charleston, South Carolina 29402
                        (803) 723-8035

DATE OF
SUBMISSION: 20 February 1992

CONTACT PERSON: Dana Beach
                        Executive Director

PROJECT BUDGET: $99,675

AMOUNT REQUESTED: $40,000

REQUESTED FOR: April 1992 - April 1994

PROJECT DESCRIPTION:

        The Sea Islands off the coast of South Carolina and Georgia are being
overtaken by rapid, poorly planned development. This poses an
environmental threat to the islands and endangers a unique African-American
culture that has flourished here for over a century. Development also causes
hardships for individual landowners. The landowners -- farmers and
fisherman, mostly black, mostly poor -- are often forced to sell land against
their will because they lack the developers' legal savvy and financial
resources. To minimize environmental damage, cultural loss, and injustice to
individuals, various groups would like to slow and regulate Sea Islands
development. So far, there has been little cooperation among them. To
remedy this, the South Carolina Coastal Conservation League, the Penn
Center, and the Neighborhood Legal Assistance Program seek two years
funding for a cooperative project based on St. Helena Island, South Carolina.
The short-term goals are to counsel individual landowners on their legal
rights, and to help local citizens groups implement strategies that have been
successful in controlling development elsewhere. The long-term goals are to
build a crucial coalition among professional organizations and citizens groups
on the Sea Islands, and to create a model for cooperative land-use planning
that could be replicated in other parts of the South.

The running head lists the project title and the participating groups, which reinforces the collaborative nature of the project on every page. Coalition work, as mentioned earlier, is often appreciated by those who give away money.

GRANTEE ORGANIZATION. This section describes the South Carolina Coastal Conservation League, fiscal sponsor for the project (they handle the money). It covers their:

◆ Mission — why they exist.

◆ Programs, with a focus on land-use planning. The use of specific names — Awendaw, Charleston, Edisto — adds a local flavor and builds credibility into their organizational resume.

◆ Total budget for the past and current years. This is important to grant-makers, because it tells them about the size and stability of the organization.

◆ Membership, which demonstrates the breadth of community support.

◆ Other funders. Foundation officers always want to know what their peers think of the group. By tallying grants received and including the names of past supporters, the authors add even more credibility to their request.

◆ Staffing level and job titles. These demonstrate the group's capacity to do the work. If you wish, you can save job titles for the personnel section, where you introduce the project staff. (See page 7 of this proposal.)

Once again, the authors have packed a lot of information into a small space, without making it *feel* packed.

BACKGROUND: LAND ISSUES. This proposal tells a story. It's dramatic. The section on land issues describes, in an expressive way, the problems this project seeks to address. Using few words and compelling descriptions, the authors set the stage for the actions needed, which are covered in subsequent portions of the proposal.

Grantee Organization

The South Carolina Coastal Conservation League, a tax exempt 501(c)(3) organization based in Charleston, was founded in 1989 to serve as an advocate for the environment throughout the South Carolina low country. We work to protect the character of rural areas, preserve coastal rivers, maintain and restore water quality, reform management practices in the local national forest, and increase public involvement in environmental issues.

Land-use planning is the area of our work most relevant to the proposed project. In this area, we have provided technical assistance to several local efforts: the 1989 Awendaw land-use plan, the 1989 Charleston 2000 plan, the 1990 Edisto Island land-use plan, and ongoing efforts on Johns Island. Our Urban Growth Project, just recently funded, will promote efficient environmentally-sound growth patterns around Charleston. We are also involved in the National Growth Management Leadership Project, a consortium of environmental groups from eighteen states that share strategies for developing and promoting innovative growth-management legislation.

Our annual budget for 1991 is $161,000. For 1992, it will be $224,000, exclusive of the proposed project. Our support comes from over 2,000 members, making us one of the largest environmental organizations in South Carolina. We have also received support from eleven private foundations, including the Pew Charitable Trusts, the Mary Reynolds Babcock Foundation, the W. Alton Jones Foundation, and the Lyndhurst Foundation.

We have four full-time staff members, one full-time land-use consultant, one part-time forestry consultant, and, during the summer, four interns. Beginning in 1992 we will add a full-time land-use planner and a forestry coordinator.

More detailed information about the Coastal Conservation League's program and budget is provided in attachments to this proposal.

Background: Land Issues

Land issues in the Sea Islands can best be understood in the context of the region's unique history. After the Civil War, the nation was divided over whether the federal government should distribute land to the newly emancipated slaves. Former slaves argued that they had earned ownership through centuries of unpaid labor, and that without land -- without some measure of economic independence -- they would be free in name only. This controversy was particularly bitter in and around the Sea Islands. There the

The authors paint a vivid picture. "...they armed themselves, barricaded the plantations, and tried to drive off their former masters..." You can practically smell the gunpowder. In less skilled hands, this would sound melodramatic, but it works.

"Chartreuse sea grasses and massive, moss-draped oaks are giving way to burger joints and rows of identical condominiums." You can almost see the transformation, and it's not a pretty sight.

What are the statistics on land transfers? If the authors can quantify the problem — number of acres sold to newcomers, percentage of land still held by descendants of emancipated slaves, and so forth — it would make the case even stronger. This section would also be improved with a map, or a series of maps, showing how land ownership on the islands has changed over the past twenty years.

Sharp, bitter irony in this description. What a startling image: the liberated plantations have become plantations once again, staffed by workers (wage slaves?) who used to be land owners.

If collaboration is the point of this project, why is it necessary? This paragraph reinforces the need for the project by describing previous efforts to address the problem and analyzing why they failed. By discussing the ways that naiveté and distrust created difficulties in the past, the authors strengthen their argument for a more savvy, cooperative approach. The analysis is blunt, but the tone is even-handed; no one group or constituency is singled out for blame.

federal government granted land to tens of thousands of freed slaves, then suddenly returned most of it to the whites who had owned island plantations before the war. To the blacks this was a terrible betrayal. On one island they armed themselves, barricaded the plantations, and tried to drive off their former masters, without success. Ultimately, there was only one place in the South where significant numbers of freed slaves emerged from the Civil War with land of their own: St. Helena and adjacent islands.

Slowly blacks acquired land on other Sea Islands. For the next century, isolated from the mainland, they farmed, fished, and wove African and American influences into a colorful, distinctive language and culture. But in the last two decades development has proceeded at a startling pace. Chartreuse sea grasses and massive, moss-draped oaks are giving way to burger joints and rows of identical condominiums. Cultural traditions found nowhere else in the world are quickly vanishing.

The transfer of land from native islanders to newcomers is not always voluntary. Many island residents are poor and have little education. They sell land because they do not know their legal rights; or because they cannot pay taxes that have skyrocketed due to nearby development; or because developers convince one person to sell a share of land owned by many heirs, then force a sale of the whole property by refusing to agree to a partition. The developers say that in exchange for land the islanders have better jobs and more opportunities. This is not the case. The developments, unabashedly called "plantations" by their residents, are guarded by uniformed patrols. Each morning they unlock gates to admit busloads of islanders, all menial workers. For the vast majority, land for opportunity has not been a fair trade.

Local citizens groups, environmentalists, and organizations interested in civil rights and cultural preservation would all like to slow and regulate development. Old patterns of communication, or miscommunication, make it difficult for them to work together. Largely black community groups have little contact with largely white legal and environmental organizations, and efforts to link groups in South Carolina with groups in Georgia have just begun. For example, in 1989 the St. Helena Citizens Committee, a group of fifty residents, spent months working with county officials to devise new zoning laws. But the Committee, operating with no professional advice, wrote laws that will probably amount to a welcome mat for developers. Miscommunication also works the other way. Professional efforts to "help" island residents have sometimes fallen flat because the projects were designed with insufficient input from the islanders themselves.

BACKGROUND: COOPERATING ORGANIZATIONS. This portion expands upon the need for collaboration and provides enough background on the participating groups to explain why each has an essential role to play. The coalition makes sense, since the partner organizations bring different strengths, skills, and contacts to the relationship. The division of labor is also described. Among other tasks, each group will provide training to the project organizer, which ensures — at least on paper — that they will all participate in developing and overseeing the program.

The Penn Center has a long and distinguished history as the Sea Islands' African-American cultural center, with experience in land retention issues. Their participation and "substantive control" guarantees that the local black community will be involved in designing and managing the project. (The Penn Center also took over fiscal sponsorship of this program during subsequent years.)

You can't serve as a land rights advocate without knowledge of the law. The Legal Assistance Program seems like the obvious choice for legal advice, given their constituency, experience, and home base at the Penn Center. With neighboring offices, it should be easy for their attorneys to train and advise the project director.

Based on what's written, a grantmaker might feel some uncertainty about the capacity of these groups. The Penn Center's previous land retention program was "curtailed due to lack of funds." Do they now have adequate resources to oversee this project? There's nothing in the budget to pay for supervisory time. The Neighborhood Legal Assistance Program has "a staff shortage," which "prevents them from spending much time on land issues." How many hours will they be able to spare for this project? How much support is expected? The proposal doesn't tell us. Were I a grant reviewer, I would pick up the phone or arrange a site visit to pursue these questions.

Background: Cooperating Organizations

The land issue in the Sea Islands has many dimensions: cultural, economic, legal, and environmental. This project therefore involves three organizations with different areas of expertise. The Penn Center's director designed the project with the person who will be its director, Nina Morais. Ms. Morais then enlisted the help of the Coastal Conservation League and the Neighborhood Legal Assistance Program.

South Carolina Coastal Conservation League: The Coastal Conservation League, the grantee organization for this project, will raise and disburse all project funds. We will also provide training for the project director, Ms. Morais, and provide technical assistance as the project progresses. The Coastal Conservation League is described above under "Grantee Organization."

The Penn Center: The Penn Center will have substantive control over the project and will provide Ms. Morais with office space, training, and community contacts. The Penn Center, located on St. Helena Island, has deep roots in the Sea Islands' black community. The Penn Center was founded during the Civil War as the nation's first school for freed slaves, part of an abolitionist experiment that historians consider a rehearsal for the project of Reconstruction that followed the war. Today, the Penn Center works to preserve the islands' cultural heritage and serves as a community center for St. Helena and surrounding islands. It conducts educational programs for children, runs a historical museum, and houses the local Head Start and Legal Assistance programs. In the 1970s, the Penn Center ran an extensive, successful land retention project. The project has since been curtailed due to lack of funds, but Penn still gives some guidance to islanders in danger of losing their land.

Neighborhood Legal Assistance Program: The Neighborhood Legal Assistance Program will provide Ms. Morais, an attorney in her own right, with legal training and community contacts. Legal Assistance, located at the Penn Center on St. Helena, defends the legal rights of impoverished island residents in cases involving, for example, public benefits, evictions, and domestic violence. The Legal Assistance attorneys have a thorough understanding of local tax and zoning laws, through a staff shortage prevents them from spending much time on land issues.

Project Description

Short-term Goals: Ms. Morais will work with residents of St. Helena on two different levels. First, she will teach individual landowners their rights under current tax laws. Native islanders often sell land because they

PROJECT DESCRIPTION. Funders often ask, "Who carries on the work after the first phase of the project is completed?" The authors answer this question indirectly — by training a network of skilled activists, they hope to ensure the long-term continuity of local land retention efforts.

This is a strong list of specific strategies. While the project organizers plan to enlist the community in choosing the best approaches, they have done a lot of groundwork to prepare for community involvement. This is a much better approach than starting out with a blank slate and saying that a plan of action will be devised later.

You can easily adapt this idea for your own proposals. Since you can't predict the future, it's acceptable to create a menu of strategies and tactics and say, "We will choose from this menu as the project develops." Just make sure that the choices are realistic. Create an action plan, not a wish list.

Here's another effective paragraph. After listing five possible strategies above, the authors discuss one of the five in detail. This shows the depth of their analysis and gives them the chance to outline an approach that worked in other communities. Notice how they describe "sliding-scale zoning" without using a lot of technical language.

By now, Nina Morais has been mentioned nine times. She is the only staff member focusing on this project, and responsibility for its success will fall squarely on her shoulders. This is a risky arrangement, for if she turns out to be the wrong person for the job, the whole thing could fall apart.

From what we can tell, Ms. Morais is the right person (her biography appears on page 6 of the proposal) and she will get lots of training and support. As mentioned in Chapter 5, Judy Austermiller of the Boehm Foundation supported this project, in part, because she met Nina Morais and felt confident about her abilities. Despite our best intentions to create community and share responsibility, our work often depends on individual talent and initiative. The right person can make a big difference.

The long-term impact of this project will depend, in part, on how many other organizations are recruited and activated. The first step is to identify possible partners, their constituencies, and their issues. The authors have done this indirectly, using phrases like "nationally prominent civil rights groups" and "disparate community groups." A specific list of organizations would be helpful here.

cannot pay rising taxes. Some of them overestimate what they owe simply because they do not understand the intricacies of the law. Ms. Morais, an attorney, will counsel individuals and hold community tax workshops on a regular basis. In time, she will train several local residents to provide this information under her supervision. Though the local residents may begin as volunteers, they will eventually become the project staff.

Ms. Morais will also work with St. Helena's community leaders, particularly the St. Helena Citizens Committee, to devise and implement a plan of action. The plan could include (1) changes in the tax laws; (2) changes in the zoning laws; (3) coordinated strategies for economic development; (4) a land trust for the benefit of the community; (5) collaboration with other organizations on statewide land-use legislation. In each of these five areas, there a many models that could be tailored to fit St. Helena's needs. Ms. Morais will bring these models to the Citizens Committee's attention, and will act as a liaison between the Committee and experts in environmental law, land-use planning, and economic development.

For example, one strategy that environmentalists have used in agricultural communities is sliding-scale zoning. Sliding scale zoning permits much greater densities of housing on small tracts than on large ones. This allows modest development and also allows farming families to divide residential land among their children, while preserving the community's rural character. Sliding-scale zoning has been extremely successful in preserving land for agricultural use. But, to our knowledge, such zoning has been adopted only where the rural population is relatively well-off, well-educated, and well-organized. The challenge would be to tailor a sliding-scale zoning initiative to St. Helena, with its widely dispersed, low-income population. There are also other models for the Citizens Committee to follow: for example, tax laws that would strongly favor agriculture, or economic development schemes that would use, but not deplete, the island's natural resources, such as a fishery owned by native islanders or direct access to urban produce markets. The point is that St. Helena residents can regain control over their land and their livelihood only by understanding what has worked elsewhere.

Long-term goals: Ultimately, the three organizations involved in this project would like to expand it into a powerful interracial, interstate coalition to protect the Sea Islands. Nationally prominent civil rights groups are now developing various Sea Island projects, primarily on Daufuskie Island near Savannah. In addition, the Penn Center is helping to organize disparate community groups into a Sea Islands Peoples Network that will focus on land-use issues. None of these organizations has staff on the islands addressing this issue full time, and none has kept in touch with local

Communication is the key to successful coalition work. Notice how they share the communication tasks: one group develops a contact list, another manages the database and designs the mailings. As a reader, you begin to see and understand the relationships among the project partners.

The greatest strength of the Land Retention Project is the way it combines and addresses multiple issues: poverty, land rights, gentrification, environmental destruction, racism, cultural loss, and economic development. This strategy makes sense "on the ground," since these issues are interwoven, but it also improves the odds of raising money. Because of the breadth of the project, the sponsors can seek grants (and individual donations) from a wide range of sources.

By reminding us, in this paragraph, of the ethnic and economic barriers that divide the environmental movement, the authors reinforce the unique multi-racial aspect of their work.

The danger of promoting your group as "a model" is that someone has to actively spread the word. Designing a project that works is the easy part — and it isn't easy. Figuring out how to package the results so others can use them, and then disseminating these lessons, is much harder.

To their credit, the authors actually have a dissemination plan, which includes ongoing contact with other groups, a final project report, and a conference. Unfortunately, there's no money budgeted for conference costs. If they're serious about hosting a conference, they will need to raise extra funds during the next two years and should describe their fundraising plan in this proposal.

environmentalists. With the Penn Center's contacts throughout the islands, and with the Coastal Conservation League's computerized mailing lists and desktop publishing capability, this project could substantially improve communication among all the groups interested in this issue. We could also help unite these groups behind certain strategies, like statewide land-use legislation. This project will enable the Penn Center, the Coastal Conservation League, and Legal Assistance to begin building a powerful coalition. It will also enable us to raise funds to hire more staff, particularly local residents, for coalition work.

This project could have a broader impact as well. It could be a model for other rural areas in the Southeast -- in Mississippi and Louisiana, for example -- whose largely black populations are just beginning to contend with aggressive development. Rural communities have few models for sensible, sustainable growth. To the extent that such models exist, they have been used only where residents are wealthy and well-educated. This project will be the first in the Southeast, and probably the first in the nation, to develop a strategy for sustainable growth in a poor and relatively powerless community. Furthermore, this project could serve as a model for organizing across race and class lines on environmental issues. Few groups in the Southeast have even tried to find common ground between white, middle-class environmentalists and the low-income, minority communities that are often the primary victims of environmental damage. This project could serve as a model for biracial organizing for both white environmentalists and black leaders throughout the South, among whom the Penn Center commands great respect.

In order to insure that this project become a replicable model, we intend to meet initially with representatives of community groups in the Sea Islands and environmental organizations throughout the Southeast. We will then stay in close touch with these people to make sure that the lessons learned on St. Helena continue to be useful elsewhere, and to make sure that what we learn is disseminated as quickly as possible. In addition, Ms. Morais will end the second year by writing an analysis of the project, describing opportunities, obstacles, and strategies for replication. This report will be the focus of a conference involving the people who have monitored the project since its inception, as well as representatives from other environmental and community groups in the Southeast.

DUTIES AND QUALIFICATIONS OF PRINCIPALS. This is a terrific personnel page, because:

1. Everyone is extremely well-qualified.

2. They bring an interesting mix of skills and experiences to the project.

3. Their qualifications are described in a straightforward manner. These biographies are neither boastful nor modest; the tone is just right.

4. The descriptions are concise. No words are wasted.

The original proposal also contains a list of advisory board members, including the director of the Land Loss Prevention Project; a board member and a staff lawyer with the NAACP Legal Defense and Educational Fund; a Sea Islands historian; and the state director of the Federation of Southern Cooperatives. These people agreed to consult with the project director as requested.

For the sake of space, I've deleted the list (though it certainly belongs in the full proposal). If you have an active advisory board, feel free to include the necessary information in your proposal.

Duties and Qualifications of Principals

Nina Morais, the project director, will undertake the tasks described above under "Proposed Project." Ms. Morais has a strong academic background in science (B.A. Amherst College), American History (M.A. Harvard University) and law (J.D. Yale University). As an intern for the NAACP Legal Defense Fund in 1987-88, Ms. Morais helped initiate a lawsuit that seeks greater equity for poor and minority children in Connecticut's public schools. Among other duties, she helped to organize and fund a statewide, grassroots coalition of minority teachers, parents, and civic leaders, then served as the liaison between the coalition and the attorneys. Since then, Ms. Morais has served as a law clerk for the Chief Judge of the United States Court of Appeals for the Second Circuit and has practiced law with Fried, Frank, Harris, Shriver, and Jacobson in Washington, D.C.

Emory Campbell, who has been Executive Director of the Penn Center for the past eleven years, will supervise the project. Mr. Campbell, a native of the Sea Islands, received his B.S. in Biology from Savannah State College and M.S. in Environmental Health Engineering from Tufts University. Before joining the Penn Center, Mr. Campbell was Director of Community Services for the
Beaufort-Jasper Comprehensive Health Service, where he worked with low-income landowners to improve housing and install water and sewage systems on St. Helena and adjacent islands.

Dana Beach, Executive Director of the South Carolina Coastal Conservation League since its founding in 1989, will provide training for Ms. Morais and technical assistance throughout the project. Mr. Beach received a B.A. in Mathematics from Davidson College and an M.B.A. from the University of Pennsylvania. He has been involved with coastal development issues in South Carolina for the past eight years: as Congressman Arthur Ravenal Jr.'s environmental assistant and as State Political Action Chair and State Conservation Chair for the Sierra Club. Mr. Beach serves on the national boards of the Coastal Alliance and the National Growth Management Leadership Project, and he is a member of the Charleston County Planning Board.

Martha Dicus, Managing Attorney at the Neighborhood Legal Assistance Program on St. Helena Island, will also provide training and technical assistance. Ms. Dicus received a B.A. from Meredith College and a J.D. from the University of South Carolina. She has worked as a legal services attorney and public defender in South Carolina for the past twelve years, and has managed the Legal Assistance office on St. Helena for the past five years. In 1989, Ms. Dicus was named Legal Services Attorney of the Year by the South Carolina Bar Association.

BUDGET. When you create your budget, restate the time frame of the project (in this case, April 1992 - April 1994) at the top of the page. This helps to put the numbers in perspective.

Note that the sponsors are contributing services in support of this project. If they could itemize the value of these services — supervisory time, office rent and utilities, bookkeeping, etc.— and show the amount as a "match," it would add up to a significant amount of money. Whenever possible, try to attach a cash value to all in-kind donations, then figure out a way to include that value in your budget as "in-kind services pledged."

Compared to many social change jobs, this salary looks generous. Keep in mind that the project organizer is an attorney who could be making a lot more money in another job, and probably did in her previous position.

Health insurance is itemized at more than $300 per month; why so much?

The travel line is also expensive, but the authors do a good job of itemizing and explaining the costs. For example, it's wise to budget money for the project organizer to visit peer organizations in other parts of the region and learn from their work. This could be the most important $2,500 in the budget.

Telephone costs exceed $200 per month, which seems high. Most of the work takes place in the local community, so why the long-distance charges? A sentence or two would adequately answer the question.

This budget is missing a revenue section, so we have no idea how much money has been raised, pledged, or requested. We don't know which foundations have been approached, or the status of these requests. It's always helpful to show where the money is coming from, not just how you plan to spend it.

Budget

This budget includes only salary and expenses for Ms. Morais. The Penn Center will absorb the cost of supervising the project and the Coastal Conservation League will absorb the cost of administering the grant.

$32,000	1st year salary
37,000	2nd year salary
7,500	Health insurance
5,175	Social Security taxes
8,000	Travel and lodging:

For Ms. Morais to spend the first three weeks of the project visiting organizations in other parts of the country that work with minority communities on interrelated environmental and economic development issues, such as the Land Loss Prevention Project in North Carolina, Mac-Sap Development in Georgia, the Highlander Center in Tennessee, and the Gulf Coast Tenant Leadership Development Project in Louisiana ($2,500)

For travel to our office in Charleston and to citizens groups and environmental organizations in South Carolina and Georgia ($3,000)

For raising funds to continue this work after the second year ($2,500)

5,000	Telephone, including call related to raising funds
5,000	Postage, office supplies, educational materials
————	
$99,675	TOTAL

Heartwood

Summary page. This proposal was submitted to the Outdoor Industry Conservation Alliance, a coalition of businesses serving hikers, skiers, rock climbers, rafters, etc. They grant a percentage of their profits to conservation groups. To apply, you need sponsorship from a member company; in this case, Patagonia. It's like going to a fancy private party — show your invitation at the door. That's why Heartwood lists their sponsor up front.

The first thing to notice is the layout. These folks know their way around a computer. The margins are generous, there's a nice mix of type faces, and the information is well-organized. While I find the boxes distracting — remember, you want to keep clutter to a minimum — the overall look is very professional.

Based on the format, it appears that they took a mandatory application form, entered it into their computer, and adapted it. Many funders require a standard form or cover sheet, but nearly all will allow you to reproduce it on your computer. This gives you the flexibility to create your own look, as Heartwood has done.

Under "total membership," they show both individuals and organizations. While 500 individual members is a respectable total for a grassroots group, the number of groups involved — 70 — is really impressive. As you'll see in the proposal, the size and scope of this coalition sets Heartwood apart. The authors are smart enough to brag about it every chance they get.

Heartwood defines their region in a way that's both precise and poetic. Perhaps they're echoing Woody Guthrie's phrasing in his populist anthem, "This Land is Your Land" — to good effect.

The funder poses an important, straightforward question. Why should *anybody* fund your project? Why should anybody care? Always take it as your challenge to answer this question as directly and clearly as it is asked.

Jargon alert: "...resource extraction, habitat fragmentation, and industrial pollution..." These phrases might be acceptable alone, but when stacked together they weigh the proposal down. Remember, technical terms are aimed at the reader's mind; simple language is more emotional and, generally speaking, more compelling. Language is a minor, but recurring, problem with this application. When in doubt, the authors tend to reach for the bigger, fancier word when a plain one will work even better. Remember, small is beautiful.

Corporate Sponsor: *Patagonia, Inc.*   December 26, 1994

LEGAL NAME OF ORGANIZATION
HEARTWOOD, Incorporated

ORGANIZATION ADDRESS
P.O. Box 402 *Paoli, Indiana 47454*

CONTACT PERSONS / TITLES / PHONE, FAX NUMBERS	
Executive Coordinator *Andy Mahler* *Voice/FAX: 812-723-2430*	*Financial Coordinator* *Phil Berck* *Voice/FAX: 812-597-5652*

PROJECT NAME **Central Appalachian Wilderness Preserve**	AMOUNT REQUESTED **$35,000**

STAFF SIZE *2 full-time, 1 half-time, 2 third-time*	TOTAL MEMBERSHIP *> 500 individuals; 70 organizations*
TAX STATUS *501(c)(3)*	ANNUAL OPERATING BUDGET (Expenses) *1993: $40,192 1994: > $100,000*

ORGANIZATIONAL PURPOSE/MISSION STATEMENT
HEARTWOOD is dedicated to the protection of the heartland hardwood forest, from the Allegheny Mountains of Pennsylvania to the Ouachita Mountains of Arkansas and Oklahoma, and from the headwaters of the Mississippi to the Tennessee River Valley.

WHY SHOULD THE ALLIANCE FUND YOUR PROJECT?

More than half of all Americans now live in cities of a million or more—many of which are located along the Eastern seaboard—far from the large public landholdings of the Western United States. Muscle-powered recreation in natural, outdoor settings continues to increase in popularity, even as wilderness opportunities and native biological diversity of Eastern hardwood forests are being diminished by resource extraction, habitat fragmentation, and industrial pollution. There now exists the will <u>and</u> the opportunity to protect the last wild places of the Central Appalachians—most of which are publicly owned—before the impending wave of industrialization irrevocably transforms these healthy forest ecosystems into degraded landscapes.

HEARTWOOD is uniquely poised to **coordinate** existing efforts, enhance public awareness, and help provide fundamental grassroots organizing. This expertise and HEARTWOOD's community of dedicated activists form the cornerstone of this funding request.

HEARTWOOD is a great name. On the surface, it combines "heartland" and "hardwood," but it evokes something deeper, with all the connotations of the words *heart* and *wood*. Heartwood is the center of the tree — as any woodworker knows, this is the oldest, toughest, and most beautiful wood.

Far too many organizations have 5- and 6-word names (which is bad enough), then they lump the first letters together into awkward acronyms. If you have the luxury of starting a new group, or you're ready to reinvigorate an old one, try to come up with a simple, evocative name.

RFP means "request for proposal." The Alliance advertised that they were offering grants for a specific purpose, and invited groups to submit applications.

PROJECT BACKGROUND AND OVERVIEW. The authors mention their sponsor, Patagonia, a second time. This serves both to thank the sponsor in front of its peer companies and to reinforce the idea that Patagonia has given both approval and money.

Weigh every adjective and adverb; keep only the words needed to make your meaning clear. Does "overarching" add anything essential to "long-term goal?" What's the difference between "a larger view" and "a larger *contextual* view?" When in doubt, edit it out.

While the term "mixed mesophytic" puts me off — I don't have a clue what it means — "Mother Forest" is pretty catchy. If you must use technical or scientific language, this is a good way to soften its impact. The authors have also increased the visual appeal of the proposal by creating a special box for this phrase.

Notice the running foot, which provides page numbers at the bottom of the page.

HEARTWOOD

DEDICATED TO THE PROTECTION OF THE HEARTLAND HARDWOOD FOREST

Andy Mahler ● PO Box 402 ● Paoli, IN ● 47454 ● Voice, FAX: (812) 723-2430

Phil Berck ● RR 3 Box 393 ● Morgantown, IN ● 46160 ● Voice, FAX: (812)597-5652

E-mail: HEARTWOOD@igc.apc.org

Response to *The Conservation Alliance* RFP:
Organizing for a Central Appalachian Wilderness Preserve
December 1994

HEARTWOOD is a cooperative network of grassroots organizations with a demonstrable record of securing protection for public forests in the Heartwood (heartland hardwood) region of North America. Our success is based on clearly articulated policy: comprehensive public forest protection; waste and demand reduction; promotion of alternative fibers such as hemp and kenaf; export restrictions; and sustainable, responsible, and profitable management of private forest land. **HEARTWOOD is requesting $35,000 from *The Conservation Alliance* for initiating and coordinating a citizen-based drive to establish a comprehensive wilderness preserve in the Central Appalachian region.**

Project Background and Overview

Through generous funding this year, *Patagonia* has helped HEARTWOOD launch the <u>Central Appalachian Organizing Project</u>, extending our coordination and support of grassroots forest protection efforts into the essential forests of this region. Working with existing groups in West Virginia, Virginia, Pennsylvania, Maryland, and eastern Ohio, our overarching long-term goal is to integrate the remaining wild places in the Central Appalachians, declare the totality a national preserve, and muster the necessary citizen support to garner federal recognition of its protected status. Along the way, a number of intermediate forest protection goals and organizing objectives will be achieved, and together they comprise the current project for which HEARTWOOD seeks funding from *The Conservation Alliance*. The budget request is tied to the first year of organizing activity. Long-term objectives and activities will be discussed when necessary to provide a larger contextual view—one that will be a key hook for attracting and motivating organizers, and influencing target outreach groups. The first-year objectives and related expenditures will be clearly delineated.

The importance of protecting forests in the Central Appalachian region cannot be overstated. The Central Appalachian bioregion contains a great diversity of forest types, including the heart of the mixed mesophytic forest—the oldest, most diverse forest in North America. Forest protection activists have fallen behind the extractive industries in this region, particularly in West

> *The mixed mesophytic is the*
> *Mother Forest—the genetic origin of all*
> *hardwood forests in the Eastern United States*

Here's a nice running head with the project title. If you use a running head, you can include the name of your group, the project title, or both. It's best to use the organization's name, since that's how the proposal will be filed and tracked.

This list of cooperating groups should appeal to funders interested in supporting community-based conservation efforts. Between the local flavor of the organizations and their offbeat names — PAWnet, Lucy Braun Association, The Volunteers — the list almost defines the word *grassroots*.

The authors use their layout skills effectively here. If these groups had been pushed into a paragraph together and separated by commas, our eyes would pass them by. Whenever you create lists — goals, objectives, collaborators — it's often helpful to indent them and define the individual items with bullets, letters, or numbers.

THE CENTRAL APPALACHIANS. Since the term "Central Appalachians" is imprecise, the authors wisely spend a paragraph defining the geographic scope of the project. (Note that this ambitious project covers only a portion of their entire region, which includes states as far away as Minnesota and Oklahoma.)

This paragraph sets up the problem statement with a brief, general discussion of environmental threats to the region. In the sections below, the authors move from the general to the specific by including the names of actual companies and towns. This strategy — defining the problem in broad terms, then using specific examples to show how the problem affects real communities — is an effective way to structure a proposal.

Their analysis of the problem is concise but sophisticated. It describes the connections between industrial development and environmental destruction, and shows how job loss drives deforestation. This analysis supports their stated goal of creating and promoting environmentally sustainable economic development, including recreation.

Footnotes are fine in a proposal, but don't overdo it. As an alternative, it's acceptable to add the note in parentheses at the end of the sentence: (see attached press clipping)

Virginia and Pennsylvania. We must use this year to catch up, establish working organizational links, and develop strategies for restoration and rehabilitation of these essential forests, which historically are the evolutionary source for all hardwood forests growing in the Eastern U.S. We will extend our virtually flat, cooperative network model, providing vitally needed *coordination*, technical assistance, and some financial support for regional organizing expenses. HEARTWOOD's expansion to the Ozarks last year has proven to be a resoundingly effective use of this strategy.

HEARTWOOD is working with several grassroots groups in the Central Appalachian region:

- West Virginia Environmental Council (WV)
- West Virginia Highlands Conservancy (WV)
- Ohio Valley Environmental Coalition (WV)
- Central Appalachian Biodiversity Project (WV)
- The Volunteers (WV)
- Virginians for Wilderness (VA)
- Buckeye Forest Council (OH)
- Lucy Braun Association (OH)
- PAWnet (PA)
- MidAtlantic Biodiversity Project (PA)
- Several student groups, including the Allegheny Defense Project (PA)

By linking these folks together through the HEARTWOOD network—and identifying additional groups and individual activists in the region—HEARTWOOD can amplify their efforts and help turn the industrial tide. Proactively, integrating and recognizing the Central Appalachian hills, coves, valleys, and ridges as the *Mother Forest*—the seed source and last refugia for hardwood species biodiversity—is, at its essence, an irresistible Noah's Ark preservation strategy.

The Central Appalachians

The principal target area includes West Virginia, central and western Pennsylvania, western Virginia, and western Maryland. Our activities will also encompass parts of the surrounding states, including eastern Kentucky, southeast Ohio, southwest New York, New Jersey, and Delaware.

The Central Appalachians are rich from a strategic political view, due to their proximity to major Eastern population centers. Right now, long-term economic well-being is being sacrificed for short-run satisfaction of greed, and most of the public remains in the dark. Imminent threats to the region's biodiversity demand immediate, potent responses if we are to save these critical pieces of landscape and protect the biological threads that connect them together.

Immediate threat—transnational extractive industries. The proposed pulp mill for Apple Grove, WV is one of the largest and potentially destructive industrial projects in the region.[1] We haven't lost this one yet, but industry is way ahead at this point. Development for at least two chip mills has begun, and TrusJoist MacMillan has initiated construction of a laminated strand lumber facility near Buckhannon, West Virginia. These projects stand to decimate large tracts of public and private forest—robbing them of their potential for regeneration—through repeated logging of large <u>and</u> small diameter tree growth. While strip mining in the Central Appalachians still exists, it is on the decline. Unfortunately, this has generated further economic pressure to create jobs; short-run solutions are politically expedient but thrive at the expense of depleted forest resources. Large-scale extractions also threaten the economic health of tourism, recreation, and existing hardwood industries.

---

[1] Press clipping enclosed

In this paragraph, the authors show common cause with the grantmakers, who work in the outdoor recreation industry — both Heartwood and the funders want to reach and involve the same constituency. The goal is stated in positive terms — "recreational forest use demonstrates the prospects for economic development which does not depend on resource extraction" — but here's the unspoken message: if there is nowhere left to hike, backpack, canoe, etc., you (the funders) will sell a lot fewer hiking boots, backpacks, and canoes. Subtle, but effective.

THE ORGANIZING PROJECT. Now we get to the nuts and bolts of the proposal. Once again, the layout — indented lists with bullets — makes it easy for the reader to find the important information. By using dynamic verbs, such as *create, cement,* and *leverage,* the authors project a sense of power and competence.

Notice how these goals are very broad. They don't say anything about how the work will be accomplished — which is appropriate. The details are described below under "objectives." Because each of these three goals relates to a corresponding section on objectives, it would help to use numbers instead of bullets. For example, the specific objectives for goal number 1 ("create and promote...") are described under the next subheading ("Framing the Preserve..."), which should also be labeled with a number 1. The second goal ("cement coalitions") would get a number 2, etc.

These objectives serve as a list of tasks to be completed. As Heartwood works through the items, the group moves closer to its goal of creating a regional wilderness plan and protecting the land. Each objective has a specific outcome: a staff member is hired, a brochure is created, mailings are prepared and sent.

While no dates are attached to these tasks, they are presented in sequence. To improve this proposal, the authors could add target dates for completion of each objective, then set some numerical goals, such as how many mailing lists they plan to obtain.

Coalition work is always attractive to grantmakers — they understand that most grassroots groups lack the resources to mount major campaigns by themselves. Coalitions can also draw on a diversity of skills, backgrounds, and perceptions to increase the impact of their work. Heartwood is working to recruit an interesting mix of constituencies under its wilderness umbrella. With 70 groups on board, the strategy seems to be working.

Once again, their coalition goals are broken down into specific objectives. They've even scheduled the organizing meetings. This proposal would be strengthened by more of these concrete milestones and numerical goals; for example, how many people do they plan to recruit for their phone tree in the first year?

Muscle-powered Recreational Access. The Central Appalachians are within a short day's drive for hundreds of thousands of East Coast hikers, backpackers, canoers, rafters, kayakers, birders, cavers, hunters, rock climbers, mountain bikers, and other outdoor enthusiasts. Prospective wilderness proponents include key decision-makers in Washington D.C. as well as many other politically influential cities and states. This geographic proximity creates natural target outreach groups, potentially receptive to the wilderness preserve concept and the recreational opportunities it affords. In addition, recreational forest use demonstrates the prospects for economic development which does not depend on resource extraction.

The Organizing Project: Goals, Strategy, and Tactical Objectives

The scope of the first year's activities encompasses essential grassroots organizing. This will set the stage for subsequent political organizing and lobbying. The first-year goals are

- ◆ create and promote the *Central Appalachian Wilderness Preserve* concept and, through grassroots organizing, garner the support of citizens in the region
- ◆ cement coalitions among existing grassroots forest protection organizations in the region, and integrate the project with the national forest reform movement
- ◆ leverage organizing activities for defensive action against immediate threats while advancing the proactive wilderness preserve solution

Framing the Preserve Concept, Organizing, and Outreach. The first-year objectives are

- • contract with two or three part-time Central Appalachian organizers to coordinate the project
- • coordinate (and initiate where necessary) citizen monitoring of all state and federal forests in the region
- • working with area naturalists and existing groups, create a vision map of the wilderness preserve
- • create a brochure (National Park genre) describing the preserve in geographic, biological, and recreational terms
- • obtain targeted mailing lists for the region
- • execute mass mailings in at least three states
- • through responses to mailings and on-the-ground organizing, recruit activist supporters in each state to promote the wilderness preserve, and to oppose industrial threats to forest integrity

Building Coalitions. One of HEARTWOOD's primary areas of expertise is in creating resilient and inclusive coalitions among smaller grassroots forest protection groups. We seek common cause with waste and recycling organizations, incinerator and landfill groups, commercial hemp and kenaf interests, groups working on chlorine and toxics issues, sustainable agriculture and trade groups, and social justice organizations. The first-year objectives here are

- • hold at least three region-wide organizing meetings (in March, May, and September 1995)
- • establish a cohesive, coordinated network with phone/fax trees in each state, assuring effective political clout when the battlefield shifts from the rural milieu to State Capital buildings and the halls of Congress
- • through example and other means, help coordinate with—and when necessary, seed—similar preserve projects around the country, coordinating with the Wildlands Project

This goal is basically reactive. Heartwood wants the flexibility to address unexpected problems as they arise. This is sensible planning but, as a result, the objectives are a bit vague and perhaps overly ambitious. For example, the group seeks to stop *all* timber sales, road building, and industrial construction in the region — is this realistic? It would be better to know how many timber sales they think they can effectively challenge in a year (but not *which* timber sales). When a group's objectives are as broad as these, their organizing capacity and pragmatism might be questioned by potential grantmakers.

EVALUATION CRITERIA. Heartwood's goals are to stop extractive industries from destroying the forest and to promote environmentally sustainable development; their strategy is community organizing. By activating thousands of people, the organizers can demonstrate success for the process (organizing) but will not necessarily achieve the desired outcome (forest preservation).

In this section, the authors would do well to separate their process evaluation — how people are activated and what they do — from their outcome evaluation — how the results, on the ground, will be measured. What, specifically, does the road to success look like after a year? This proposal needs to define short-term success in a more concrete way.

They use nice language here: "map it, name it, and claim it ... the old rules no longer apply ... energy, enthusiasm, a sense of urgency, and clarity of vision ... citizens as caretakers of the wilds." Indeed, this language could be used earlier in the proposal, when the authors introduce their solutions.

HEARTWOOD BACKGROUND. This brief overview does a nice job of describing Heartwood's recent accomplishments and evolving strategy. Because of space limitations, the authors have attached an outline of recent successes, as indicated in footnote 3. The main point — the group has halted most of the logging in their region — is stated up front, just in case the reviewer doesn't read the attachment. (Remember, proposal attachments are not always distributed to grant reviewers, so make sure you get all the essential information into the body of the proposal.)

If allowed by the funder's guidelines, this section would work even better at the beginning of the proposal. Heartwood's accomplishments inspire confidence and make their ambitious goals (see above) seem more attainable.

Uncompromising Defense. Organizing, outreach, and coalition building not only build support for the establishment of the wilderness preserve, but create a comprehensive strategy for defending against the invasive industrial conversion of public assets to private profits. The objectives here are

- through administrative appeals and citizen-based litigation, block all timber sales on public land
- seek to close existing logging roads, and to prevent all proposed road building
- through grassroots organizing (and when appropriate, administrative appeals and litigation), block all proposed paper and chip mills, manufactured lumber facilities, and other transnational industrial invasions

Evaluation Criteria and Future Prospects

The criteria used for monitoring progress and evaluating project outcomes derive directly from the listed objectives, i.e., press clipping files, logs of appeals attempts and results, counts of expanded mailing lists and phone trees, minutes of organizational meetings, records of court appearances, etc. Ultimately, the success of this initiative will be measured by organized citizen groups enjoying broad-based support in their local communities as they forge bonds of common purpose and trust. With a communications and coordination infrastructure in place, resource sharing, cooperative planning, specialization, and the division of labor will help generate the strategic political support necessary to sustain long-term protection and expansion of the Central Appalachian wildlands. In the process, HEARTWOOD will provide examples of how non-extractive forest use can be an important component of sustainable economic development in rural, forest-dependent communities.

Regional groups around the country have, for some time, been exploring coordinated national forest protection strategy which can be characterized as **"map it, name it, and claim it**." Options being discussed include the possibility of transferring jurisdiction over forest preserves from the Forest Service to another federal agency.[2] These bold ideas presume that the old rules no longer apply. We must generate sufficient energy, enthusiasm, a sense of urgency, and clarity of vision to create a new forest protection paradigm based on citizens as caretakers of the wilds.

HEARTWOOD Background

HEARTWOOD has accomplished amazing forest protection feats within a relatively meager budget over the past year.[3] Our coalition has halted virtually all logging on National Forests in Indiana, Illinois, Ohio, and Kentucky, and we have suspended or ended major forest-destroying projects in Missouri, Arkansas, and Tennessee. HEARTWOOD is in the midst of a bioregional, organizational, and financial expansion. We are now shifting our clout from a defensive posture to a more proactive stance. Among other advances, this move will encompass public education focused on wood products demand reduction, and promotion of alternatives to wood fibers. We are also expanding our network to provide services to forest protection groups in the Eastern and Southern United States (Forest Service Regions 8 & 9). The intent is not to dictate policy or establish central authority, but rather to build upon the solid foundation of communication,

---

[2] See attached sample brochure prepared by *RESTORE: The North Woods.*

[3] see *Recent Successes...* attachment.

It's okay to boast, but be careful not to overstate your case. When the authors claim that Heartwood "will create unprecedented synergistic power and change the face of the forest protection movement," the language is far too fancy. We change the world inch by inch, meeting by meeting, task by boring, sweaty task. These people are good organizers; let's see them create an unprecedented amount of sweat among their members and colleagues.

FUNDING REQUEST. This is a decent budget — simple and clear — but it would be improved by more details. A few unanswered questions:

1. How many people and staff hours do they plan to pay for with $16,000? Is this enough staff time to implement their ambitious list of objectives? (For a partial answer, see footnote 4.)

2. Considering the size of their region, the travel budget seems small. What's the basis for this amount?

3. How many names and/or mailing lists will they purchase for $3,000? How many pieces of mail can they send for another $3,000?

4. What do they mean by "administrative support for local groups?" Does that include training, bookkeeping, newsletter production, membership tracking, fundraising, or anything else?

These question can be addressed with a sentence beneath each line item, or in a separate budget narrative. One or two paragraphs would be plenty.

It's appropriate to list attachments, as the authors have done here, but be selective. If you're not sure which enclosures to send, read the funder's guidelines. Restrict yourself to the minimum number of items requested and avoid duplication. For example, how much material in the *Recent Success* flyer is also covered in the *Heartwood Annual*?

coordination, and support represented by HEARTWOOD's more than 70 participating member organizations. We are providing the model for forest protection grassroots organizing throughout the country, nurturing strong regional coalitions, and **growing** the interconnections among us. This national *Network Cooperative* will create unprecedented synergistic power and change the face of the forest protection movement.

Funding Request

HEARTWOOD is requesting $35,000 to support this project's first-year activities as described above.[4] Funds will cover compensation for the Central Appalachian organizers, travel, printing and mailing costs, phone and fax, and some administrative support for financially strapped forest activist groups in the region. This money will not only be used to achieve the outlined objectives—important milestones in and of themselves—but will help construct the foundation for pursuing the larger goal of establishing a permanent *Central Appalachian Wilderness Preserve*.

BUDGET SUMMARY

	REQUEST
Central Appalachian Organizers–Service Contracts	16,000
Travel and Mileage	3,000
Mailing List Purchase	3,000
Postage	3,000
Printing	3,000
Phone, Fax, and E-mail	2,000
Administrative Support for Local Groups	5,000
TOTAL REQUEST	**35,000**

Thank you for your consideration of this request.

Phil Berck, *Financial Coordinator*

Andy Mahler, *Executive Coordinator*

Attachments
HEARTWOOD Board of Directors; HEARTWOOD Member Organizations
Recent Success, Activities, and Impending Threats to the Region*
HEARTWOOD 1994 Annual (published May 1994)*
HEARTWOOD's *Citizens' Guide To Protecting Your National Forests**
Central Hardwoods Fact Sheet*
Apple Grove press clipping
RESTORE: The North Woods sample brochure
501(c)(3) letter
*Printed on tree-free kenaf paper

---

[4] Additional funds are being sought to support broader mailings and more expansive outreach tactics. In-kind donations of printing and layout services will also help stretch this budget.

MONO LAKE COMMITTEE

The experience of the Mono Lake Committee proves that long-term battles can be fought and won. For nearly 50 years, the city of Los Angeles diverted water from the lake, almost 300 miles to the north, for urban use. Since Mono Lake is fed by a few small streams, these diversions lowered the water level, destroying lake and riparian habitat and exposing the unique mineral towers (tufa) represented in the group's logo.

The Mono Lake Committee fought for 16 years to end these diversions and restore the watershed. During the last round of hearings, supporters and allies sent 4,000 letters to the Water Board. I doubt that the original members planned on a 16-year campaign, but the group persevered, organized and eventually won.

In September 1994, after the project presented in this proposal was underway, the California State Water Resources Board ordered Los Angeles to stop diverting water from the basin until the lake level rises seventeen feet — which will take decades. To replace water it formerly removed from the lake, the city must develop local water conservation and reclamation projects.

COVER LETTER. The proposal begins with a cover letter, which is included so you can see how the letter and proposal fit together.

This project is built on a compelling concept: take the kids out of East Los Angeles and other inner-city neighborhoods and show them, in person, where their tap water comes from. This is an interesting strategy to involve communities of color in water resource issues.

"Approximately $36,129..." Does that sound approximate? Also, $17,000 seems like an unusual request, which makes me wonder how these numbers were produced. A foundation officer might skip ahead to the budget page and look for answers. Unfortunately, the budget doesn't address these questions, either.

The direct tone of this appeal is effective: "We have five reasons..." This cover letter serves as an excellent summary by discussing the need for the project, its intended results, and why this particular foundation is being asked to support it — all in brief, clear paragraphs set off with effective use of bold type and indented text.

Be careful with words like "overwhelming." As an alternative, try to quantify the demand. How many groups have requested water education programs? How many requests have been turned down due to lack of money or staff? How many groups are asking for repeat programs? What's the trend — how do the number of requests, and the turnout for education programs, compare to previous years?

MONO LAKE
C O M M I T T E E
1207 West Magnolia Blvd.,
Suite D
Burbank, CA 91506
(818) 972-2025

February 27, 1994

Board of Directors

Co-Chairs:
Sally Gaines
Ed Manning

Todd Berens
Libby Ellis
Patrick Flinn
Susana Fousekis
Ed Grosswiler
Dian Grueneich
Barbara Blake Levine
David Marquart
Tom Soto

Directors Emeriti
Grace de Laet
Helen Green
Genny Smith

Executive Director
Martha Davis

**Mono Lake Office &
Information Center**
P. O. Box 29
Lee Vining, CA 93541
(619) 647-6595

Mr. James R. Compton, President
Compton Foundation, Inc.
545 Middlefield Road, Suite 178
Menlo Park, CA 94025

Dear Mr. Compton,

On behalf of the Mono Lake Committee, I am submitting the enclosed proposal to develop a public education program on California water issues for Los Angeles city youth. Our funding request is for seed money to help us transform a successful pilot project into a permanent, self sustaining program serving our Southland community.

Under this proposal, the Mono Lake Committee will join with community groups in Los Angeles for the purpose of educating inner city youth about California water and the special places that lie at the other end of our water taps. As part of the program, participants will visit Mono Lake and see for themselves one example of example of the magnificent ecosystems with which they share their water.

This collaborative project will help make one of the most important communities in the Southland a player in addressing the water problems facing our state. The result: support for the protection of distant places like Mono Lake and the San Francisco Bay Delta will be voiced by an inner city constituency who knows and cares about the connection between their city's water use and the health of these resources.

Our proposal is budgeted at approximately $36,129 for this year. We ask that the Compton Foundation support this project by providing $17,000 in seed money for 1994.

We have five reasons for coming to the Compton Foundation for this project.

* **First, wise water use policies in Los Angeles are critical to the protection of Mono Lake and the San Francisco Bay Delta.**

Water demand will continue to grow in California. Alternatives such as water conservation and recycling must be promoted by local residents if this demand is to be met in a way that does not cause further harm to the State's precious natural resources.

* **Second, there is overwhelming demand by Los Angeles inner city service organizations for the proposed water education program.**

The Mono Lake Committee co-sponsored a pilot water education project with Los Angeles community groups last year. This project was an overwhelming success, with many of the participants becoming outspoken promoters of water conservation and the protection of special places like Mono Lake. Many inner city service organizations are now asking the Committee to repeat the program.

"We need the money" is an honest part of any appeal. The authors have done a wise thing, however; by placing this reason in the middle of the list, they don't appear desperate. Never begin your proposal with, "Give us money because we don't have any." First focus on what the community wants and needs — then describe how your group can and will respond, if funded.

Be wary about praising the grantmaker in the cover letter. If done poorly, it sounds like naked flattery. You want to treat foundation officers as colleagues, not royalty. Here, the authors are modest in their praise, so it works. They also demonstrate how this project would build on the foundation's previous efforts by "shifting the water debate in California."

(By the way, the Compton Foundation turned down this proposal because it fell outside their area of interest. According to Suzanne Michell, program associate for the foundation, they fund national education programs, but traditionally have supported neither local nor youth education — though these restrictions are not mentioned in their published guidelines. A phone call would have saved the authors a lot of work. On a happier note, the World Wildlife Fund, Southern California Gas Company, and other grantmakers supported these outdoor education programs.)

JARGON ALERT: "...results-oriented." This sounds impressive, but what group doesn't strive for results? The authors might rephrase this item as, "Fifth, the project will achieve measurable results, as follows." The important word is *measurable*.

An excellent list — specific and realistic. Note that they state how many trips they plan to organize during the grant year.

For this final item, the authors should attach a number to the outreach goal. How many groups will receive their materials?

Watch for repetition. This letter begins and ends with the catchy phrase, "...the special places that lie at the end of our water taps." Nearly identical wording is used on the first and last pages of the proposal. Once is great, twice is okay, but four times in one application wears out the freshness of the phrase.

In most cases, the executive director (or other lead staff) should sign the cover letter. It's acceptable for the project director, development director, or a board officer to sign, especially if he or she has a relationship with the funder. (Sometimes you will be asked to include a separate letter, signed by an officer of the board, stating that the board of directors has approved the application.)

* **Third, we need a special investment to help us jump start the proposed public education program.**

Although several organizations will be involved in the proposed program, all are short of ready capital for the planning and curriculum development needed for this education effort. The Mono Lake Committee is also carrying an enormous financial burden from the recent legal hearings on Mono Lake. The grant of seed money from the Compton Foundation will enable the Committee to build on the success of our pilot project and develop a comprehensive, self-sustaining program which integrates targeted educational materials with support for Mono Lake tours.

* **Fourth, the Compton Foundation has been a leader in supporting bold efforts to protect California's water resources and has provided pathbreaking support for environmental justice programs.**

We believe that our program is unique among state-wide environmental education efforts and has enormous potential for shifting the water debate in California. For too long, the Southland's inner city community has not had a voice in water decisions that directly impact their future.

* **Fifth, the project is results oriented.**

The Mono Lake Committee has long been a leader in the development of L.A.-based water conservation and reclamation programs. Drawing upon this experience and our successful pilot project last year, we are poised to achieve the following results in 1994:

* production of a water education curriculum, targeting inner city youth, which connects water use to the natural environments of California;

* co-sponsorship of at least three to five trips to Mono Lake for inner city youth organizations;

* provision of a comprehensive education program for these groups at Mono Lake;

* distribution of materials and information about our program to a wide range of service groups, community based organizations, schools and public agencies involved in water conservation education.

To achieve these results, all we need is a modest seed investment. We hope you share our sense of the importance of working with Los Angeles' inner city community to develop a unique coalition which will support protection of all the special places that lie at the end of our water taps. The Mono Lake Committee is a 501 (C)(4) organization. The Mono Lake Foundation serves as our 501 (C)(3) fiscal agent. Enclosed is a copy of the Foundation's 501 (C)(3) status.

Thank you for the consideration of our proposal. Please call me if you have any questions.

Sincerely,

Martha Davis
Executive Director

THE OPPORTUNITY. The proposal itself begins on this page. Unfortunately, there's no headline identifying the *Mono Lake Committee* or even *Inner City Water Education Project*. The cover letter is designed to serve as a summary page, but if it gets separated from the proposal, the readers will be confused.

These subheadings — THE OPPORTUNITY, THE STRATEGY, etc. — work well. What would normally be called a "problem statement" is, in fact, an opportunity statement. They also use a great quotation to introduce the problem. To find out what LACC stands for, however, we have to read through to the next page. Always spell out the full name of an organization the first time you use it.

Notice the words "last week." In a subtle way, this makes the proposal more immediate and shows that the group is working on the issue *right now*.

Conceptually, this section is very strong. It's concise, compelling, and well written. They've done a good job framing the issue. By defining the problem as one of ignorance — people don't know the source of their drinking water — the obvious solution is education ... and this is an education project.

The authors have overlooked one major point, however. Why save Mono Lake? They don't describe the basin's unique ecology and beauty, its seasonal populations of migrating birds, how much water is pumped to Los Angeles, the effects of these diversions, how much water is wasted by the city, and so on.

Perhaps the Compton Foundation has a relationship with the Mono Lake Committee, so the authors assume that foundation staff and board are knowledgeable about the issue. Board members retire, however, and staff take on new jobs, and everyone reads hundreds of proposals. Even if you're applying to a foundation filled with seasoned activists, it's wise to devote a few paragraphs to the "big picture." Never assume that the funder knows as much about the issue as you do.

This "low-cost, high yield opportunity" is an attractive pitch. All foundation officers want to see a significant return on their "investment," so this appeal is presented in investor's language.

THE STRATEGY. You can begin to see the shape of the proposal: subheading (in capital letters), quote, discussion. This excellent format can be easily adapted for your own work.

The authors effectively quote both kids and parents (next page) involved with the program. Whenever possible, request letters of support from your clients, then get permission to use any appropriate excerpts. For even better results, interview your clients and try to capture their spoken words. The quote at the top of the page works best because it sounds spontaneous. The one at the bottom of the page is more formal — it may have been written in a thank-you letter.

THE OPPORTUNITY

"Our water comes from San Francisco????"
Members, LACC Clean and Green Program

Tragically, most people in California don't know where their water comes from. Because they are unaware of the connection between their water use and the special places like Mono Lake and the San Francisco Bay Delta, they have no idea of the devastating impact that water diversions have had on these ecosystems.

This is particularly true in Los Angeles. Even after seven years of drought and an aggressive water conservation campaign, most Southlanders believe their water comes "from under the house." L.A. teenagers active in conservation were stunned to hear in a water program presented last week by the Mono Lake Committee that much of "their" water came from such distant places as San Francisco and Colorado.

California's environmental community has long recognized the importance of educating the Los Angeles public about the sources of their water supply. If we are to be successful in protecting places like Mono Lake and the San Francisco Bay Delta, Southlanders must understand and appreciate the special resources that lie at the other end of their taps.

However, making the connection is difficult. Los Angeles is a diverse, fragmented community, with its inner city being the largest and most isolated population. Most of these people lack the resources to leave the City and experience nature, and so have no concept of the damage Northern Californian ecosystems have sustained as a result of L.A.'s water diversions.

The Mono Lake Committee is one of the leading voices for water conservation and wise water use policies in the State. We have worked in Los Angeles for 15 years and, drawing upon our experience, we have developed an innovative plan for reaching the inner city community with the message that water conservation and resource protection matter.

The main thrust of our plan is to bring inner city youth to Mono Lake so they can experience for themselves one of the places that their water comes from. Just like putting a face to a name, Mono Lake is a real life example of the impact that unwise water use policies have had on the environment. This knowledge helps to empower these young people, providing them with the opportunity to voice their opinion and the incentive to change their own water use.

Our plan is being developed on a shoestring budget. This proposal offers a low cost, high yield opportunity to reach a vital constituency that is usually overlooked in California's water debates. All that is needed is a modest seed grant to invest in the development of a water education program which targets at-risk inner city youth in Los Angeles.

THE STRATEGY

"The issues that concern [Mono Lake] should get people thinking about where water comes from and its effect in nature. People should stop to think about what we are leaving our future generations."
Fernando Gomez, Age 18, after visiting Mono Lake.

The Mono Lake Committee is committed to informing the Los Angeles public about their water alternatives. These people are a vital part of solving California's water problems. If they join in the process, they stand to gain not only a sound, reliable water supply for the future, but also a sense of pride and ownership for the magnificent places with which they share their water.

No running heads or page numbers. Remember to number your pages and tag them with the name of your group or project.

By detailing the history of the project, and naming their collaborators, the authors build credibility into the proposal.

This is an interesting approach: comparing expectations to reality. The authors highlight this information by indenting their columns and using asterisks to mark each item.

Be as specific as you can. This list would work even better if it tallied how many kids attended the public hearings, or how many testified. And how — specifically — did they change their water consumption at home?

As you read the proposal, you can see that the organization knows how to learn from experience and adapt its programs to meet the needs of the community. The story is told in a simple, conversational tone. You can sense the small victories. The tone of the writing is inclusive.

Some people wince at the now-clichéd concept of building "self-esteem." But it takes guts for a kid from Compton or East L.A. to stand up and testify in front of the state water board.

THE PROPOSAL. The participation of Mothers of East Los Angeles, which began as an anti-gang organization, is intriguing. Their involvement adds an extra level of authenticity and uniqueness to this project. When a neighborhood group such as M.E.L.A. becomes active in conservation issues, it goes a long way toward democratizing the environmental movement.

The terms "pilot project" and "seed money" are confusing here. In most cases, you request a seed grant (the first grant) to start a pilot project (the first phase of the project), not after the pilot is completed. In this case, the Mono Lake Committee successfully completed phase one and is now asking for money to further develop the project and make it self-sufficient. They would do better to drop the word "seed" and just ask for a grant.

Here's the essential news: demand for their inner-city education programs exceeds the supply. They don't have enough staff or money to serve all the people who want to participate. If they can quantify the difference between supply and demand — how many groups were turned down in the last year — it would make a very strong case for the grant.

As part of the Committee's ongoing public education efforts, we initiated a special pilot project in response to a growing demand by L.A. groups for a more active water education program. In 1992 and 1993, we teamed up with community groups and inner city service organizations in Los Angeles (including the Mountains Education Program and Los Angeles Conservation Corps) to show young people one of the places from where their water comes -- Mono Lake.

Our staff provided training seminars for community educators and sponsored trips to Mono Lake for inner city youth groups involved in water conservation programs. The trips blended recreation and fun with seminars about wetland ecology, water conservation and California history.

Our expected goals were to:

* educate young people about the sources of their water;
* demonstrate the value of protecting these special places;
* encourage young people to conserve water at home;
* provide a meaningful experience in nature; and,
* build self-esteem.

The unexpected results from this project was that these inner city youth:

* sent over 40 letters to the State Water Resources Control Board supporting Mono Lake's protection;
* attended and testified at an L.A. public hearing on the future of Mono Lake;
* returned with their families, neighbors and friends to Mono Lake; and,
* incorporated water conservation techniques into their daily lives.

This experience taught us that: (1) seeing and learning about Mono Lake effectively communicates the need to change water policies that needlessly damage the State's environment; (2) in Los Angeles there is a constituency which is eager to be a part of solving water supply problems; (3) there are established groups in the City who want us to work with them and who can act as messengers to schools and neighborhoods to spread the water conservation message; and, (4) offering at-risk inner city youth the opportunity to experience nature builds their self-esteem and adds to their quality of life.

In summary, there is a large untapped network of people and groups in Los Angeles who can and should be a part of solving California's water problems.

THE PROPOSAL

"We have a lot of kids in our program who are very hard workers and very devoted to water conservation. It would be wonderful to reward them with a trip to Mono Lake."
Juana Gutierrez, Mothers of East Los Angeles.

The Mono Lake Committee is requesting a seed grant from the Compton Foundation to help us turn our successful pilot project into a public education program on California water issues specifically targeting at-risk inner city youth in Los Angeles.

Until now, we have responded to requests for seminars and trips to Mono Lake as best as we could, using available staff and a curriculum that we developed for a wide range of visitors to the Mono Basin. However, following last year's successful pilot project, we have received multiple requests from various inner city service organizations for similar programs. Thus, despite the Committee's tight financial situation, we created a new staff position that is dedicated to the development of a program which is designed to serve our Los Angeles audience.

Here's a list of objectives for the next phase of their project. Once again, the items are clear and specific, and each objective is fleshed out with a task list or a description of its components. This adds credibility to the plan.

The authors wisely restate the names of their collaborators and potential partners. By involving these groups, they can reach a much larger audience without hiring lots of staff or spending lots of money. This is sometimes called "leverage" or "leveraging your resources"; in other words, making a little money go a long way. See Chapter 8 for more information on leverage.

The trips to Mono Lake are the most interesting — and perhaps the most challenging — aspect of the project, since that's where the most profound learning takes place. This section gives enough detail about what happens at the lake to convince the reader that the time spent there will be educational and productive.

Somewhere in the proposal, it would be helpful to enhance the emotional content with a story or two: how the kids reacted when they first saw the lake, an unexpected comment around the campfire, etc. A few photos, used as attachments or incorporated into the proposal itself, would also work well.

Here is another strong image — it links the beginning of the water supply system (Mono Lake) with the end (Santa Monica Bay).

This is a good description of the group's capacity to do the work, but this paragraph would have been more appropriate in the next section, Organization Resources.

ORGANIZATION RESOURCES. Fernando is the star of this proposal. He's quoted twice (from the same letter?). If you can, try to use quotations from different people. If you plan to use quotes, start gathering testimonials long before the proposal deadline.

To expand on the collaboration section, and to show how these partnerships are helping to leverage extra resources, the authors detail the nuts-and-bolts contributions that each participating group has offered or is being asked to organize.

To create an effective, integrated and self-sustaining program, we will need to accomplish the following in 1994:

1. Strengthen our connections with community based groups, schools and water conservation programs in Los Angeles. We are currently working with the Los Angeles Conservation Corps, the Mountains Education Program and the Mothers of East Los Angeles, and have received inquiries from the Metropolitan Water District of Southern California Southern California, West Basin Municipal Water District, EXPERT and others;

2. Develop a curriculum targeted to Los Angeles inner city youth which will:
    (a) explain the sources of the region's water supplies;
    (b) convey the importance of protecting these areas;
    (c) identify the range of water alternatives available to L.A. and promote
        development of sustainable supplies; and,
    (d) teach water conservation techniques;

3. Co-sponsor with inner city service organizations a minimum of 3-5 integrated multi-day programs at Mono lake which include:
    (a) interactive educational activities teaching ecosystem dynamics, natural
        history and water history;
    (b) recreational activities including hikes, Mono Lake canoe tours and evening
        campfire programs;
    (c) ecosystem restoration activities, possibly including field work projects; and,
    (d) transportation, meals and lodging/camping.

4. Produce two teacher's packets targeting grammar and high school levels which will link water conservation with the protection of the State's natural ecosystems. The packets will be designed so that they can be adapted to other regions of the State using L.A.'s water supply as the primary model. In addition, the packets will encourage classes to visit Mono Lake and the Santa Monica Bay (both ends of the L.A. Aqueduct) to learn about the impacts of water use on natural systems.

Because the Mono Lake Committee has been active in water conservation and natural history education since its founding in 1978, we have substantial resources on which to draw for the development of the proposed program. These existing resources include a general Mono Lake curriculum, conservation brochures ("You are the Connection"), natural history canoe tours at the Lake (featured last year in Sunset Magazine) and interpreter-led walks on Mono's shores.

Our request for seed money from the Compton Foundation is tied specifically to funding the expansion and tailoring of our existing successful program to the needs of our inner city Los Angeles audience. Upon completion of the above work in 1994, the Committee will be prepared to co-sponsor with inner city service organizations an extensive array of L.A. based workshops and Mono Lake tours.

ORGANIZATION RESOURCES

"I would like to thank LACC...and the Mono Lake Committee for giving city people a chance to see what we need to see. I would encourage the Committee to keep opening more opportunities like this..."

Fernando Gomez, Age 18, after visiting Mono Lake.

One of the unique features of the proposed Mono Lake program is the level of cooperation and resource commitment among the participating inner city service organizations. The Los Angeles Conservation Corps (LACC) has offered to make its vans and drivers available to bring the youth groups up to Mono Lake. In addition, LACC has tents and other camping equipment which it can provide for the outdoor portions of the trips. We are talking with other groups, such as Mothers of

This biography is brief, yet it covers all the necessary information. The job title creates a small problem: Stacy Simon is called the Project Coordinator here, but in the next section (under Public Education Team) and on the budget page, she's called the Public Education Coordinator.

Grantmakers always want to know, "How does this project fit into the broader work of the organization? How important is it?" Six staff members are working on the water education program, which shows that the Mono Lake Committee has made the project a high priority.

From the people quoted in the proposal, it appears that most of the "inner city youth" are Latino. How about the staff? What's the cultural mix? This is the place to discuss staff diversity issues.

CONCLUSION. The conclusion simply restates the problem, then describes the plan for addressing the need. For many proposals this is optional, but if you'd like to add a conclusion to your grant application, this is a good model.

East L.A., about sources of funding to help cover the costs of food and transporting the youth to Mono Lake. We are also exploring possible financial support for these expenses from the Metropolitan Water District of Southern California and West Basin Municipal Water District.

The Mono Lake Committee will provide the staff and educational materials needed to conduct the Mono Lake trips and seminars. The Committee has an outstanding staff which is qualified to accomplish the proposed program. Our staff resources include:

* Project Coordinator: Stacey Simon, MLC Public Education Coordinator

Stacey Simon has been both an educator and an administrator for our summer public education program at Mono Lake. Last year, she was the lead organizer for the pilot project to bring inner city youth to Mono Lake. She is now working half the year in our Los Angeles office and half the year at Mono Lake.

Stacey has a bachelor's degree from Occidental College. She has taught in public schools in California and Costa Rica. She also developed environmental education programs for two Costa Rican schools. Stacey is fluent in both English and Spanish.

* Public Education Team

The Mono Lake Committee created the public Education Team in 1993 to ensure that the entire organization played a role in education programming and outreach. The Team is composed of our Public Education Coordinator, Executive Director, Publications Editor and Visitor Center Manager. In addition, two interns, each with ten years of experience in outdoor education and curriculum development, have joined our staff this year specifically to assist with curriculum planning and development.

CONCLUSION

[The Mono Lake Committee has] "literally forced Los Angeles to pay attention and seek out [water] alternatives they would not otherwise have done."
Assemblyman Phil Isenberg, California Legislature.

There is little doubt that water demand in Southern California will continue to rise. As environmentalists, it is essential that we prepare, through water conservation and recycling programs, to meet that demand in a way that does not cause additional harm to Mono Lake, the San Francisco Bay Delta or other ecosystems.

The people of Los Angeles need to be part of developing these solutions for California's water problems. The most effective way to reach the L.A. public with this message is to show them the special places that lie on the other end of their taps. For most Southlanders, Mono Lake is a powerful symbol of the beauty and the vulnerability of the distant ecosystems with which they share their water.

By targeting at-risk inner city youth as the audience for our proposed public education program, the Mono Lake Committee is seeking to achieve two goals. The first is the development of a new, culturally diverse constituency who can and will advocate conservation and wise water use policies. Our second goal is to offer city youth the opportunity to experience the natural world and add to their quality of life.

With a small investment in the development of this program, we can lay the foundation for such a future. We hope the Compton Foundation will join us in making this a new program a resounding success.

BUDGET. The Public Education Coordinator, who's been with the Mono Lake Committee for at least a year, would be making $18,500 annually if she were employed full-time. That seems low for Los Angeles, even by movement standards. (As it turns out, she has since received a raise.)

While some foundations will admire the Mono Lake Committee's thrift, others may raise the issue of staff turnover. How long can you keep good people at low salaries? How will wage levels influence the effectiveness and stability of the group over the long run? Every nonprofit must address this question, and most groups need to find ways to raise wages and improve benefits.

Wages for the canoe guides and interns also seem unrealistically low; a grantmaker might well question these salaries. When writing budgets, wages should be itemized by the individual; for example, the intern line could be shown as:

> 2 interns @ $1,105   . . . . $2,210

Their hours are also confusing. Does each intern work quarter-time (.25 FTE), or do their combined hours add up to .25 FTE? And where did the Mono Lake Committee find two people, "each with ten years experience in outdoor education and curriculum development," who will work for this salary? Are they students who receive credit for their internships? One extra sentence would answer the question.

When itemizing benefits, you also have the option of adding the cost of benefits to each person's salary line and calling it "salary and benefits" or "salary and fringe." (For an example of how this works, see the Native Seeds/SEARCH diabetes project budget on page 88.)

How many trips do they plan to take and how many people will be involved? This information is partially covered in the proposal, but should be restated in the budget. For example:

> Trip food   (8 meals/person x 30 people x $2.50/meal) $600

Of course, you need to do the math correctly and check your proposal for typos. The subtotal for direct costs should be $5,860, not $5,578. The correct amount, however, is reflected in the total costs, since $30,269 + $5,860 = $36,129.

Most funders would be pleased to learn that the Mono Lake Committee and its coalition partners are providing more than half the funds needed for this project. The budget should include a "status report" on these contributions. How much will each group raise? How much of the $19,129 goal has been pledged or received?

INNER CITY WATER EDUCATION PROGRAM BUDGET

Staffing

Public Education Coordinator	$14,040 (75% FTE)
Publications Editor (20 days)	$ 2,083
Visitor Center Manager (30 days)	$ 3,250
Executive Director (10 days)	$ 1,732
3 Canoe Guides (5 days)	$ 900
2 Interns	$ 2,210 (25% FTE)
Benefits/Overhead	$ 6,054
Total Employee Costs	**$30,269**

Direct Costs

Printing/Postage	$ 3,000
Mileage	$ 250
Materials	$ 500
Trip lodging	$ 500
Trip Transportation	$ 1,010
Trip Food	$ 600
Total Direct Costs	**$ 5,578**
Total Costs	**$36,129**

Compton Foundation Contribution	$17,000

Mono Lake Committee & Coalition Contributions
    Los Angeles Conservation Corps
    Mothers of East LA
    Mountains Education Program
	$19,129

Total Project Funds	**$36,129**

FTE = full time equivalent

PINEROS Y CAMPESINOS UNIDOS DEL NOROESTE

INTRODUCTION. This organizational summary is handled very efficiently. In just three sentences, we learn:

- How many years PCUN has been organized
- The English translation of their Spanish name
- Their geographic territory, including the group's home base
- Their constituency
- Their main organizing goal

This is a clear, concise statement of project goals. Goal statements tend to be lofty, but this one is practical enough to cover the day-to-day needs of the organization in item 2, "to provide actual support..." Since most groups are short-handed, interns are a great source of inexpensive labor and, over the long run, a good way to recruit and train permanent staff. As evidenced by this proposal, social change groups can sometimes convince grantmakers to pay for the extra help.

The obvious question raised in these early paragraphs is: why limit these internships to Jews? The authors address this issue on pages 3-4 of the proposal by describing the long history of Jewish involvement in the farm labor movement and discussing the need to build a community of progressive activists to help bridge ethnic divisions.

ORGANIZATIONAL BACKGROUND. In this section, the authors divide their work into seven subheadings. This is a sensible approach, given the breadth of their programs. The task of describing the organization is more manageable when split into separate pieces.

Statistics are used effectively to define PCUN's membership (3,700 people, 98% immigrants) and dues structure. By choosing to calculate total dues paid over eight years, the authors produce an impressively large number. If they were to divide this number by eight and say, "Since PCUN was founded, dues income has averaged $32,000 per year," it would look a lot less significant. Remember, statistics are flexible. Figure out how to best interpret or present them to make your case.

This proposal contains no "problem statement." The authors have chosen to spread their analysis of the problem throughout the document. Each subheading begins with a discussion of the relevant problem — the difficulties faced in organizing farmworkers, pesticide exposure, lack of decent housing, and so on. Each section then describes steps taken by PCUN to solve these problems. The format is unusual, but it provides enough information for grant reviewers to evaluate PCUN's proposed solutions. (PCUN also uses a similar format with their general support proposals.)

1

Pineros y Campesinos Unidos del Noroeste (PCUN)
A Year in the Movement": A Cross-Cultural Leadership Development Project
Funding Narrative

I. Introduction

Founded in April 1985, PCUN (Northwest Treeplanters and Farmworkers United) is Oregon's union of farmworkers, nursery and reforestation workers, and is also the state's largest *Latino* organization. Our most fundamental goal is to empower farmworkers to understand and take action against dsystematic exploitation and all of its effects. PCUN is based in the mid-Willamette Valley town of Woodburn, the farmworker center of Oregon's largest agricultural county.

"A Year in the Movement" is a new project which will recruit Jews to work in Oregon's farmworker movement for a one-year period. The project and the internships have three basic goals: (1) to strengthen "movement" leadership by creating and sustaining opportunities for Jews with progressive values to gain in-depth, hands-on experience in the movement for social and economic justice; (2) to provide actual support for PCUN's organizing and service activities; and (3) to stimulate others in both communities to recognize the commonalities in our respective struggles, a step in an ongoing process of alliance building between the Jews and Latino farmworkers in Oregon.

II. Organizational Background

PCUN's primary focus is to change the agricultural labor system in a manner that guarantees better working and living conditions, redresses the power imbalance between growers and workers, and gestablishes respect, fairness and dignity as the bases for employment relationships. Our efforts have often faced sharp resistance from Oregon agribusiness, a $3,000,000,000-per-year enterprise; surviving nearly ten years in a hostile climate is itself a major accomplishment.

As described below, pursuing our goal has meant undertaking a wide variety of activities, all intended to build capacity, hope, respect, visibility, and make manifest in Oregon a movement which requires and sustains these qualities:

Membership and Infrastructure
"No nos unimos" ("We don't unite") is an oft-heard lament in the farmworker community. 3,900 farmworkers have contradicted that saying and become PCUN members, joining the original 80 who founded PCUN in 1985. 98% of PCUN members are immigrants from Mexico or Central America; about half reside in Oregon year-round. Membership dues, now at $5.00 per month, have totalled $254,000 since 1986. At annual conventions, the membership sets clear direction and policy and elects a nine-member board of directors every other year. A stable and strong board, including PCUN officers as an Executive Committee, have provided solid management of long-term development and day-to-day affairs, respectively. PCUN has a permanent headquarters facility with 6,000 square feet of office and meeting hall space, plus an adjacent house now used for full-time volunteers. Since 1988, some 200 members and supporters volunteered thousands of hours to refurbish and repair these structures.

Field Organizing and the Tenth Anniversary Organizing Campaign
For decades, the agriculture industry has used its economic and political power to keep farm workers isolated, unorganized, underpaid and unassertive by encouraging frequent and massive labor turnover and oversupply, by convincing lawmakers to exclude farmworkers from federal and state labor legislation, by pressuring for weak or nonexistent enforcement of the limited legal rights afforded farmworkers, and by undercutting worker activism with firings, blacklisting, eviction from employer-controlled housing, threats, and even violence.

Since 1988, our Farmworker Labor Rights Project has challenged the discrimination and injustice

PCUN has been organizing farmworkers for several years. By reviewing their history, with dates and details, the authors show the evolution of PCUN's organizing strategy. Because they've had success in their work, this paragraph builds their credibility.

This proposal wins no awards for layout. To comply with the 5-page limit on the narrative, the authors chose a dense type face and filled the pages. The subheadings work pretty well, but once we've glanced over them, our eyes don't know where to go. To solve these layout problems, the authors could:

- Edit out 10-15% of the text to free up some space.

- Indent the first word in each paragraph. (You'll be surprised how much room this creates on the page.)

- Add space below the subheadings to make them stand out even more.

- Stack and indent all lists, such as the one on the right describing the strawberry harvest. These items are thoughtful and thorough and deserve the attention they would receive in the center of the page.

Once again, details help to ground this proposal in reality. Instead of saying, "We serve the farmworker community beyond the fields," the authors describe and quantify the services provided.

This combination of labor organizing and community service sets Pineros y Campesinos Unidos del Noroeste apart, and shows them to be a savvy, hands-on organization. The numbered section at right describes the reasons why. (When was the last time you saw "honesty, effectiveness, and *militancy*" used together in a sentence?)

This proposal is filled with numbers: members, people served, organizations endorsing their boycott, etc. PCUN puts a lot of effort into collecting data. These numbers are then used to improve the group's credibility and bolster its case in grant proposals, brochures, press releases, membership recruitment information, newsletters, and other items. Make it a priority to measure your work and keep track of the numbers.

institutionalized against farmworkers in labor laws and their enforcement, and in prevailing labor practices, and worked to bring growers to the collective bargaining table. In 1989, we led a high profile but unsuccessful legislative fight to enact a collective bargaining rights law and we co-led a coalition which won an increase in Oregon's minimum wage to $4.75. In 1990, our lawsuit invalidated a state law restricting workplace picketing during harvests. In 1991, we led the first ever organized strike in Oregon agriculture. Grower retaliation against strikers prompted us to launch a nationwide boycott in 1992 against grower-owned NORPAC, Oregon's largest food processor. The boycott is endorsed by over 60 organizations, honored by 20 stores and a major college, and has more than doubled our supporter list.

To escalate our challenge to the growers' continued intransigence, we decided to take our organizing—indeed our entire struggle—to a new level and go on the offensive to create the critical mass which can overcome workers' isolation and fear and catalyze the boycott. To do this, our membership, gathered at a special assembly on November 6, 1994, unanimously mandated undertaking the biggest farmworker organizing drive ever attempted in the Northwest. After sixth months of Planning, preparation and community organizing, the **"Tenth Anniversary Organizing Campaign"** broke new ground in June by winning the first ever crop-wide wage increase. Two major strikes and a dozen work stoppages sent shock waves through the grower community and established a new wage "floor", boosting the "piece-rate" paid in the strawberry harvest from 10¢ to 12¢ per pound—a rate stagnant for ten years—to 13¢ to 15¢ in the first picking. We estimate that these increases generated an aggregate of $1,000,000 in higher earnings for Western Oregon's 25,000 strawberry workers. The Campaign involved thousands of workers, hundreds of supporters band serves as a model for how "community unionism" can marshal resources, and can mobilize, train and deploy volunteer organizers drawn from the workforce, the community, and progressive sectors.

The Campaign also reinvigorated pride in and identification with the farmworker movement, especially among ex-farmworkers within the Mexican community. To build on this momentum, PCUN has, among other things, initiated a broad-based drive to re-name Woodburn's First Street for Cesar E. Chavez; the first such effort anywhere in Oregon.

Services and Service Center-Related Campaigns
As immigrants, most farmworkers speak little English, have limited formal education, and lack reliable sources of information. To address the day-to-day needs that result, and to help sustain and build organization capable of withstanding the long haul (where tangible victories can be few and far between), PCUN operates a service center and provides a death benefit for members in good-standing. Center staff perform some 4,000 services annually (including immigration and income tax orientation and assistance, basic legal advice and referral, advocacy on consumer and government agency matters) in a manner which: (1) creates trust, confidence and motivation by setting an example of honesty, effectiveness, and militancy, (2) helps members understand how this country's economic, legal and social systems work, (3) promotes the member's participation in solving his orher own problem, and (4) generates information for and participation in special campaigns, such as to eliminate discriminatory barriers workers face when seeking public benefits.

In every generation, gaining immigration status and reuniting families have been high on the priority list in immigrant communities. The Service Center's immigration programs have ranged from assisting 1,300 members and family legalize during the "amnesty" of 1987 and 1988, helping 600 of these members petition to immigrant for 1,700 family members since 1990, and holding numerous forums on legislative or political developments related to immigration—promptly, with accurate information (to combat rumors and charlatans) and provide clear, concrete analysis. Our next project will likely be citizenship/English classes beginning next Fall, again incorporating political analysis.

Pesticide Project
Farmworkers in Oregon suffer chronic and acute exposure to numerous carcinogenic pesticides due to lack of protective gear, improper storage, inadequate posting and fear of grower retaliation

It's useful to know that PCUN is collaborating with farmworker groups in other regions. Are they affiliated with the United Farm Workers? Cesar Chavez appears throughout the proposal, but his union is mentioned a lot less. Perhaps the authors assume that we know, but assumptions are often wrong. The relationship needs to be spelled out.

Their ambitious media program is covered in just one paragraph, yet we still get a strong picture of the work.

Their housing efforts are equally impressive. Note that PCUN's involvement continues past the construction phase to encompass tenant organizing. Throughout this proposal, the focus is always shifting from workplace issues — wages, safety, worker rights — to larger community issues — immigration, housing, racism, and sexism (as demonstrated by the Women's Project). These changes in focus reinforce the idea that PCUN is a broad-based social justice organization and not merely a trade union. This sets the stage — and demonstrates the need — for the project presented in this proposal.

"A YEAR IN THE MOVEMENT." These three premises effectively frame the discussion of why PCUN needs Jewish interns, and why the Jewish community needs to be involved with Latino farmworkers. The authors emphasize that both communities benefit from participating in the project.

against those who question pesticide practices. Our Project to Stop Pesticide Poisoning, seeks to quantify the amount, type, and effects of dangerous agricultural chemicals, to document pesticide exposures, and to educate farmworkers to alert PCUN about pesticide use or exposure, and to understand pesticides as an economic and labor issue. The Project has worked to enact effective "right-to-know" legislation, video-taped dozens of unsafe practices, assembled a medical and legal team to pursue exposure cases, and organized three major trainings by international pesticide expert Dr. Marion Moses, our chief pesticide consultant, who directs the Pesticide Education Center in San Francisco.

Media & Communications

PCUN's Farmworker Media Project encompasses our work in video, radio, print, photography, visual art and mass-media monitoring. The Project publishes a quarterly newsletter, *PCUN Update* circulated to more than 2,700 supporters, trains farmworkers to film and produce videos, and has roduced three video features (*Nuestra Lucha: Our Struggle for Justice, Boycott for Justice in the Fields*, and *Homage to Cesar Chavez*). From March 1990 to June 1994, we also produced and aired *La Hora Campesina*, a weekly radio show in Spanish, first on a Woodburn AM station and later on Portland's listener-sponsored FM station. In collaboration with the Western States Center, we are producing a full-length video documentary on the Tenth Anniversary Organizing Campaign, seeking to stimulate interest in and understanding of grassroots organizing and present the anatomy of a major organizing campaign.

Farmworker Housing

Workers generally live in overcrowded, substandard and exorbitantly-priced housing, located either in Valley towns or in labor camps on company land. The severe shortage of quality, affordable housing has become even more acute in recent years as more workers have brought their families to Oregon and reside here year-round. Since its founding in 1991, we have played a leadership role in the Farmworker Housing Development Corporation (FHDC). In March 1994, FHDC completed construction of 48 apartments at a cost of $2,6000,000, the first phase of the Nuevo Amanecer project in Woodburn. The Project won the 1994 Governor's Award and serves as a national model for farmworker housing. We exercise our influence within FHDC to ensure a strong commitment to tenant organizing and control, and to situating farmworker housing in town—rather than remote areas—as a step to break vulnerability to exploitation and de facto segregation. Phase Two, including 40 more units plus a multi-purpose center, is scheduled for ground breaking in late 1995.

Women's Project

In addition to all of the indignities and injustices faced by their male counterpart, women in farm labor deal with sexual harassment and pay inequity, spousal and child abuse, sexist cultural norms, and the lack of institutional support for fundamentally addressing these problems. The Women's Project is a new PCUN initiative dedicated to filling that void. The Project has just hired an organizer who will work with a core group of women members to survey their peers, assess the needs and opportunities for mutual support, leadership and economic development, and issue-specific campaigns, resulting in a specific plan of action by Fall, 1995.

III. "A Year in the Movement": Building Bridges Today and Leaders for the Future

The establishment of this Project flows from these three premises: (1) to win the rights we deserve, farmworkers need allies in and alliances with other communities; (2) to combat anti-Semitism and the change the system which perpetuates and exploits it, Jews need to reinforce their progressive traditions and build alliances, especially with communities of color; (3) building stronger Jewish-farm worker collaboration is particularly appropriate and timely given conditions generally, recent developments in each community, and the history of that collaboration.

The history of farmworker organizing in the U.S. amply demonstrates that outside support has

As they have done earlier in the proposal, the authors begin this section with a description of the problem — in this case, an analysis of why farm-workers can't win on their own and have historically depended on other communities for assistance. This helps to demonstrate the need for the kind of outside support an intern program could provide.

The authors then report on threats facing the progressive Jewish commu-nity. The depth of their analysis, plus the fact that the Jews in Portland are well organized and committed to the project, builds the case for this grant.

Unfortunately, the tone is intellectual and distant, which makes this discus-sion less compelling than it could be. If the authors could describe the expe-rience of a specific family, and how the family tradition of activism has been changed or lost — and then show how this story is indicative of the broader Jewish community — it would make the proposal more persuasive.

This paragraph, which discusses the terms of the alliance between the Latino farmworker and Jewish communities, is the heart of the proposal. It begins to answer the question, why Jewish interns? Because this discus-sion is so important, it deserves a more prominent place in the proposal. The authors could:

- ◆ Summarize this information and include it in the introduction on page 1.

- ◆ Give this paragraph its own subheading; for example, "Why Jewish Interns?"

- ◆ Indent the paragraph to make it stand out.

This portion really nails down the argument. Even readers knowledgeable about U.S. social change history will learn a lot about the involvement of Jews in the farmworker movement. By naming names and providing titles, the authors take a broad statement ("hundreds of Jews volunteered") and make it tangible. Seen in the light of this history, PCUN's internship pro-gram builds on a 30-year relationship. It's a tradition worth honoring and renewing.

Finally, a story to leaven all the serious talk of discrimination and injustice. Indeed, this proposal would be improved with an anecdote or two about the day-to-day working relationships between Latinos and Jews in PCUN. Now we get a story, and it's a good one.

played an indispensable role in attaining and sustaining meaningful advances. That support has taken many forms: honoring and promoting boycotts, contributing funds, applying political pressure, defending field actions, and much more. Among PCUN's most natural allies are those from communities who share the experience of the outsider and manifest a tradition of solidarity with the victims of injustice. At this, a critical time in PCUN's struggle, we must call and count on such allies more than ever. The ascendancy of the anti-immigrant movement, and its likely success in nationalizing the California 187 campaign, underscores our need to forge the most consistent and effective alliances possible.

The progressive wing of the Jewish community finds itself at a crossroads as well. In Portland, a gathering" of forty or so Jewish activists has convened monthly meetings for nearly a year, coming to grips with the political changes in the world and in Oregon which are producing new dangers and opportunities. Though this group has just formally organized as the Progressive Jewish Gathering and is developing a long-term analysis and program which will serve as their basis to act visibly and collectively in response to the Right's ascendancy and a growing threat of Fascism.

The Gathering has resolved that concertedly promoting leadership development among the younger eneration of Jews is essential to preserving the Jewish tradition of progressive activism and to srengthening Jewish identity. In the 1990's, younger people are not coming as spontaneously to activism as they did in the 1960's. Most young Jews who came to activism in the civil rights and anti-War movements developed in isolation from the legacy of immigrant labor struggles of earlier decades and their spoken or unspoken lessons about organizing, combating defeatism, and the process of passing on leadership responsibilities. McCarthyism actively or passively silenced most of the activists in their parents' or grandparents' generation. Simultaneously, Post-War opportunities for upward economic mobility made continued activism seem less necessary and put more at risk. This class shift opened a deeper gulf between Jews and communities of color. Today's activist Jews must act to overcome these trends which threaten to undermine a new generation of potential activists.

One persistent myth about Jewish/people-of-color alliances is that the respective needs must be asymmetrical. Racism has prevented the children of most immigrant farmworkers from attaining the economic standing of many Jewish immigrants' children. Race and class dynamics have left the Jewish and farmworker communities in different conditions and created different needs. A genuine alliance, therefore, would only contemplate sending farmworker interns to work for Jewish organizations if such a need actually existed. The Gathering, however, has identified the reverse arrangement—young Jews experiencing movement work and building cross-cultural relationships—as one of their needs, believing that the Jewish people can only be genuinely secure in a just society and that the fight to create that society will require new leaders with cross-cultural experience.

Jews' historical and contemporary ties with the farmworker movement provide a specific context for this Project. Since the mid '60's, hundreds of Jews volunteered as field organizers, staffed boycott committees, and raised money for United Farm Workers. The UFW accepted Jews into leadership roles, such as legal counsel (Jerry Cohen), Cesar Chavez's spokesman (Marc Grossman), and organizing director (Marshall Gans). Today, Irv Hershenbaum serves as the UFW's Second Vice-President. In PCUN, this tradition has continued. Larry Kleinman, a co-founder of both the Willamette Valley Immigration Project (precursor to PCUN) and PCUN, has served as PCUN's Secretary-Treasurer since 1988. Steve Goldberg and Gene Mechanic provide us legal counsel and Jews comprise a substantial portion of PCUN's most loyal financial and volunteer supporters. As an organization, PCUN recognizes that the impetus for much of this involvement stems from the Jewish people's own immigrant legacy and history of resistance to persecution.

The common thread of immigrant communities' struggles underlies PCUN's decision to name its meeting hall for Sonia and Edward Risberg, Russian Jewish immigrants and grandparents of Larry Kleinman. The Risbergs were active in union and tenant movements in Chicago during the 1930's and 40's, and members of the International Workers Order, a mutual support organization which offered services and benefits, some similar to PCUN's. In 1988, the Risberg's estate of $15,000

This description — hundreds of Mexican and Central American farmworkers cheering a pair of deceased Jewish immigrants from Chicago — makes an emotional impact. With a bit more detail, the authors could really sharpen the focus to enliven this scene. A brief excerpt from one of the speeches, or a comment from a union member, would work nicely. A photograph of the rally could also be attached to the proposal or reproduced on one of the pages, in the same way that maps or graphs are sometimes used. (For an example, see page 68.) The rally is covered in PCUN's newsletter — which was attached to the proposal — but there's no guarantee that the newsletter will be circulated to the grant reviewers. These details should be presented in the body of the proposal.

INTERN PROGRAM SPECIFICS. This is a good title, because the plan is very specific. The high level of detail — salary and benefits, living arrangements, job description, and supervisors — demonstrates that PCUN has done its homework, and inspires confidence in their ability to manage the project.

PCUN has lots of experience with interns, as detailed here. The diversity of the group, and the fact that six out of sixteen joined the permanent staff after completing their internships, speaks well of the organization.

Unfortunately, this proposal doesn't include an evaluation plan. We know what the interns will do, but we don't know how many people they are expected to serve, how their presence will improve PCUN's organizing capabilities, or how many community presentations they will make. In a proposal with so much data, this is an unexpected oversight. Without benchmarks, it's tough to evaluate the short-term impact or cost-effectiveness of the project (see budget).

The authors made this choice, in part, because of space limitations and their strong relationship with the funder. To help them better manage the project, however, they should consider editing other sections to make room within the page limit, then include some evaluation points.

The original proposal also contains a list of advisory board members from the local Jewish community. The group includes community and union organizers, writers, educators, and a lawyer, many of whom have been active in farmworker issues. "Together," the proposal states, "these 11 activists bring to this project a total of over *three hundred years* of experience in movement work." (For the sake of space, I've deleted their names.)

was donated in their memory toward purchase of the building. At PCUN's 1993 annual convention, the membership voted unanimously to dedicate the hall to their memory as a conscious act of class solidarity crossing cultural and generational lines. A formal dedication ceremony was held on April 28, 1994, the ninth anniversary of PCUN's founding and the 98th anniversary of Sonia's birth. More than 400 farmworkers and supporters attended the ceremony, together with Pete Seeger, UFW co-founder Richard Chavez, and Oregon Governor Barbara Roberts. As described in more detail in the attached copy of the May, 1994 issue of PCUN Update, the event and the entire campaign which it culminated, has cemented an enduring bridge of mutual understanding.

IV. Intern Program Specifics

Our plan calls for interns to commit one year of full-time service and be sufficiently bi-lingual to function in the community. Although we expect that most candidates will be under 30 years of age, no formal age limit will be established. The intern will be paid $100 per week, have medical insurance, access to a car, and live with a farmworker family (expenses paid by the organization).

The intern will work primarily in the Service Center which operates four days per week. This assignment provides the most structured environment to interact with PCUN members, see and understand the wide range of problems which members encounter in daily life, learn the union's methods for addressing those problems, and see close up how this country's legal and economic system actual produces its many unjust results. The intern will have an organizing assignment and participate in strategy and evaluation meetings. During the second half of the year, the intern will make presentations to student and community groups, especially in the Jewish community, to raise awareness about the program and its premises, encourage support for them, and invite participation.

PCUN's President and General Coordinator, Cipriano Ferrel, will oversee the overall project and Service Center Coordinator Susan Dobkins will supervise the intern's day-to-day work. PCUN has assembled a Project Advisory Committee composed of Jewish activists to serve as a resource and support for both the intern and the organization. Committee members bring a wealth of experience in dealing with class and race contradictions from the Jewish side, and will assist with recruitment, arranging and participating in presentations, and strategizing on replicating this model.

PCUN has had considerable experience with interns. Our summer internship program has had a life-altering impact on the most of the 16 individuals who participated over the past five years. Fifteen of them were under 25 years of age, only four had any prior "movement" experience, and six went on to join the PCUN staff. Eight of the 16 are Mexican, ten are women, and two are Jewish. From our experience, we recognize that this internship will be challenging and sometimes intense. Advisory Committee members, PCUN staff and full-time volunteers (especially the Jews) will play a crucial role in providing personal support to the intern on difficult and deeply-felt issues of class and race, and fostering the intern's Jewish pride and identity which flows from acting in the Jewish tradition of progressive values and solidarity with others.

V. Conclusion

PCUN is one of the modern day successors to the immigrant-based organizations and unions in which Jews predominated earlier this century. Organizations like PCUN are all that today's immigrants' really have. As a people in America, Jews now have much more but, as history has repeatedly shown, stand to lose it all when the inevitable crisis of an unjust system boils over. Therefore, Jews have a stake in every farmworker movement gain that makes the system more just because it makes our society that much more secure for all.

"A Year in the Movement" is admittedly a modest effort but, we believe, a powerful and significant done. As far as we know, no other program like it exists. With sufficient backing, the Project can serve as a model for other organizations and communities and a permanent source of leadership.

BUDGET. This simple budget handles the finances effectively. Notice how the authors have calculated the total costs of the project, then divided them into two columns. By itemizing in-kind contributions — goods or services donated by staff, members, and supporters — they show that PCUN is investing lots of organizational resources to make this project work. In-kind donations always impress foundation officers and reduce the fundraising chores. In this case, one-third of the costs are covered before PCUN submits a single proposal.

Here are a few questions and suggestions to help improve this adequate budget.

1. How did they calculate "other staff time?" How many staff hours will $3,000 buy?

2. What's the mileage rate? How will the intern use these miles: work, recreation, presentations, shopping?

3. For "Advisory Committee Time & Travel," what's the basis for this amount?

4. Funders sometimes calculate the number of people served or activated for the money spent. If the point of this proposal is to activate 1.25 interns, the cost per unit might seem high, especially when you include in-kind costs. Somewhere in this proposal, the authors need to describe the "ripple effect" these interns will have on the organization and the movement: "By funding this project, we will be able to increase our membership by ___ % and provide services to ___ additional people."

(In his defense, grantwriter Larry Kleinman of PCUN says, "In ten years of writing proposals no one has ever asked for that level of detail." It's a valid point — why invest the extra effort? If you can provide these details without a lot of work, however, it will make your proposal a bit more professional. In other words, it might help and it certainly won't hurt.)

These comments, linked to the budget with asterisks, help to explain the numbers. The same system could be used to address the questions raised above, or the authors could gather all this information into a few paragraphs at the bottom of the budget page.

PINEROS Y CAMPESINOS UNIDOS DEL NOROESTE (PCUN)
"A Year in the Movement" Project

1995-96 Project Budget *

EXPENDITURES

Purpose		Sought from Foundations	Inkind
Salaries & Fringe		$19,500	
Intern (full-time, 12 months)	10,000		
Intern (full-time, 3 months) **	2,500		
Other staff time	3,000		
Fringe Benefits & Payroll Taxes	4,000		
Advisory Committee Time & Travel			$5,000
Intern Housing			4,500
Intern Transportation (auto)			1,500
Intern Mileage		500	
Sub-Total		$20,000	$11,000
Project Total			**$31,000**

* The budget represents total costs for the first full year of operation. The Project is scheduled to begin in April, subject to funding.

** Funding for the subsequent intern, whose internship will overlap the first intern's term by three months.

BUDGET NARRATIVE AND FUNDING HISTORY. This page does a great job of putting their funding request in perspective. The authors might reverse the title phrases, however, since the first five paragraphs describe their "Funding History" and the last paragraph is devoted to the project budget.

Once again, they've put the best face on these numbers by combining eight years' worth of dues, service fees, and donations. The level of in-kind support is also terrific. It would strengthen this discussion to include a figure for total grant support. If grant income is historically the largest source of funding for PCUN, the other types of support might look less impressive in comparison. Given the diversity of their funding, however, they should itemize their foundation success, too. (PCUN has chosen to do this in recent proposals.)

An organization of PCUN's size and sophistication should hire a CPA to conduct an annual audit. Generally speaking, all groups with annual budgets over $100,000 should be audited. It's the best way to ensure proper bookkeeping and also increases the confidence level of prospective funders. Audits normally cost $3,000 to $5,000 (unless you can find a sympathetic accountant who will donate the service), but it's money well spent.

While the level of detail is impressive, all these numbers start to run together. To make them more accessible, the information can be organized in a different way. For example,

	GRASSROOTS REVENUE	FOUNDATION GRANTS	TOTAL
1993	$ 67,000	$109,000	$176,000
1994	$129,500	$146,500	$276,000

The grassroots revenue could also be subdivided into dues, service fees, donations, and benefit events. If tabulated over five years, this would give a brief but effective history of PCUN's fundraising program.

Foundation staff always want to know which of their peers you plan to approach. This is a fine list, but it would work better in columns marked *foundation, project, amount requested*, and *status* (funded, pledged, pending, or to be submitted). Columns take up more space, but use less text and are easier to grasp. The foundation prospect list might require its own page.

The total project budget of $22,250 does not match the $20,000 shown on the budget page. Budgets tend to change as proposals are revised; two drafts may have been combined without the benefit of a good proofreader. Perhaps you also noticed that the total dues listed at the top of this page ($257,000) differs from the total on page one of the application ($254,000).

These kinds of errors probably won't sink a proposal, but they won't help, either. Find *someone who has not been involved in developing the proposal* to proofread it before you submit it.

Budget Narrative and Funding History

PCUN has consistently generated the majority of needed resources from grassroots and in-kind sources. Over the past eight years (1987 through 1994), our members have paid dues totaling $257,000, and another $186,000 for services. Some 560 supporters have donated $152,000. Nearly 200 individuals contributed in 1994, all but four donating less than $1,000 each. In the first six months of 1995, more than 300 individuals and organizations have already contributed. We estimate the value of in-kind goods and services received since 1986 at $500,000!

Since 1985, 27 foundations have supported our work, 22 providing funding more than once. To help facilitate foundation and donor support for PCUN's education and research activity, the Willamette Valley Law Project, a 501(c)(3) corporation, continues to operate the Oregon Farmworker Research, Education and Legal Defense Fund and acts as fiscal sponsor for foundation grants or individual contributions requiring tax-exempt status. Neither PCUN nor the Law Project undergo a ormal annual audit, but copies of each corporations IRS 990 forms are available upon request.

In 1991, 1992, and 1993, we sustained our work on an annual average of $180,000, covering seven full-time staff plus overhead. Meeting new challenges means expanding our staff and accelerating leadership develop throughout the organization. Coordination responsibilities for the boycott, the organizing committee and the new women's project have been assigned to younger, newer staff, and a position of general coordinator was established to better facilitate internal communication, planning and strategizing. Adding three new staff positions, plus fulfilling our ongoing commitment to improve staff salaries and benefits, are boosting our personnel costs from about $139,000 in 1993 to $186,000 in 1994 and a projected $216,000 in 1995.

In order to carry out this plan, we successfully intensified our fundraising efforts. We began 1994 by raising the $20,000 needed for building repairs and a special dedication ceremony. Pete Seeger and others performed without fee at a benefit concert for PCUN in Portland on April 27, 1994; the event netted $27,000. Overall, we raised more than $275,000 in 1994—$100,000 more than in 1993—with all-time highs in individual donations, membership dues, special events proceeds, and foundation grants. We increased grassroots revenues to $129,000, **93% above 1993 levels.** Foundation grants totaled just under $147,000, a 34% increase over 1993.

These figures do not include a dramatic rise in in-kind resources which we estimate will reach $154,000 in 1995. Volunteer staff now comprise the equivalent of five full-time positions or one-third of the organization's regular staff. In 1995, we expect to sustain our grassroots income at or above the elevated 1994 levels, and increase foundation support by almost $30,000. Grants have already been committed for the Women's Project (ATR), for the Tenth Anniversary Organizing Campaign (Peace Development Fund, McKenzie River Gathering, Franciscan Charities, Veatch Program, and Stern Family Fund), for the Pesticide Project (Ruth-Mott and Public Welfare), and for general support (Threshold Network, Ralph L. Smith, and Harburg).

The one year budget for the "A Year in the Movement" Project calls for $20,000 from foundations, but we can get the project started with a minimum of $10,000, covering one intern's stipend plus room and board with a farmworker family. The budget includes a portion of a second intern's stipend; overlapping the new intern's service by six months with the first intern's term will facilitate a better transition and make the best use of peer experience. The Kongsgaard-Goldman Foundation in Seattle has indicated that it will make a grant to the Project of between $1,000 and $5,000 in early summer, 1995. Shefa Fund has selected the Project for its funding docket and already secured a $1,000 commitment. A grant from the Jewish Fund for Justice would in two very significant ways. First it could provided the remaining amount needed to actually make it operational. Second, it would send a signal of support from an institution regarded as in the vanguard of innovative cross-community work.

Foundations, like all of us, like to think they are getting a good deal. Show them how efficiently their money will be used or how it will leverage other money.

— Pam Rogers, Haymarket People's Fund

Leverage, or How to Use Money to Create More Money

Most fundraising books and magazines are filled with terms like *database-driven telemarketing*, *resource stewardship*, *human capital*, and *charitable remainder trusts*. I try to avoid this kind of fundraiser-speak, since I don't know what most of these phrases mean, but there's one word I can't get around: *leverage*. Leverage refers to creative ways to use money on hand, or already pledged, to raise additional money. Here's how it works.

MATCHING AND CHALLENGE GRANTS

Some foundations and many government agencies give grants on a matching basis. For every dollar they provide, you are required to raise another dollar from a different source, such as your membership or another foundation. In a 2-for-1 match, you must raise two dollars for every one they pledge. Sometimes these are called *challenge grants* because you use the promise of funding to challenge other donors to give.

Matching grants might seem like extra work for everyone, but they serve as a kind of insurance policy for the funder and can actually help you raise more money. Let's say you need $15,000 for a project, and Foundation A pledges $5,000 on a 2-for-1 matching basis. First, they're protected. They write the check only if you solicit enough money to complete the project, so their grant won't be wasted on a partially funded, less-than-effective program. Second, you can use their pledge as a lever to pry loose donations from other sources. You go to Foundation B and Major Donor C and say, "Listen, we have $5,000 already committed. If you'll contribute $5,000 each, we can collect the five grand waiting in the bank and the project will be fully funded." With the first commitment in hand, your request carries a lot of credibility.

Challenge grants are also a great way to motivate your regular donors to make additional gifts. When I worked at Native Seeds/SEARCH, we used challenge grants to begin and end a capital campaign for a new seed bank, library, and grow-out garden. One of our regular foundation supporters pledged $10,000 on the condition that we raise an equal amount from our members. We promoted this challenge in our newsletter and sent a special mailing to the entire membership requesting gifts for the match. We also phoned selected donors. The result: nearly $30,000 in member contributions!

This strategy worked so well, we tried it again two years later when we neared our final fundraising goal. We approached the same funder with a similar request: you helped us initiate the campaign, now help us finish it. They obliged with another $10,000 grant and once again we prepared a mailing and announced the new challenge on the front page of our newsletter. Our members came through with an additional $22,000 in gifts. Overall, nearly one thousand members — one-quarter of the membership — made donations to the capital campaign, which eventually raised more than $250,000.

If you do receive a challenge grant, it's often possible to "draw" some of the money before the match is completed. With both grants described above, we requested half the total — $5,000 — once we were able to demonstrate $5,000 in matching contributions. We photocopied all appropriate checks as they came in, then sent the folder of photocopies to the foundation when we reached the threshold.

For most projects, the first grant is the hardest to secure. You might improve your odds by *suggesting a challenge grant* in your proposal, especially if you are confident you can raise the match from your members or the people you serve. Grassroots support sends a powerful signal that your work is valued by the community.

In-kind Donations

In-kind donations are any goods or services you receive for free. For many groups, this area is an unexplored gold mine. Other organizations do a great job of collecting non-cash contributions but keep poor records, so they can't tabulate the cash value of these gifts. Just to get you thinking about how you might improve your work life at little or no cost, here's a short list of possible in-kind goods and services.

Goods: artwork, audiovisual equipment, books and magazines, cars and trucks, computer equipment, construction materials, food and drink (for events or volunteers), furniture, house plants, landscaping plants, mailing lists, office supplies, pagers, photocopy machines, tools, telephones.

Services: accounting, advertising, banking and investment, catering, computer support and networking, construction, entertainment (for events), graphic design and layout, housing (for interns, consultants, or staff), landscaping, legal, mailing, office space, payroll, printing, storage, travel, training and consulting.

Notice that most of these goods and services are best provided by businesses. In-kind gifts are a great way to involve your local small business community, since it's always easier to solicit goods or services than cash donations. Even if you're turned down, you might be able to negotiate a substantial discount, which will reduce your expenses. You won't get anything for free, or at a discount, unless you ask.

Many groups request free items — airplane tickets, bicycles, hotel rooms, restaurant meals, whatever — to use in their fundraising raffles and auctions. Businesses want their generosity to be publicized, so be sure to acknowledge their gifts in your newsletter and annual report, at your benefit events, in your news releases, and any other way you can.

Like challenge grants, in-kind contributions are another opportunity to show community support for your work. Many funding agencies will allow you to use in-kind donations to fulfill a percentage of your matching grant requirements. Appropriate non-cash contributions can include outside gifts, such as free consulting services, or donations from within your organization, like supervisory staff time not funded by grant money. For an example of how to present in-kind gifts in your project budget, see the Pineros y Campesinos Unidos del Noroeste (PCUN) proposal on page 149.

Most groups do a poor job keeping track of their non-cash gifts. If you take time to itemize and tally the value of all in-kind donations, your group will benefit in several ways.

1. **BY PUTTING A CASH VALUE ON THESE CONTRIBUTIONS, YOU WILL IMPRESS YOUR MEMBERS, DONORS, AND FOUNDATION PROSPECTS.** This, in turn, will help you secure additional in-kind gifts, cash donations, and grants. PCUN, for example, received an estimated $500,000 in non-cash gifts over eight years. Given their modest annual budget of $180,000, free goods and volunteer labor greatly increased the number of people they were able to organize and serve.

2. **VOLUNTEERS ARE OFTEN TAKEN FOR GRANTED.** Most of us immediately understand the value of donated legal fees or accounting support, but the people who stuff envelopes are worth a lot, too. Convert hours into dollars and it's harder to overlook their contributions. For example, Native Seeds mails four catalogs per year, with twenty volunteers working an average of four hours at each mailing party. According to the local volunteer center, general volunteer support is worth $4.50 per hour, which works out to $1,440 in free labor for this one task. (The volunteers are fed very well, which is a great way to say, "Thank you.")

3. **AS MENTIONED ABOVE, THESE GIFTS CAN BE USED TO MEET THE MATCHING REQUIREMENTS ON SOME GRANTS.** Remember to include a brief explanation of how you calculate the cash value of in-kind gifts.

PROGRAM-RELATED INVESTMENTS AND LOANS

Foundations have traditionally earned money from stocks, bonds, real estate, and other investments, then used the earnings to fund their grant programs. Some funders also support nonprofits through *program-related investments (PRIs)*. Charitable investing has been used to underwrite low-income housing, historic preservation, small business development, community revitalization, and other program areas. In addition to their typical portfolios, PRIs provide funders with a way to invest directly in social change and earn a small return. (For more information on how PRIs work, see the Bibliography.)

Involving investors in your programs — even when those investors are foundations — is a tricky strategy. A program-related investment is not, technically speaking, a loan, but from the perspective of the grantee organization it functions like a loan: the principal must be repaid with interest. If you are unable to repay the funder, you will have a hard time getting grants in the future. Make sure you have sufficient collateral to cover the debt, or have another *guaranteed* source of income lined up for the near future. Many worthy organizations have failed due to unwise borrowing. If you can't pay for it, don't do it. Even better, find another way to do it that requires less cash.

Having said that, there are times when a well established, broadly funded organization can successfully manage a program-related investment or even a traditional bank loan. If your group is spinning off a small business to earn money for your programs, you might need a loan to get started. Income from the business would then be used to retire the debt. Capital campaigns offer another good example, because land and buildings purchased with investment or loan money can serve as collateral. If you were unable to raise the necessary funds to cover the loan, you could sell the property — as a last resort — and repay the lender.

To illustrate how this works, let's review the recent capital campaign at Native Seeds/SEARCH described earlier in this chapter. The group received two challenge grants to help buy and restore two old adobe buildings and the adjacent land for a new seed bank and grow-out garden. The same foundation also invested $40,000 through a PRI at 3.5% interest, a much lower rate than we would have received from a commercial lender. We combined this investment with money from a bequest and bought the property outright for $90,000.

While we were obligated to repay the investor within 15 years, we planned to do it in three years. Most of the money we raised from members and other grantmakers went directly into renovation costs, but a portion was set aside for payments to the foundation. Whenever our capital campaign account had a big enough cushion, we made another $5,000 payment on the principal. As I write this, nearly three years into the campaign, $30,000 has been repaid and the debt should be retired soon.

This brief description makes the process look simple. In fact, it took tremendous time and energy. To put things in perspective, consider this:

the $40,000 PRI was only 16% of the total project budget. We raised the rest as we went along. After receiving this initial investment, we spent only what we had available and incurred no additional debt.

If you have a diverse funding base and can manage your money this prudently, your group might be ready for a program-related investment or a loan. If not, raise it before you spend it.

Be careful what you ask for — you might get it!
Then you'll have to do the work and be responsi-
ble for it.

      — Tia Oros, Seventh Generation Fund

Grants Administration

Many grant proposals — indeed, some of the best grant proposals — are nothing more than dreams committed to paper. Even the most practical, well-planned projects always include a big dose of uncertainty. Dreaming dreams is easy, but designing a project — diagramming the dream — is hard work. Writing the proposal is even harder. Convincing someone to pay for it is harder still. Each stage of the process is progressively more difficult.

Congratulations! You won the grant. The money is in the bank. Now you've reached the *really* hard part: testing your dream against reality. To pass the test, you need to run the program effectively, handle the money scrupulously, and keep the donor informed.

The goal of this entire process — creating a project, writing a proposal, winning a grant, implementing your plan — is to make a real, measurable difference in the real world. It's tempting to fixate on the money, but remember: you apply for grants to fund your work, not to beef up your bank account. Money in the bank does not guarantee success in the community.

If you manage the project well and get the work done, you will find it easier to raise money in the future. Do a sloppy job and you may not be considered for future funding. Even worse, word will get around that your organization is disorganized and irresponsible. This brings us back to one of the first questions to ask yourselves when designing a new program: *Do we have the capacity to both implement and manage it properly?* Be realistic in your assessment. This chapter focuses on how you can best manage your grant money and keep the grantmaker happy.

RECORD-KEEPING AND REPORTING

If you receive grants, you will write reports. This is one of the great truths of nonprofit life. A few small family foundations want nothing more than a newsletter, but everyone else insists on a formal accounting of your work. Many foundations request an *interim report* — say, six months into a one-year grant — and virtually all require a *final report* at the end of the project.

Grant reports fill several functions:

1. **ACCOUNTABILITY.** The people who pay for your work have a right to know what you accomplished (and didn't accomplish) with their money. Foundation staff are accountable to their boards and grantmaking committees, and the foundations themselves must report to the Internal Revenue Service. Your report is part of a very long paper trail designed to ensure that the community is being served through the grantmaking process.

2. **MANAGEMENT OVERSIGHT.** Most people behave more cautiously when someone important is looking over their shoulder. By requiring grant reports, funders help their grantees stay on schedule, honor the work plan, and avoid impulsive behavior.

3. **PUBLICITY.** Foundations use reporting information in their annual reports, press releases, and other publications, which helps your group gain added exposure and recognition.

4. **FUNDRAISING.** Some grantmakers — especially community foundations — solicit donations from the community to pass through to their grantees. If these foundations can demonstrate effective grantmaking, their credibility improves and they raise more money. This, in turn, helps local organizations by increasing the pool of funds available for grants.

The key to grants administration is common sense. Invest a little thought and effort along the way and everything will work to your advantage. The following ideas will help you stay on track.

1. **REVIEW PROGRESS PERIODICALLY.** Project organizers should meet on a regular basis to evaluate their work. For some projects, quarterly meetings are adequate; for others, you'll need to get together every week. Ask tough questions. How does the actual program compare with your proposal? Are you sticking with the timeline? Do you need to make changes? Are you spending money at an appropriate rate?

Minor adjustments are normal, since grant proposals always contain an element of improvisation. *If you find that you require a major change of program, however, notify the grantmaker and negotiate these changes.* A grant proposal is a contract and any significant alterations must be approved by both parties — grantor and grantee. Better to adapt and achieve a good result than stick with the original program and accomplish less. Foundation officers understand this and want you to succeed.

2. **TAKE LOTS OF NOTES.** You can't write an accurate final report unless you keep track of what you do all year. Without documentation, you'll also find it difficult to analyze your work. How many people are you reaching? What's working and what isn't? What are you learning? If your proposal includes numerical objectives or evaluation points (and it should), how are you doing with the numbers? Collect lots of data. Document everything.

3. **SAVE ALL ARTICLES, REVIEWS, BROCHURES, ETC.** If your project is written up in the local newspaper, clip and save the article. If the grant pays for production of publications, save copies. These items should be enclosed with the relevant reports.

4. **ACKNOWLEDGE THE GRANTMAKERS.** Mention foundation supporters in your publications and relevant news releases, unless they wish to remain anonymous.

5. **FOLLOW INSTRUCTIONS.** Foundations always tell you what to include in your final report. Give them what they want.

6. **KEEP IT SIMPLE.** Grants officers don't have time to wade through piles of paper. Be selective about what you write and attach. For most grant reports, two pages of narrative, a budget detailing actual spending, and one or two attachments is plenty of information.

7. **DON'T EXPECT A REACTION FROM THE FOUNDATION** — unless you do something wrong or leave something out. In most cases, a staff member will flip through the grant report, extract whatever information he or she needs, and file it. Your report will sit in the file cabinet until the editor starts gathering material for the foundation's annual summary. When you submit your next proposal, someone will pull the file to see if you fulfilled the reporting requirements. That's about it.

In his essay, "Foundation Leadership," which appears in *Environmental Leadership* (Island Press, 1993), Jon Jensen of the George Gund Foundation tells a cautionary tale.

> Most foundations are primarily in the business of making grants, as opposed to following up on grants and evaluating how they worked.... Following up on the progress and impact of funded projects takes on lower priority in the day-to-day activities of the staff person...

> For example, I once asked a colleague in another foundation what grants were on the agenda that had just been voted on by his board a few weeks ago. I received, in reply, a blank stare.... He was already so focused on the next set of grants, he had forgotten those he had just finished.

> The pressure to keep moving forward is so great that looking back becomes a luxury. As might be expected, grantees may feel neglected because they receive few if any follow-up calls from the foundation, and get little or no comment in response to the lengthy and carefully crafted progress reports they submit.

The moral of this story is, no news is good news. Do a careful, competent job with your grant reports, but don't expect much in the way of praise or criticism. Follow the lead of foundation staff — write it, submit it, and don't worry about it.

On the opposite page is a grant report prepared for the Albuquerque Community Foundation, which provided funds for Native Seeds/SEARCH in New Mexico. It's brief, detailed, and specific, giving foundation staff a clear, measurable idea of how their money was spent. In just two pages, this report:

◆ Restates the goals and objectives of the project. (This format is required by the foundation, but it's a good idea for all grant reports.)

◆ Identifies 14 community groups that participated in outreach programs.

◆ Lists 15 traditional crops grown in the demonstration garden.

◆ Names seven indigenous communities where staff collected seeds and cuttings from heirloom fruit trees.

◆ Describes the group's upcoming projects and next steps.

◆ Includes an excerpt from an article by Brett Bakker, Native Seeds/ SEARCH New Mexico field manager.

By naming names and providing details, Brett's work is made real for the reader. We could have written, "We offered educational programs to 14 organizations and grew 15 traditional crop varieties," but the lists of crops and cooperating groups paint a much more vivid picture. The work of Native Seeds is embodied in these names because they reflect the diversity of the group's constituency and the crops they grow. That sense of connection with the community and the land is reinforced at the bottom of the last page, in the words of the man who did the work.

MANAGING GRANT MONEY

Financial management is the weak link in many grassroots groups. Planning and budgeting combine all the money taboos — money is evil, dirty, corrupting, etc.— with that common ailment, "math phobia." Put a spread sheet in front of most activists and they will run screaming from the room. As financial management trainer Terry Miller writes in his book, *Managing for Change*, "For people driven to work in the nonprofit sector ... there is often the sense that managing money is tantamount to making a deal with the devil."

Your bookkeeping skills will have a big impact on your ability to raise money and do your program work. Many otherwise successful groups have folded because they didn't take the necessary steps to put their books in order. "If you try to avoid financial management," Miller says, "the ironic thing is that you may spend more of your time on it than you would have otherwise — like any good discipline, good financial management systems make life more systematic, easier to get the work done."

Native Seeds • SEARCH

2509 N. Campbell Ave. #325
Tucson, AZ 85719
520/327-9123
FAX: 520/327-5821

New Mexico office:
PO Box 4865 (144 Harvard SE)
Albuquerque, NM 87196
505/268-9233
October 26, 1994

TO: Laura Hueter Bass, Albuquerque Community Foundation
FR: Andy Robinson, Development Director, Native Seeds/SEARCH
RE: Final Grant Report

In September 1993, the Foundation granted $1,500 to Native Seeds/SEARCH to support our community education and outreach programs in Albuquerque and northern New Mexico. An interim report was submitted in April 1994; this report should complete our requirements for the grant. Financial documentation is enclosed.

Goals and Objectives (as outlined in proposal): Brett Bakker, our New Mexico staff, will assist Native American farmers by distributing seeds, providing technical support for local and tribal seed-saving, and networking growers through the Traditional Native American Farmers Association. Through outreach programs, seed sales, gardening workshops, and contacts with the local news media, he will educate the public about the need to preserve genetic diversity and support indigenous culture and agriculture. He will also manage a small demonstration and grow-out garden in Albuquerque, while keeping the office open one day each week for walk-ins.

Results: Brett continues as a half-time employee for Native Seeds/SEARCH (he makes his real living maintaining the grounds at the University of New Mexico). In the past year, he provided educational programs and consultation to a variety of community groups across the region, including:

Albuquerque Organic Gardening Association
Santo Domingo Pueblo Senior Citizen Project
Flowering Tree Permaculture Institute, Santa Clara Pueblo
Huichol Center for Cultural Survival and Traditional Arts
Ramah Navajo Weavers Association
High Desert Research Farm
Albuquerque Public Library

Indian Pueblo Cultural Center
Albuquerque Master Gardeners
Jefferson Middle School
Uptown Garden Club
Cornstalk Institute
UNM Anthropology Department
La Montanita Food Co-op

A non-profit organization working to conserve traditional crops, seeds, and farming methods that have sustained native peoples throughout the Greater Southwest.

We had another successful year in our grow-out garden, with land and water donated by Shepherd of the Valley Presbyterian Church at Rio Grande and Montano. Among the winners:

Alvarón temporal peas	Hopi white lima beans	Taos brown beans
Punta Banda tomatoes	Wenk's yellow hot pepper	Hopi black sunflowers
Cuartelas fava beans	New Mexico melons	Jemez mission grapes
Mostaza roja	Acoma mixed gourds	Orach
San Juan squash, chiles, and watermelons		

Seeds from the harvest will be sold to interested gardeners through our catalog, distributed for free to indigenous farmers, and preserved in our seed bank. While Brett was unable to organize any formal gardening workshops at the site, several volunteers helped out informally throughout the growing season with planting, weeding, and harvesting.

Brett collected seeds and cuttings from heirloom fruit trees at San Felipe, Isleta, Santo Domingo, Zia, Jemez, and San Juan Pueblos, and the Spanish community of El Guique. Thanks to a grant from the Educational Foundation of America, Brett will be able to focus more of his time on collecting endangered crops. He is preparing for a series of trips throughout northern New Mexico, southern Colorado and southern Utah. His goal: bring in at least 50 uncollected varieties over the next eighteen months. The first trip, a collaboration with the High Desert Research Farm at Ghost Ranch, will take place next month.

Brett continues as our local liaison to the Traditional Native American Farmers Association (TNAFA), an all-indigenous group convened by Native Seeds/SEARCH to support traditional agriculture in New Mexico and Arizona. Brett met with TNAFA staff about ten times during the past year, attended their last annual conference at Camp Verde, Arizona, and will participate in their 1994 conference next month in Santa Fe.

The news media was once again supportive and interested in our conservation efforts. Brett was interviewed on KUNM Radio and showed off our crops on *The New Garden*, a program syndicated nationally on PBS. (TNAFA director Calvin Aragon, of Acoma, was also profiled on the show.) Our work was mentioned in *The New Mexican* and *Arellano*, a quarterly publication from Embudo, New Mexico. Brett also writes a regular column for La Montanita's *Co-op Connection* newsletter; here's a recent excerpt:

"There's a sense of wholeness journeying the backroads. Piles of corn wait to be shucked; there's a new way to learn of tying red chile into ristras. The cattle will soon be brought down from the hills to clear the cornstalks. Even with the harvest tasks, no one's too busy not to offer a cup of coffee around the kitchen table and talk of the year's crops, recipes for chile caribe, and how's Tio Florencio feeling lately?"

In this season of plenty, we thank you — again! — for your enthusiastic support.

For detailed information on accounting systems and evaluating what level of complexity is appropriate for your organization, I refer you to Miller's book, which is listed in the bibliography. "There is no magic or secret to financial management," Miller writes. "You know more about it than you think you do." To start you thinking about the subject, and to reinforce your better instincts, here are a few broad suggestions.

1. **IF YOU NEED HELP, HIRE A PROFESSIONAL.** For many grassroots groups, it makes sense to hire a bookkeeping service. Contract bookkeepers don't cost that much because you pay only for the hours you use each month and in return you get a breadth of experience. If you can find someone who supports your mission, she or he might donate the service or offer a discount. Select a bookkeeper with nonprofit experience. Ask other groups in your community for recommendations.

2. **SET UP YOUR BOOKS TO TRACK INCOME AND EXPENSES BY DEPARTMENT OR PROGRAM.** Don't try to track expenses by individual grant. You will create unnecessary work for yourself, since most funders don't want or need that level of detail. (See number 6 below.) For the same reason, don't open a separate bank account for each grant unless required by the funder to do so.

   When you track your expenses by program (and not by individual grant), you are more likely to seek grant support for your own priorities and initiatives, rather than responding to the grantmaker's priorities. This is one of the subtle ways that financial management systems influence your program work. All successful fundraising strategies address the interests of both funder and recipient to some degree, but if you want your group to be successful over the long run, you need to stick to your mission and not get sidetracked in pursuit of money.

3. **SPEND GRANT MONEY ON RELEVANT PROGRAM EXPENSES ONLY.** Most grants are restricted to the activities outlined in your proposal, according to the financial plan reflected in your project budget. Unless you receive general support money, don't treat your grant as an emergency slush fund or rewrite the budget as you go. Minor changes are fine, but if your project budget needs significant adjustments, notify the funder and negotiate the alterations. If you have the foresight to anticipate these changes and the diligence and honesty to initiate the contact, the grantmaker is bound to be impressed. This makes for an easy, straightforward negotiation.

4. **REVIEW PROJECT EXPENSES EACH MONTH.** Track your cash flow. Be careful you don't spend all your grant funds long before the project is supposed to end (unless you finish the work early).

   If you receive multiple grants for a project, you may be able to exhaust the first grant before the work is complete and still have money in the bank from the second or third grant. In this situation — depending upon your relationship with the funder — you could submit an early final report and perhaps even apply for a follow-up grant while the project continues. If you're not clear about how to proceed, check with foundation staff. In many cases, they will ask you to stick with the original reporting schedule.

5. **KEEP RECEIPTS FOR ALL EXPENSES.** You won't need to submit them with your grant report, but it's useful to have receipts on hand in case you run into questions from foundation staff. More important, receipts and appropriate documentation help to maintain an "audit trail" and demonstrate your stewardship of community funds. Good internal control has a big impact on your effectiveness and credibility; saving documentation for all expenditures is the most important part of good control.

6. **ONCE AGAIN, KEEP IT SIMPLE.** The following expense statement, which was attached to the Albuquerque Community Foundation grant report on page 163, is more than adequate. The foundation provided $1,500 toward a $15,000 project budget; like most grantmakers, they weren't worried about which specific line items were covered by their grant, so we didn't bother to track or report that information.

An important addition to this budget would have been an *income report* detailing, in three or four lines, how the balance of the project funds were raised. Income reports give you an opportunity to brag about other grants you receive, and demonstrate community support for your work through membership donations, program fees or other earned income, and in-kind gifts from local businesses.

Native Seeds/SEARCH   **New Mexico Field Office**

EXPENSE REPORT   SEPTEMBER 1, 1993–AUGUST 31, 1994

Salary and payroll taxes	$11,359
Rent and office supplies	1,583
Garden supplies and seed purchase	849
Printing and postage	210
Telephone	428
Travel	440
Professional fees	606
Miscellaneous	74
Total	**$15,549**

Several years ago I was involved with "the little project that couldn't." Every problem spawned three new problems, delay led to delay, and after a year of doing nothing it was time to submit our final report. We wrote to the foundation, detailing our troubles, and described our plan to revive the project. After explaining the financial situation — we had spent only $3,000 of their $20,000 grant — we requested a nine-month extension.

Their response arrived in the mail a few weeks later. One of my co-workers was expecting a letter addressed, "You stupid jerks," but the tone was respectful and supportive. "Thank you," the foundation officer wrote, "for being so careful with our money. Your extension is approved. Good luck."

It's easy to think of foundation staff as "them," especially if they work in another city. It's easy to withhold information, especially if it makes you look bad. It's easy to rearrange the truth. But remember: funders are your partners and peers. If you lie, you put that partnership at risk.

There is no such thing as a flawless project. Grantmakers understand this, which is why they value honesty. As Linda Reymers of the McKenzie River Gathering says, "We'd rather hear the reality *and* what the group is doing to respond and improve the situation." Pam Rogers of the Haymarket People's Fund says,

> If your organization is getting over a bad image problem (like the director stole a bunch of money), be really honest and up front about how the organization is rectifying its mistakes.

Every problem has a solution; describe yours. Don't run around like Chicken Little shouting, "The sky is falling! The sky is falling!" Tell them about your strategy — you've hired an engineer and you're building a scaffold and you plan to prop it up while you figure out what to do next. Show your ingenuity.

THE VALUE OF HONESTY

Once, at a conference, I heard a grants officer lecturing a room full of grant recipients. He was angry because so few of them had bothered to add his name to their mailing lists. "If I gave you twenty dollars," he said, "you would send me a newsletter. I give you $1,000 and never hear from you again. What's wrong with this picture?"

Once you receive the grant, your relationship with the grantmaker enters a new phase. Up to that point, all your communications — phone calls, proposal, site visit — are a form of courtship. When that check is written, the relationship gets serious. Unfortunately, many groups deposit the check and become deadbeat partners — they're silent and invisible until it's time to ask for more money. Listen to Betsy Taylor of the Merck Family Fund:

> Keep in touch once you receive a grant. Don't send heavy reports and piles of paper. I won't read them. Send a short note, a post card, a press clip. The majority of grantees fail to communicate and stay on my radar screen.

YOUR MOTHER WAS RIGHT: THE VALUE OF GOOD MANNERS

It takes very little work to "stay on the radar screen" and maintain healthy foundation relations. As Jon Jensen indicates, you probably won't get a reaction, since foundation staff are so busy, but they'll appreciate your effort. Down the road, when you apply for another grant, you will see the results. Keep these suggestions in mind:

1. **SEND A THANK YOU LETTER AS SOON AS YOU ARE NOTIFIED OF THE GRANT.**

2. **PUT ALL FUNDERS ON YOUR MAILING LIST.** Make sure they receive your newsletter, annual report (if you produce one) and other publications.

3. **IF SOMETHING EXCITING HAPPENS, MAIL A POSTCARD OR A BRIEF HANDWRITTEN NOTE.** "I thought you might like to hear about..." E-mail is also effective, but if you send paper it is more likely to end up in your grant file. Your good manners will be remembered when the file is pulled for the next proposal review.

4. **SHARE YOUR PRESS COVERAGE.** When the International Shadow Project was featured in *Time Magazine*, I photocopied the article and sent it to all major donors and foundation supporters. (Be selective — *do not* distribute a three-sentence calendar announcement of your next event, or a 15-second video clip from the local evening news.)

5. **SEND PHOTOGRAPHS WHERE RELEVANT.** A good photo packs a lot of emotional appeal and provides a nice break from all the words.

6. **IF YOU'RE TRAVELING AND PLAN TO BE IN THE NEIGHBORHOOD, OFFER TO MEET WITH FOUNDATION STAFF AND GIVE THEM A PROGRESS REPORT.** You might be turned down, but the offer will be appreciated.

7. **DON'T OVERDO IT.** Three or four extra contacts per year — press clips, postcards, etc. — are plenty. If, however, you have questions about your current project or need assistance with your upcoming proposal, don't be shy about calling for help.

When I reviewed this list with one of my classes, a student raised her hand and said, "So, we're supposed to do all the things our mothers taught us to do." That sums it up pretty well, at least in the case of my mother. Treat foundation officers like respected peers. Say thank you. Use your manners. Be a credit to your mother and your organization, too.

Over the years I've noticed that proposals that say, "Give us money or something terrible will happen," don't do nearly as well as those that say, "This is great work and we're going to do it with or without you. Here is your chance to join in and make it better."

— Martin Teitel, CS Fund

The Long Haul: Stamina, Persistence, Resilience

In Tucson, we have a popular line of t-shirts decorated with images from the Mexican card game *loteria*. My favorite, *El Mundo*, features a picture of Atlas balancing the world on his shoulders. He's the same fellow, sculpted in bronze, who towers over Rockefeller Center in New York — knees bent, biceps bulging, head bowed, a look of intense concentration on his face.

Whenever I needed extra energy, I used to dress in my *El Mundo* shirt. I would often wear it to the fundraising workshops I teach, hidden beneath a shirt and tie. At the end of class, when it was time for the customary pep talk, I'd flip the tie over my shoulder and start unbuttoning my shirt. This action was always greeted by a nervous silence, since most people had never seen a teacher undress in class. After unfastening four or five buttons, I would stretch the shirt open across my chest, revealing Atlas, and ask, "Anybody feel like this guy?" The students laughed and cheered. They understood.

I wore *El Mundo* a lot. Changing the world is a hard, sweaty business, and I needed all the energy — real or imagined — I could get. I wore that shirt until it was a rag. It literally fell off my back. I still teach people how to raise money, but I draw my energy from other sources.

Nearly every day I feel profoundly grateful for my work. That doesn't mean I'm not tired or angry or discouraged, because I am. Still, I persevere. I've learned that real social change takes generations, and unless we're in it for the long run, we just skim the surface and nothing really changes.

Maggie Kuhn, founder of the Gray Panthers, wrote, "I outlived my enemies and so can you!" We are often our own worst enemies, besieged by inner voices of doubt. "Who appointed you Atlas? Are you crazy? What makes you think you can save the world?"

Take it as your goal to outlive that voice. Be persistent, be tough, be flexible — especially in your fundraising. Here are a few humble suggestions to help you redesign your mind for the long haul.

DEALING WITH REJECTION

When I worked as a door-to-door canvasser for Oregon Fair Share, I was expected to talk with 40 people per shift and recruit five members. For every enthusiastic person who said, "Great, let me write you a check," seven others said, "Get lost." Some nights were much easier, others were brutal. I spent very little time arguing or convincing; my job was to find the right people and leave everyone else alone. In some ways, rejection was helpful. The quicker the refusal, the sooner I could move on to the next house. The law of averages eventually bailed me out.

The odds of having your grant proposals approved are about the same: one in eight. At some point in your grantwriting life — probably very early — you will face rejection. Perhaps you just received a rejection letter, which is why you're reading this book.

You've heard this before, but if you're like me, you need to hear it again: *Don't take it personally.* As Peter Bahouth of the Turner Foundation says,

> If we turn you down, it doesn't mean you're a bad person. Everyone is doing good work, regardless of whether we can provide funds. The trick for any foundation is to find the excellent among the good.

Martin Teitel puts it this way: "Maybe it would help people to understand that our job is more of a matching task than one of judging people's worth."

For many activists, however, it's hard to separate the personal from the professional. Jon Jensen of the George Gund Foundation acknowledges reality in his essay, "Foundation Leadership," *(Environmental Leadership*, Island Press, 1993):

> The most important part of being a good grantmaker is being respectful of grantseekers and the work they are doing.... They are not just presenting a project; they are setting in front of you their dreams, hopes, and, more than likely, a big part of their livelihood.

Given this situation, how can you *not* take it personally?

As a first step, you need to sort out the things you can, and can't, control. Most proposals are rejected due to lack of money, which has nothing to do with you, your organization, your project, or your writing skills. The vast majority of funders can't (or won't) allocate sufficient funds for every proposal they receive. If you send out grant applications, you will accumulate your share of rejection letters. That's the way it works.

Of course, the best antidote for rejection is success. By targeting your proposals, you can greatly improve your odds. Over the past few years at Native Seeds/SEARCH, nearly 50% of our proposals were funded. Our terrific batting average was based, in part, on our program, reputation, relationships, and the quality of the proposals we submitted, but the biggest factor was our *research*. Before we knocked on a foundation door with our proposal, we knew who was inside, what they cared about, and how they wanted to be approached. If we knew in advance that they wouldn't be interested in our work, we didn't knock.

If you take one message from this book, let it be this: *do your homework*. You will raise more money, waste less time, and feel better about your efforts. (For more information on grants research, see Chapter 5.)

There's another, more subtle reason for doing a thorough job on the research. During five years at Native Seeds, I built a prospect base of 250 foundations, corporations, and other funding sources. Over time, we applied to perhaps half the list. Several others we tracked for our long-term project, a conservation farm. The remaining prospects were fairly marginal, but that file cabinet, stuffed to the limit with foundation guidelines and annual reports, was a great comfort to me. As I filed away each rejection letter, I would think, "Okay, if you don't want to work with us, we'll find someone else who does." In many cases, "someone else" was right at my fingertips. Rejection doesn't feel so bad when you have other options.

DIVERSIFYING YOUR FUNDING

I read an article in the *Chronicle of Philanthropy* (November 30, 1995) that described how the environmental movement is trying to revitalize itself by rebuilding from the grassroots up and increasing the emphasis on community fundraising. Sam Hitt, who heads Forest Guardians in Santa Fe, New Mexico, was quoted as saying, "Foundation support is like a drug. You get that check in the mail and you are on the ceiling for the rest of day, but then it goes away." Any grantee organization — environmental or otherwise — knows this feeling.

Most addictions will eventually kill you, and grant money is no exception. If your organization survives on foundation grants, it will die without them. Who, then, controls the fate of your group? No foundation can underwrite your work forever. Very few will fund you for more than two or three years in a row. You can improve your financial health by developing relationships with several grantmakers, but that won't protect you if their priorities shift. Issues rise and fall on the public agenda, and a lot of foundation money moves with the trends.

If you're serious about creating real change in your community, you must develop grassroots financial support. Change takes time and requires a steady stream of money. A diverse funding base of individual gifts, major donors, benefit events, and earned income is the best way to ensure the long-term survival and success of your organization.

Unlike most foundations, individuals have been known to support specific groups for decades. When I went to work at the local Planned Parenthood affiliate in 1988, we began transferring donor information from file cards to a computer database. Some of those cards had been marked on for twenty years! Many $10 and $20 contributors had, over the years, become major donors, giving annual gifts of $500 or more. Their commitment increased as their financial situation improved and they became more involved with the group and saw how their money was being used. In some cases, their children (and even grandchildren) were also donors. This happens when an organization lives to be sixty years old and maintains its relevance and vitality.

If you'd like a quick refresher on the whys and hows of diversifying your funding, take another look at Chapter 2.

USING YOUR TIME AND ENERGY EFFECTIVELY

I once wrote on a job application, "I've learned to keep my sense of balance and my sense of humor under the usual constraints of not enough time and never enough money." It's a clever sentence, but in one sense it's a lie. When I wrote it, I felt overwhelmed by the problems we face, and I still do.

Take an honest look at the world — it's easy to be overwhelmed. Your goal, as activist-for-life, is to put that feeling in perspective and enjoy the victories you earn along the way. You need both balance and humor to survive, but mostly you need faith — faith in the power of change and your ability to create change. The following ideas will help you keep the faith and get the work done.

1. **HONOR YOUR PRIORITIES.** When I first met my wife, I told her the two things I couldn't tolerate were gross injustice and moldy dishes. In the intervening ten years, nothing has really changed. I've washed a lot of dishes and devoted most of my waking hours to organizing and raising money. Work is the biggest part of my life, because it gives me a sense of community and purpose. I am sustained by what I do all day.

   Your priorities may be different. Learn what they are and honor them. If you spend time in meetings thinking about your children, go to fewer meetings and enjoy your kids more. If you feel the need to make things grow, put your hands in the dirt. If your faith is wavering, find quiet time and space to strengthen yourself spiritually. If you're exhausted, take a nap.

   The main point is, figure out what moves you most and then do it. Burnout is caused by people doing what they *should* instead of what they *want*. Give your favorite organization whatever time you can afford — give it wholeheartedly and passionately — then draw the line. In the long run, you will have more time and energy to share.

2. **PICK YOUR FIGHTS.** It pains me to say this, but you must develop an aversion to lost causes. If you can't see your way to victory — even if that victory won't occur for years or decades — pick another fight. To maintain your sanity and stamina, focus your energy where it will do the most good.

3. **GO EASY ON THE IDEOLOGICAL PURITY.** Don't get sucked into petty arguments with co-workers and allies. The history of the social change

movement is filled with campaigns that failed because allies could only agree — only! — on 90% of the program. If you're spending a lot of time arguing about turf, or the wording of your news release, or how to divide up the credit, something is wrong. Check your ego at the door and focus on areas of agreement, not disagreement.

4. **LEARN HOW TO JUGGLE.** Sort through the pile on your desk daily and put the most pressing items on top; deal with them first. Buy a calendar and use it. Don't go to meetings just for the sake of being there. Spend some time each day raising money. Keep track of the bank balance, but don't be obsessed. Say "thank you" whenever possible, for any reason. When you make a mistake, accept responsibility and solve the problem. Most of all, keep your wits about you. When in doubt, think.

5. **CREATE SOMETHING GOOD, THEN USE IT AGAIN AND AGAIN.** At Native Seeds/SEARCH, we submitted proposals to 62 funders in 1995. That sounds like a lot of work (it was), but not nearly as much work as you might think. We wrote proposals for eight projects, plus general support, then adapted them to meet the specific requirements of each foundation. Creating and refining these proposals took time, but once we had the right words, it was relatively easy to change the length, move the paragraphs around, and fit them into the required format. (For the record, 26 were funded, 20 were turned down, and 16 are pending as of January 1996.)

Recycling your work will save you vast amounts of time. In fact, you can take this strategy even further by pulling paragraphs or phrases from your proposals and using them in your direct mail solicitations, news releases, brochures, newsletters, and any other written materials. At Native Seeds, the membership renewal letters (six per year) were built from language first created for grant proposals.

6. **DON'T BE A DRUDGE.** Last and best, give yourself lots of credit, then take a long break. Hike, swim, sleep, dance, ride a bike, go see a movie, make love with your sweetheart, cook an extravagant meal, stay up all night and read a good book. (Not *this* book; this is work.) Forget about the sorry state of the world for a few hours, and revel in the wondrous state of the world. To quote the late author and troublemaker Edward Abbey,

> Be as I am — a reluctant enthusiast, a part time crusader, a half-hearted fanatic. Save the other half of yourselves and your lives for pleasure and adventure. It is not enough to fight for the land; it is even more important to enjoy it.

I am the worst person to offer this advice, since I'm usually the last one to heed it. When this book is finished, however, I plan to take a long hike into mountains, swim in my favorite creek, and lay on a big rock in the sun. You should do the same.

THE PERFECT ORGANIZATION...

Doesn't exist.

People rarely call a doctor when they're healthy, and nobody looks for a consultant when their nonprofit is running smoothly. I spend a lot of time talking with folks who feel that their organizations are sick, and it makes them feel sick.

The first thing I ask is, "When you walked into the office this morning and flipped the switch, did the lights go on?"

"Sure."

"Aha! That's a victory. You found enough money to pay the electric bill. How about the phone?"

"We're talking, aren't we?"

"Terrific. Another victory."

This is a useful strategy for a therapist — my unofficial job title — but it's probably cost me some consulting work. People don't want to spend money to learn what they're doing right; they want me to fix what's wrong. Most of us tend to ignore the things we accomplish just by showing up each day, answering the phone, digging through the pile on the desk, pushing the work forward, and flying the flag of hope for everyone to see and admire.

Corporate gurus have a name for this strategy. They call it "muddle-through management," and it's gaining respect as a legitimate way to run a small business or even a nonprofit. It's especially effective for small, overworked, underfunded social change organizations with big ideas. Muddle-through management might be the best way save the world, which is a very muddled place.

In the perfect world, every group would have a comprehensive strategic plan, an ample budget, a hard-working board, and lots of staff. Everyone would be paid a living wage. All problems would have obvious solutions.

Alas, there is no perfect world, except the one we carry inside our hearts. The perfect organization doesn't exist, except in our fantasies. Every nonprofit — even the most pragmatic, diverse, visionary, well-funded group — has a truckload of troubles. So don't assume that your group is the only one that's broke and disorganized. You're in excellent company, and you're doing good work in spite of everything.

It's okay to strive for perfection, but don't let your fantasies or frustrations interfere with that pile on your desk. Keep digging.

Appendices

FOUNDATION CENTER COOPERATING COLLECTIONS   FREE FUNDING INFORMATION CENTERS

The Foundation Center is an independent national service organization established by foundations to provide an authoritative source of information on foundation and corporate giving. The New York, Washington, D.C., Atlanta, Cleveland, and San Francisco reference collections operated by the Foundation Center offer a wide variety of services and comprehensive collections of information on foundations and grants. Cooperating Collections are libraries, community foundations, and other nonprofit agencies that provide a core collection of Foundation Center publications and a variety of supplementary materials and services in areas useful to grantseekers. The core collection consists of:

THE FOUNDATION DIRECTORY 1 AND 2, AND SUPPLEMENT	THE FOUNDATION GRANTS INDEX QUARTERLY	THE LITERATURE OF THE NONPROFIT SECTOR
THE FOUNDATION 1000	FOUNDATION GRANTS TO INDIVIDUALS	NATIONAL DIRECTORY OF CORPORATE GIVING
FOUNDATION FUNDAMENTALS	GUIDE TO U.S. FOUNDATIONS, THEIR TRUSTEES, OFFICERS,	NATIONAL GUIDE TO FUNDING IN. . . . (SERIES)
FOUNDATION GIVING	AND DONORS	USER-FRIENDLY GUIDE
THE FOUNDATION GRANTS INDEX	THE FOUNDATION CENTER'S GUIDE TO PROPOSAL WRITING	

Many of the network members make available for public use sets of private foundation information returns (IRS Form 990-PF) for their state and/or neighboring states. A complete set of U.S. foundation returns can be found at the New York and Washington, D.C., offices of the Foundation Center. The Atlanta, Cleveland, and San Francisco offices contain IRS Form 990-PF returns for the southeastern, midwestern, and western states, respectively. Those Cooperating Collections marked with a bullet (■) have sets of private foundation information returns for their state and/or neighboring states.

Because the collections vary in their hours, materials, and services, *it is recommended that you call the collection in advance.* To check on new locations or current information, call toll-free 1-800-424-9836, or visit our Web site at http://fdncenter.org/library/library.html.

REFERENCE COLLECTIONS OPERATED BY THE FOUNDATION CENTER

THE FOUNDATION CENTER 8th Floor 79 Fifth Avenue New York, NY 10003 (212) 620-4230	THE FOUNDATION CENTER 312 Sutter St., Rm. 312 San Francisco, CA 94108 (415) 397-0902	THE FOUNDATION CENTER 1001 Connecticut Ave., NW Washington, DC 20036 (202) 331-1400	THE FOUNDATION CENTER Kent H. Smith Library 1422 Euclid, Suite 1356 Cleveland, OH 44115 (216) 861-1933	THE FOUNDATION CENTER Suite 150, Grand Lobby Hurt Bldg., 50 Hurt Plaza Atlanta, GA 30303 (404) 880-0094

ALABAMA

■ BIRMINGHAM PUBLIC LIBRARY
Government Documents
2100 Park Place
Birmingham 35203
(205) 226-3600

HUNTSVILLE PUBLIC LIBRARY
915 Monroe St.
Huntsville 35801
(205) 532-5940

■ UNIVERSITY OF SOUTH ALABAMA
Library Building
Mobile 36688
(205) 460-7025

■ AUBURN UNIVERSITY AT
MONTGOMERY LIBRARY
7300 University Drive
Montgomery 36117-3596
(334) 244-3653

ALASKA

■ UNIVERSITY OF ALASKA AT
ANCHORAGE
Library
3211 Providence Drive
Anchorage 99508
(907) 786-1848

JUNEAU PUBLIC LIBRARY
Reference
292 Marine Way
Juneau 99801
(907) 586-5267

ARIZONA

■ PHOENIX PUBLIC LIBRARY
Business & Sciences Unit
12 E. McDowell Rd.
Phoenix 85004
(602) 262-4636

■ TUCSON PIMA LIBRARY
101 N. Stone Ave.
Tucson 87501
(520) 791-4010

ARKANSAS

■ WESTARK COMMUNITY
COLLEGE—BORHAM LIBRARY
5210 Grand Avenue
Ft. Smith 72913
(501) 788-7200

■ CENTRAL ARKANSAS LIBRARY SYSTEM
700 Louisiana
Little Rock 72201
(501) 370-5952

PINE BLUFF-JEFFERSON COUNTY
LIBRARY SYSTEM
200 E. Eighth
Pine Bluff 71601
(501) 534-2159

CALIFORNIA

■ HUMBOLDT AREA FOUNDATION
P.O. Box 99
Bayside 95524
(707) 442-2993

■ VENTURA COUNTY COMMUNITY
FOUNDATION
Funding and Information Resource
Center
1355 Del Norte Rd.
Camarillo 93010
(805) 988-0196

■ CALIFORNIA COMMUNITY
FOUNDATION
Funding Information Center
606 S. Olive St., Suite 2400
Los Angeles 90014-1526
(213) 413-4042

OAKLAND COMMUNITY FUND
Nonprofit Resource Center
1203 Preservation Pkwy., Suite 100
Oakland 94612
(510) 834-1010

■ GRANT & RESOURCE CENTER OF
NORTHERN CALIFORNIA
Building C, Suite A
2280 Benton Dr.
Redding 96003
(916) 244-1219

LOS ANGELES PUBLIC LIBRARY
West Valley Regional Branch Library
19036 Van Owen St.
Reseda 91335
(818) 345-4393

RIVERSIDE CITY & COUNTY PUBLIC
LIBRARY
3021 Franklin Ave.
Riverside 92502
(714) 782-5201

NONPROFIT RESOURCE CENTER
Sacramento Public Library
828 I Street, 2nd Floor
Sacramento 95814
(916) 264-2772

■ SAN DIEGO COMMUNITY
FOUNDATION
Funding Information Center
101 West Broadway, Suite 1120
San Diego 92101
(619) 239-8815

NONPROFIT DEVELOPMENT CENTER
Library
1922 The Alameda, Suite 212
San Jose 95126
(408) 248-9505

■ PENINSULA COMMUNITY
FOUNDATION
Funding Information Library
1700 S. El Camino Real, R301
San Mateo 94402-3049
(415) 358-9392

LOS ANGELES PUBLIC LIBRARY
San Pedro Regional Branch
9131 S. Gaffey St.
San Pedro 90731
(310) 548-7779

VOLUNTEER CENTER OF GREATER
ORANGE COUNTY
Nonprofit Management Assistance
Center
1901 E. 4th St., Ste. 100
Santa Ana 92705
(714) 953-1655

SANTA BARBARA PUBLIC LIBRARY
40 E. Anapamu St.
Santa Barbara 93101
(805) 962-7653

SANTA MONICA PUBLIC LIBRARY
1343 Sixth St.
Santa Monica 90401-1603
(310) 458-8600

SONOMA COUNTY LIBRARY
3rd & E Streets
Santa Rosa 95404
(707) 545-0831

SEASIDE BRANCH LIBRARY
550 Harcourt St.
Seaside 93955
(408) 899-8131

COLORADO

PIKES PEAK LIBRARY DISTRICT
20 N. Cascade
Colorado Springs 80901
(719) 531-6333

■ DENVER PUBLIC LIBRARY
General Reference
10 West 14th Ave. Pkwy.
Denver 80204
(303) 640-6200

CONNECTICUT

DANBURY PUBLIC LIBRARY
170 Main St.
Danbury 06810
(203) 797-4527

■ GREENWICH LIBRARY
101 West Putnam Ave.
Greenwich 06830
(203) 622-7910

■ HARTFORD PUBLIC LIBRARY
500 Main St.
Hartford 06103
(203) 293-6000

D.A.T.A.
70 Audubon St.
New Haven 06510
(203) 772-1345

DELAWARE

■ UNIVERSITY OF DELAWARE
Hugh Morris Library
Newark 19717-5267
(302) 831-2432

FLORIDA

VOLUSIA COUNTY LIBRARY CENTER
City Island
Daytona Beach 32014-4484
(904) 257-6036

■ NOVA SOUTHEASTERN UNIVERSITY
Einstein Library
3301 College Ave.
Fort Lauderdale 33314
(305) 475-7050

INDIAN RIVER COMMUNITY
COLLEGE
Charles S. Miley Learning Resource
Center
3209 Virginia Ave.
Fort Pierce 34981-5599
(407) 462-4757

■ JACKSONVILLE PUBLIC LIBRARIES
Grants Resource Center
122 N. Ocean St.
Jacksonville 32202
(904) 630-2665

■ MIAMI-DADE PUBLIC LIBRARY
Humanities/Social Science
101 W. Flagler St.
Miami 33130
(305) 375-5575

■ ORLANDO PUBLIC LIBRARY
Social Sciences Department
101 E. Central Blvd.
Orlando 32801
(407) 425-4694

SELBY PUBLIC LIBRARY
Reference
1001 Blvd. of the Arts
Sarasota 34236
(941) 951-5501

■ TAMPA-HILLSBOROUGH COUNTY
PUBLIC LIBRARY
900 N. Ashley Drive
Tampa 33602
(813) 273-3628

■ COMMUNITY FOUNDATION OF
PALM BEACH & MARTIN COUNTIES
324 Datura St., Suite 340
West Palm Beach 33401
(407) 659-6800

GEORGIA

■ ATLANTA-FULTON PUBLIC LIBRARY
Foundation Collection—Ivan Allen
Department
1 Margaret Mitchell Square
Atlanta 30303-1089
(404) 730-1900

■ DALTON REGIONAL LIBRARY
310 Cappes St.
Dalton 30720
(706) 278-4507

■ THOMAS COUNTY PUBLIC LIBRARY
201 N. Madison St.
Thomasville, GA 31792
(912) 225-5252

HAWAII

■ UNIVERSITY OF HAWAII
Hamilton Library
2550 The Mall
Honolulu 96822
(808) 956-7214

HAWAII COMMUNITY FOUNDATION
Hawaii Resource Center
222 Merchant St., Second Floor
Honolulu 96813
(808) 537-6333

IDAHO

■ BOISE PUBLIC LIBRARY
715 S. Capitol Blvd.
Boise 83702
(208) 384-4024

■ CALDWELL PUBLIC LIBRARY
1010 Dearborn St.
Caldwell 83605
(208) 459-3242

ILLINOIS

■ DONORS FORUM OF CHICAGO
53 W. Jackson Blvd., Suite 430
Chicago 60604-3608
(312) 431-0265

■ EVANSTON PUBLIC LIBRARY
1703 Orrington Ave.
Evanston 60201
(708) 866-0305

ROCK ISLAND PUBLIC LIBRARY
401 - 19th St.
Rock Island 61201
(309) 788-7627

■ UNIVERSITY OF ILLINOIS AT
SPRINGFIELD
Brookens Library
Shepherd Road
Springfield 62794-9243
(217) 786-6633

INDIANA

■ ALLEN COUNTY PUBLIC LIBRARY
900 Webster St.
Ft. Wayne 46802
(219) 424-0544

INDIANA UNIVERSITY NORTHWEST
LIBRARY
3400 Broadway
Gary 46408
(219) 980-6582

■ INDIANAPOLIS-MARION COUNTY
PUBLIC LIBRARY
Social Sciences
40 E. St. Clair
Indianapolis 46206
(317) 269-1733

IOWA

■ CEDAR RAPIDS PUBLIC LIBRARY
Foundation Center Collection
500 First St., SE
Cedar Rapids 52401
(319) 398-5123

■ SOUTHWESTERN COMMUNITY
COLLEGE
Learning Resource Center
1501 W. Townline Rd.
Creston 50801
(515) 782-7081

■ PUBLIC LIBRARY OF DES MOINES
100 Locust
Des Moines 50309-1791
(515) 283-4152

■ SIOUX CITY PUBLIC LIBRARY
529 Pierce St.
Sioux City 51101-1202
(712) 252-5669

KANSAS

■ DODGE CITY PUBLIC LIBRARY
1001 2nd Ave.
Dodge City 67801
(316) 225-0248

■ TOPEKA AND SHAWNEE COUNTY
PUBLIC LIBRARY
1515 SW 10th Ave.
Topeka 66604-1374
(913) 233-2040

■ WICHITA PUBLIC LIBRARY
223 S. Main St.
Wichita 67202
(316) 262-0611

KENTUCKY

■ WESTERN KENTUCKY UNIVERSITY
Helm-Cravens Library
Bowling Green 42101-3576
(502) 745-6125

■ LEXINGTON PUBLIC LIBRARY
140 E. Main St.
Lexington 40507-1376
(606) 231-5520

■ LOUISVILLE FREE PUBLIC LIBRARY
301 York Street
Louisville 40203
(502) 574-1611

LOUISIANA

■ EAST BATON ROUGE PARISH LIBRARY
Centroplex Branch Grants Collection
120 St. Louis
Baton Rouge 70802
(504) 389-4960

■ BEAUREGARD PARISH LIBRARY
205 S. Washington Ave.
De Ridder 70634
(318) 463-6217

■ NEW ORLEANS PUBLIC LIBRARY
Business & Science Division
219 Loyola Ave.
New Orleans 70140
(504) 596-2580

■ SHREVE MEMORIAL LIBRARY
424 Texas St.
Shreveport 71120-1523
(318) 226-5894

MAINE

■ MAINE GRANTS INFORMATION
CENTER
University of Southern Maine
P. O. Box 9301, 314 Forrest Ave.
Portland 04104-9301
(207) 780-4411

MARYLAND

■ ENOCH PRATT FREE LIBRARY
Social Science & History
400 Cathedral St.
Baltimore 21201
(410) 396-5430

MASSACHUSETTS

■ ASSOCIATED GRANTMAKERS OF
MASSACHUSETTS
294 Washington St., Suite 840
Boston 02108
(617) 426-2606

■ BOSTON PUBLIC LIBRARY
Soc. Sci. Reference
666 Boylston St
Boston 02117
(617) 536-5400

WESTERN MASSACHUSETTS
FUNDING RESOURCE CENTER
65 Elliot St.
Springfield 01101-1730
(413) 732-3175

■ WORCESTER PUBLIC LIBRARY
Grants Resource Center
Salem Square
Worcester 01608
(508) 799-1655

MICHIGAN

■ ALPENA COUNTY LIBRARY
211 N. First St.
Alpena 49707
(517) 356-6188

■ UNIVERSITY OF MICHIGAN-ANN
ARBOR
Graduate Library
Reference & Research Services
Department
Ann Arbor 48109-1205
(313) 764-9373

■ WILLARD PUBLIC LIBRARY
7 W. Van Buren St.
Battle Creek 49017
(616) 968-8166

■ HENRY FORD CENTENNIAL LIBRARY
Adult Services
16301 Michigan Ave.
Dearborn 48126
(313) 943-2330

■ WAYNE STATE UNIVERSITY
Purdy/Kresge Library
5265 Cass Avenue
Detroit 48202
(313) 577-6424

■ MICHIGAN STATE UNIVERSITY
LIBRARIES
Social Sciences/Humanities
Main Library
East Lansing 48824-1048
(517) 353-8818

■ FARMINGTON COMMUNITY LIBRARY
32737 West 12 Mile Rd.
Farmington Hills 48018
(810) 553-0300

■ UNIVERSITY OF MICHIGAN—FLINT
Library
Flint 48502-2186
(810) 762-3408

■ GRAND RAPIDS PUBLIC LIBRARY
Business Dept.—3rd Floor
60 Library Plaza NE
Grand Rapids 49503-3093
(616) 456-3600

MICHIGAN TECHNOLOGICAL
UNIVERSITY
Van Pelt Library
1400 Townsend Dr.
Houghton 49931
(906) 487-2507

SAULT STE. MARIE AREA PUBLIC
SCHOOLS
Office of Compensatory Education
460 W. Spruce St.
Sault Ste. Marie 49783-1874
(906) 635-6619

■ NORTHWESTERN MICHIGAN
COLLEGE
Mark & Helen Osterin Library
1701 E. Front St.
Traverse City 49684
(616) 922-1060

MINNESOTA

■ DULUTH PUBLIC LIBRARY
520 W. Superior St.
Duluth 55802
(218) 723-3802

■ SOUTHWEST STATE UNIVERSITY
University Library
Marshall 56258
(507) 537-6176

■ MINNEAPOLIS PUBLIC LIBRARY
Sociology Department
300 Nicollet Mall
Minneapolis 55401
(612) 372-6555

ROCHESTER PUBLIC LIBRARY
11 First St. SE
Rochester 55904-3777
(507) 285-8002

ST. PAUL PUBLIC LIBRARY
90 W. Fourth St.
St. Paul 55102
(612) 292-6307

MISSISSIPPI

■ JACKSON/HINDS LIBRARY SYSTEM
300 N. State St.
Jackson 39201
(601) 968-5803

MISSOURI

■ CLEARINGHOUSE FOR
MIDCONTINENT FOUNDATIONS
University of Missouri
5110 Cherry, Suite 310
Kansas City 64110
(816) 235-1176

■ KANSAS CITY PUBLIC LIBRARY
311 E. 12th St.
Kansas City 64106
(816) 221-9650

■ METROPOLITAN ASSOCIATION FOR
PHILANTHROPY, INC.
5615 Pershing Avenue, Suite 20
St. Louis 63112
(314) 361-3900

■ SPRINGFIELD-GREENE COUNTY
LIBRARY
397 E. Central
Springfield 65802
(417) 837-5000

MONTANA

■ MONTANA STATE
UNIVERSITY—BILLINGS
Library—Special Collections
1500 North 30th St.
Billings 59101-0298
(406) 657-1662

■ BOZEMAN PUBLIC LIBRARY
220 E. Lamme
Bozeman 59715
(406) 582-2402

■ MONTANA STATE LIBRARY
Library Services
1515 E. 6th Ave.
Helena 59620
(406) 444-3004

■ UNIVERSITY OF MONTANA
Maureen & Mike Mansfield Library
Missoula 59812-1195
(406) 243-6800

NEBRASKA

■ UNIVERSITY OF
NEBRASKA—LINCOLN
Love Library
14th & R Streets
Lincoln 68588-0410
(402) 472-2848

■ W. DALE CLARK LIBRARY
Social Sciences Department
215 S. 15th St.
Omaha 68102
(402) 444-4826

NEVADA

■ LAS VEGAS-CLARK COUNTY LIBRARY
DISTRICT
1401 E. Flamingo
Las Vegas 89119
(702) 733-3642

■ WASHOE COUNTY LIBRARY
301 S. Center St.
Reno 89501
(702) 785-4010

NEW HAMPSHIRE

■ NEW HAMPSHIRE CHARITABLE FDN.
37 Pleasant St.
Concord 03301-4005
(603) 225-6641

■ PLYMOUTH STATE COLLEGE
Herbert H. Lamson Library
Plymouth 03264
(603) 535-2258

NEW JERSEY

■ CUMBERLAND COUNTY LIBRARY
New Jersey Room
800 E. Commerce St.
Bridgeton 08302
(609) 453-2210

■ FREE PUBLIC LIBRARY OF ELIZABETH
11 S. Broad St.
Elizabeth 07202
(908) 354-6060

■ COUNTY COLLEGE OF MORRIS
Learning Resource Center
214 Center Grove Rd.
Randolph 07869
(201) 328-5296

■ NEW JERSEY STATE LIBRARY
Governmental Reference Services
185 W. State St.
Trenton 08625-0520
(609) 292-6220

NEW MEXICO

■ ALBUQUERQUE COMMUNITY
FOUNDATION
3301 Menual NE, Ste. 30
Albuquerque 87176-6960
(505) 883-6240

■ NEW MEXICO STATE LIBRARY
Information Services
325 Don Gaspar
Santa Fe 87501-2777
(505) 827-3824

NEW YORK

■ NEW YORK STATE LIBRARY
Humanities Reference
Cultural Education Center
Empire State Plaza
Albany 12230
(518) 474-5355

SUFFOLK COOPERATIVE LIBRARY
SYSTEM
627 N. Sunrise Service Rd.
Bellport 11713
(516) 286-1600

NEW YORK PUBLIC LIBRARY
Bronx Reference Center
Fordham Branch
2556 Bainbridge Ave.
Bronx 10458
(718) 220-6575

BROOKLYN IN TOUCH
INFORMATION CENTER, INC.
One Hanson Place—Room 2504
Brooklyn 11243
(718) 230-3200

BROOKLYN PUBLIC LIBRARY
Social Sciences Division
Grand Army Plaza
Brooklyn 11238
(718) 780-7700

■ BUFFALO & ERIE COUNTY PUBLIC
LIBRARY
Business & Labor Dept.
Lafayette Square
Buffalo 14203
(716) 858-7097

HUNTINGTON PUBLIC LIBRARY
338 Main St.
Huntington 11743
(516) 427-5165

QUEENS BOROUGH PUBLIC LIBRARY
Social Sciences Division
89-11 Merrick Blvd.
Jamaica 11432
(718) 990-0761

■ LEVITTOWN PUBLIC LIBRARY
1 Bluegrass Lane
Levittown 11756
(516) 731-5728

NEW YORK PUBLIC LIBRARY
Countee Cullen Branch Library
104 W. 136th St.
New York 10030
(212) 491-2070

■ PLATTSBURGH PUBLIC LIBRARY
19 Oak St.
Plattsburgh 12901
(518) 563-0921

ADRIANCE MEMORIAL LIBRARY
Special Services Department
93 Market St.
Poughkeepsie 12601
(914) 485-3445

■ ROCHESTER PUBLIC LIBRARY
Business, Economics & Law
115 South Ave.
Rochester 14604
(716) 428-7328

ONONDAGA COUNTY PUBLIC
LIBRARY
447 S. Salina St.
Syracuse 13202-2494
(315) 435-1800

UTICA PUBLIC LIBRARY
303 Genesee St.
Utica 13501
(315) 735-2279

WHITE PLAINS PUBLIC LIBRARY
100 Martine Ave.
White Plains 10601
(914) 422-1480

NORTH CAROLINA

■ COMMUNITY FDN. OF WESTERN
NORTH CAROLINA
Learning Resources Center
14 College St.
P.O. Box 1888
Asheville 28801
(704) 254-4960

■ THE DUKE ENDOWMENT
100 N. Tryon St., Suite 3500
Charlotte 28202
(704) 376-0291

DURHAM COUNTY PUBLIC LIBRARY
301 North Roxboro
Durham 27702
(919) 560-0110

■ STATE LIBRARY OF NORTH CAROLINA
Government and Business Services
Archives Bldg., 109 E. Jones St.
Raleigh 27601
(919) 733-3270

■ FORSYTH COUNTY PUBLIC LIBRARY
660 W. 5th St.
Winston-Salem 27101
(910) 727-2680

NORTH DAKOTA

■ BISMARCK PUBLIC LIBRARY
515 N. Fifth St.
Bismarck 58501
(701) 222-6410

■ FARGO PUBLIC LIBRARY
102 N. 3rd St.
Fargo 58102
(701) 241-1491

OHIO

■ STARK COUNTY DISTRICT LIBRARY
Humanities
715 Market Ave. N.
Canton 44702
(216) 452-0665

■ PUBLIC LIBRARY OF CINCINNATI &
HAMILTON COUNTY
Grants Resource Center
800 Vine St.—Library Square
Cincinnati 45202-2071
(513) 369-6940

COLUMBUS METROPOLITAN LIBRARY
Business and Technology
96 S. Grant Ave.
Columbus 43215
(614) 645-2590

■ DAYTON & MONTGOMERY COUNTY
PUBLIC LIBRARY
Grants Resource Center
215 E. Third St.
Dayton 45402
(513) 227-9500 x211

■ MANSFELD/RICHLAND COUNTY
PUBLIC LIBRARY
42 W. 3rd St.
Mansfield 44902
(419) 521-3110

■ TOLEDO-LUCAS COUNTY PUBLIC
LIBRARY
Social Sciences Department
325 Michigan St.
Toledo 43624-1614
(419) 259-5245

■ YOUNGSTOWN & MAHONING
COUNTY LIBRARY
305 Wick Ave.
Youngstown 44503
(216) 744-8636

MUSKINGUM COUNTY LIBRARY
220 N. 5th St.
Zanesville 43701
(614) 453-0391

OKLAHOMA

■ OKLAHOMA CITY UNIVERSITY
Dulaney Browne Library
2501 N. Blackwelder
Oklahoma City 73106
(405) 521-5072

■ TULSA CITY-COUNTY LIBRARY
400 Civic Center
Tulsa 74103
(918) 596-7944

OREGON

OREGON INSTITUTE OF
TECHNOLOGY
Library
3201 Campus Dr.
Klamath Falls 97601-8801
(503) 885-1773

■ PACIFIC NON-PROFIT NETWORK
Grantsmanship Resource Library
33 N. Central, Suite 211
Medford 97501
(503) 779-6044

MULTNOMAH COUNTY LIBRARY
Government Documents
801 SW Tenth Ave.
Portland 97205
(503) 248-5123

■ OREGON STATE LIBRARY
State Library Building
Salem 97310
(503) 378-4277

PENNSYLVANIA

NORTHAMPTON COMMUNITY
COLLEGE
Learning Resources Center
3835 Green Pond Rd.
Bethlehem 18017
(610) 861-5360

ERIE COUNTY LIBRARY SYSTEM
27 S. Park Row
Erie 16501
(814) 451-6927

DAUPHIN COUNTY LIBRARY SYSTEM
Central Library
101 Walnut St.
Harrisburg 17101
(717) 234-4976

LANCASTER COUNTY PUBLIC
LIBRARY
125 N. Duke St.
Lancaster 17602
(717) 394-2651

■ FREE LIBRARY OF PHILADELPHIA
Regional Foundation Center
Logan Square
Philadelphia 19103
(215) 686-5423

■ CARNEGIE LIBRARY OF PITTSBURGH
Foundation Collection
4400 Forbes Ave.
Pittsburgh 15213-4080
(412) 622-1917

POCONO NORTHEAST
DEVELOPMENT FUND
James Pettinger Memorial Library
1151 Oak St.
Pittston 18640-3755
(717) 655-5581

READING PUBLIC LIBRARY
100 South Fifth St.
Reading 19602
(610) 655-6355

■ MARTIN LIBRARY
159 Market St.
York 17401
(717) 846-5300

RHODE ISLAND

■ PROVIDENCE PUBLIC LIBRARY
225 Washington St.
Providence 02906
(401) 455-8088

SOUTH CAROLINA

■ ANDERSON COUNTY LIBRARY
202 East Greenville St.
Anderson 29621
(803) 260-4500

■ CHARLESTON COUNTY LIBRARY
404 King St.
Charleston 29403
(803) 723-1645

■ SOUTH CAROLINA STATE LIBRARY
1500 Senate St.
Columbia 29211
(803) 734-8666

SOUTH DAKOTA

NONPROFIT GRANTS ASSISTANCE
CENTER
Dakota State University
Business and Education Institute
3534 Southwestern Ave.
Sioux Falls 57105
(605) 367-5380

■ SOUTH DAKOTA STATE LIBRARY
800 Governors Drive
Pierre 57501-2294
(605) 773-5070
(800) 592-1841 (SD residents)

■ SIOUX FALLS AREA FOUNDATION
141 N. Main Ave., Suite 310
Sioux Falls 57102-1132
(605) 336-7055

TENNESSEE

■ KNOX COUNTY PUBLIC LIBRARY
500 W. Church Ave.
Knoxville 37902
(615) 544-5700

■ MEMPHIS & SHELBY COUNTY
PUBLIC LIBRARY
1850 Peabody Ave.
Memphis 38104
(901) 725-8877

■ NASHVILLE PUBLIC LIBRARY
Business Information Division
225 Polk Ave.
Nashville 37203
(615) 862-5843

TEXAS

ABILENE CENTER FOR NONPROFIT
MANAGEMENT
Funding Information Library
500 N. Chestnut, Suite 1511
Abilene 79604
(915) 677-8166

■ AMARILLO AREA FOUNDATION
700 First National Place
801 S. Fillmore
Amarillo 79101
(806) 376-4521

■ HOGG FOUNDATION FOR MENTAL
HEALTH
3001 Lake Austin Blvd.
Austin 78703
(512) 471-5041

TEXAS A & M UNIVERSITY AT
CORPUS CHRISTI
Library
Reference Dept.
6300 Ocean Dr.
Corpus Christi 78412
(512) 994-2608

■ DALLAS PUBLIC LIBRARY
Urban Information
1515 Young St.
Dallas 75201
(214) 670-1487

EL PASO COMMUNITY FOUNDATION
201 E. Main St., Suite 1616
El Paso 79901
(915) 533-4020

■ FUNDING INFORMATION CENTER
OF FORT WORTH
Texas Christian University Library
2800 S. University Dr.
Ft. Worth 76129
(817) 921-7664

■ HOUSTON PUBLIC LIBRARY
Bibliographic Information Center
500 McKinney
Houston 77002
(713) 236-1313

■ LONGVIEW PUBLIC LIBRARY
222 W. Cotton St.
Longview 75601
(903) 237-1352

LUBBOCK AREA FOUNDATION, INC.
1655 Main St., Suite 209
Lubbock 79401
(806) 762-8061

■ FUNDING INFORMATION CENTER
530 McCullough, Suite 600
San Antonio 78212-8270
(210) 227-4333

■ NORTH TEXAS CENTER FOR
NONPROFIT MANAGEMENT
624 Indiana, Suite 307
Wichita Falls 76301
(817) 322-4961

UTAH

■ SALT LAKE CITY PUBLIC LIBRARY
209 East 500 South
Salt Lake City 84111
(801) 524-8200

VERMONT

■ VERMONT DEPT. OF LIBRARIES
Reference & Law Info. Services
109 State St.
Montpelier 05609
(802) 828-3268

VIRGINIA

HAMPTON PUBLIC LIBRARY
4207 Victoria Blvd.
Hampton 23669
(804) 727-1312

■ RICHMOND PUBLIC LIBRARY
Business, Science & Technology
101 East Franklin St.
Richmond 23219
(804) 780-8223

■ ROANOKE CITY PUBLIC LIBRARY
SYSTEM
Central Library
706 S. Jefferson St.
Roanoke 24016
(703) 981-2477

WASHINGTON

■ MID-COLUMBIA LIBRARY
405 South Dayton
Kennewick 99336
(509)586-3156

■ SEATTLE PUBLIC LIBRARY
Science, Social Science
1000 Fourth Ave.
Seattle 98104
(206) 386-4620

■ SPOKANE PUBLIC LIBRARY
Funding Information Center
West 811 Main Ave.
Spokane 99201
(509) 626-5347

■ UNITED WAY OF PIERCE COUNTY
Center for Nonprofit Development
734 Broadway
P.O. Box 2215
Tacoma 98401
(206) 597-6686

GREATER WENATCHEE COMMUNITY
FOUNDATION AT THE WENATCHEE
PUBLIC LIBRARY
310 Douglas St.
Wenatchee 98807
(509) 662-5021

WEST VIRGINIA

■ KANAWHA COUNTY PUBLIC LIBRARY
123 Capitol St.
Charleston 25301
(304) 343-4646

WISCONSIN

■ UNIVERSITY OF
WISCONSIN-MADISON
Memorial Library
728 State St.
Madison 53706
(608) 262-3242

■ MARQUETTE UNIVERSITY MEMORIAL
LIBRARY
Funding Information Center
1415 W. Wisconsin Ave.
Milwaukee 53201-3141
(414) 288-1515

■ UNIVERSITY OF
WISCONSIN—STEVENS POINT
Library—Foundation Collection
99 Reserve St.
Stevens Point 54481-3897
(715) 346-4204

WYOMING

■ NATRONA COUNTY PUBLIC LIBRARY
307 E. 2nd St.
Casper 82601-2598
(307) 237-4935

■ LARAMIE COUNTY COMMUNITY
COLLEGE
Instructional Resource Center
1400 E. College Dr.
Cheyenne 82007-3299
(307) 778-1206

■ CAMPBELL COUNTY PUBLIC LIBRARY
2101 4-J Road
Gillette 82716
(307) 682-3223

■ TETON COUNTY LIBRARY
320 S. King St.
Jackson 83001
(307) 733-2164

ROCK SPRINGS LIBRARY
400 C St.
Rock Springs 82901
(307) 352-6667

PUERTO RICO

UNIVERSITY OF PUERTO RICO
Ponce Technological College Library
Box 7186
Ponce 00732
(809) 844-8181

UNIVERSIDAD DEL SAGRADO
CORAZON
M.M.T. Guevara Library
Santurce 00914
(809) 728-1515 x 4357

Participants in the Foundation Center's Cooperating Collections network are libraries or nonprofit information centers that provide fundraising information and other funding-related technical assistance in their communities. Cooperating Collections agree to provide free public access to a basic collection of Foundation Center publications during a regular schedule of hours, offering free funding research guidance to all visitors. Many also provide a variety of services for local nonprofit organizations, using staff or volunteers to prepare special materials, organize workshops, or conduct orientations.

The Foundation Center welcomes inquiries from libraries or information centers in the U.S. interested in providing this type of public information service. If you are interested in establishing a funding information library for the use of nonprofit organizations in your area or in learning more about the program, please write to: Judith Margolin, Vice President for Public Services, The Foundation Center, 79 Fifth Avenue, New York, NY 10003-3076.   11/95

Appendix B:
Resources for
Canadian Organizations

CANADIAN CENTRE FOR PHILANTHROPY, 425 University Ave., Suite 700, Toronto, Ontario M5G 1T6, (416) 597-2293 or (800) 263-1178, www.ccp.ca.

The Canadian Centre for Philanthropy operates a free nonprofit resource library in Toronto and also publishes books and pamphlets on grants research, fundraising, and nonprofit management. A partial list of titles:

Resource Guide, 1994. 52 pages. Free upon request. Lists sources for publications, consultants, videos, training materials, periodicals, books, and funding research.

Canadian Directory to Foundations, 1994. Approx. 475 pages. $220 plus shipping and tax. Profiles more than one thousand Canadian foundations.

The Grant Report: Foundation Granting Activity in Canada, 1995. 362 pages. $80 plus shipping and tax. Lists recent grants over $5,000 provided by Canadian foundations.

NATIONAL COUNCIL OF WELFARE, 1010 Somerset Street West, 2nd Floor, Ottawa, Ontario K1A 0J9, (613) 957-2963.

The National Council of Welfare is a federal citizens' group established to advise the Minister of Human Resources Development on matters of concern to low-income Canadians. The agency publishes a series of free booklets and reports in both English and French, including the following titles:

Bookkeeping Handbook for Low-Income Citizen Groups, 1973. 103 pages. How to create and/or refine your accounting system.

Organizing for Social Action, 1975. 78 pages. A description of three successful organizing campaigns with analysis by the participants.

SELF-COUNSEL PRESS, 1481 Charlotte Road, North Vancouver, British Columbia, V7J 1H1, (604) 986-3366.

This press offers several books for nonprofits, including:

Fundraising for Non-Profit Groups, Joyce Young and Ken Wyman, 1995. 264 pages. $10.95 plus shipping and tax. Fourth edition of this popular text, which is especially useful for social change organizations.

Forming and Managing a Non-Profit Organization in Canada, Flora MacLeod, 1995. 216 pages. $19.95 plus shipping and tax. Outlines the steps needed to create and manage a healthy organization.

Faith-based grantmaking is based on a tradition of radical questioners, challenging authority, encouraging debate. Jesus, along with Jewish martyrs, resistance fighters, and the prophets, spoke out forcefully against injustice, often at great danger. As funders we are committed to supporting those who follow in their footsteps.

— Marjorie Fine, Unitarian Universalist Veatch
Program at Shelter Rock

Appendix C:
Raising Money from
Faith-Based Grants Programs

Religious funders are a good source of money for social change. According to *Responsive Philanthropy* (Winter 1996), the newsletter of the National Committee for Responsive Philanthropy, organized religion donated $7.1 billion for non-religious purposes in 1992, including $1.3 billion to charities outside religious denominations.

While a few faith-based funders resemble foundations in their operations and proposal review processes, the vast majority do not. In trying to define the difference, Marjorie Fine describes an old advertisement for kosher hot dogs. In the Summer 1994 issue of *Network*, the newsletter of the National Network of Grantmakers, she wrote, "While the U.S. Government had certain standards, the [kosher butchers] had even stricter ones because, 'They had to answer to an even higher authority.'" She adds, "Do we [religious funders] have a spiritual high ground that other grantmaking institutions and funders do not?"

Here's another significant difference. According to Mary Eileen Paul and Andrea Flores, editors of the *1995 Religious Funding Resource Guide*, "Religious institutions rarely consider themselves as 'grantmakers.' Their giving capacity is often part of a larger social justice component in their structure, and staff managing the giving program have multiple other responsibilities.... Religious institutions or churches will give support only if they see you and your work as part of their work."

Faith-based grants programs draw their ideals and values from deep historical roots, so they tend to have a long-term perspective on social change. They also have a broad base in community. Gary Delgado, one of the founders of the Center for Third World Organizing, addresses this issue in his essay, "Leveraging God's Resources from her Representatives on Earth," which appears in *The Activists' Guide to Religious Funding*. "More than 40 percent of the U.S. population attends church regularly," he writes. "The percentage of church attendees in low-income organizations is often higher. Our members are their members." This combination of depth and breadth (not to mention spiritual height) makes faith-based funders a unique resource for social justice.

If you think religious funding might fit with your programs, do your homework. For further information and strategies for approaching faith-based funding programs, three excellent resource books are included in the Bibliography on page 186. On the local front, most community churches are listed in the Yellow Pages. You should also contact your local Council of Churches and ask for a directory of congregations.

If you choose to pursue funding from religious sources, keep the following points in mind.

1. **RELATIONSHIPS COUNT.** This is true in the foundation world, but even more critical in the religious funding arena. The importance of relationships is based, in part, on the intricate pathways through which money and accountability flow — from local congregations through regional dioceses and judicatories to national denominational offices, and then back down to the local level. In many cases, decision makers rely on the opinions of colleagues who are above, below, or beside them in the hierarchy. To raise money successfully from these sources, you need a few advocates within the denomination — pastors or rabbis, administrators, lay leaders, members of congregation social action committees. Clergy can also help you involve their peers in other denominations.

   "One thing to remember," says Gary Delgado, "is that working with churches is a two-way street. If you develop the relationships and really pay attention to what the clergy people have to say, the collaboration will work for both parties. If you just go for the money, you might get it — once. So pay attention to the self-interest of individual clergy."

2. **FAITH-BASED FUNDRAISING IS A FORM OF COMMUNITY ORGANIZING.** According to Mary Eileen Paul and Andrea Flores, "Churches or Temples in your local community are more than likely to be concerned about the same issues you are. They can represent powerful allies if you involve them in planning and implementation of strategies for change. As a grantseeker you need to learn the social justice agenda and focus of the religious institution, and to understand that fundraising is basically an organizing task ... because you have an additional constituency and institutional structure to relate to, to educate, and to involve in your work."

3. **START WITH LOCAL CONGREGATIONS.** It is possible to go straight to the national religious giving programs, but most prefer an endorsement at the community level before providing a grant. Even if you receive fund-

ing from the national office, you might offend the local clergy, which will hurt your efforts in the community.

Of course, you can raise a lot of money directly from local churches, synagogues, and other religious institutions. Many congregations contribute to grassroots groups without going through regional or national offices. They can also help with donated office space, furniture, photocopying, free publicity in their newsletters, volunteers, public endorsements of your work, and perhaps an opportunity to give a guest sermon about your issue.

4. **CHOOSE QUALITY OVER QUANTITY.** Unless you live in a very small town, you won't have time to develop strong relationships with all the local clergy. You're unlikely to have the stamina or patience to apply to all religious funding programs — the *1995 Religious Funding Resource Guide* includes guidelines and application materials for 35 grant and loan programs, while *Church Philanthropy for Native Americans and Other Minorities* lists 67 sources of grants and 34 loan programs. As Mary Eileen Paul and Andrea Flores write, "Rather than trying to get to know all the religious bodies ... at once, pick one or two to start with. That way, the relationships are fewer, more maintainable, and more likely to result in lasting support."

5. **FOLLOW THE GUIDELINES!** Nearly all faith-based funders require forms — lots and lots of forms. Fill them out carefully and completely. Provide only the attachments requested.

6. **FAITH-BASED FUNDRAISING IS A LONG-TERM STRATEGY — SO PLAN ACCORDINGLY.** To raise money (and make friends) among clergy, you must invest the time up front. According to Gary Delgado, it can take anywhere from six months to two years to receive a grant. On the other hand, Delgado says, religious funders have a long-range perspective and "do not expect your organization to change the world in a year or two or express your measurable progress in quarterly reports." If you build solid relationships and involve the religious community in your work, you stand a good chance of receiving financial support over several years.

Bibliography

This bibliography includes books, magazines, and CD-ROM products I have reviewed and, in many cases, used. Hundreds of additional books and periodicals are also available to help you with fundraising, proposal development, and other organizational needs. I urge you to visit your nearest Foundation Center Cooperating Collection (see Appendix A) and spend some time browsing through the stacks. The Internet is also a growing resource for nonprofits; for a brief directory of Internet resources, see page 48.

Before ordering any of these materials, *call to confirm availability and current price*. Most publishers also require *an additional small charge for shipping and handling*.

BOARD DEVELOPMENT

THE BOARD OF DIRECTORS, Kim Klein and Stephanie Roth, 1995. 32 pages. $10. Chardon Press, 3781 Broadway, Oakland CA 94611, (888) 458-8588.

> This booklet includes nine articles reprinted from the *Grassroots Fundraising Journal*, including several on board fundraising responsibilities and strategies. My favorite: "Fifty-Six Ways that Board Members Can Raise $500."

BOARDS FROM HELL, Susan M. Scribner, 1995. 50 pages. $15. Scribner & Associates, 49 Coronado Avenue, Long Beach, CA 90803, (310) 433-6082.

> A humorous look at everything that can go wrong with your board of directors. Includes sections on how to create a healthy, productive board and then involve board members in strategic planning.

COMMUNITY-BASED FUNDRAISING

FUNDRAISING FOR SOCIAL CHANGE, Kim Klein, 1994. 351 pages. $25. Chardon Press, 3781 Broadway, Oakland CA 94611, (888) 458-8588.

> One of the best books on fundraising, and one of the few that addresses the needs and concerns of progressive groups. Excellent sections on direct mail and major donor fundraising.

GETTING MAJOR GIFTS, Kim Klein and Lisa Honig, 1999. 34 pages. $12. Chardon Press, 3781 Broadway, Oakland CA 94611, (888) 458-8588.

> This booklet includes ten articles reprinted from the *Grassroots Fundraising Journal*. Contains enough information to design and initiate a major donor program.

THE GRASS ROOTS FUNDRAISING BOOK: HOW TO RAISE MONEY IN YOUR COMMUNITY, Joan Flanagan, 1995. 342 pages. $16.95. Contemporary Books, Two Prudential Plaza, Suite 1200, Chicago, IL 60601-6790, (312) 540-4500.

> One of the classics of fundraising literature, this book is humorous, practical, and fun to read. The material on benefit events is especially thorough and wise.

COMPUTER PRODUCTS FOR GRANTS RESEARCH

For a brief evaluation of these products, including price information, see page 47.

CHRONICLE GUIDE TO GRANTS, Chronicle of Philanthropy, 1255 23rd Street, NW, Washington, DC 20037, (800) 287-6072.

FC SEARCH, The Foundation Center, 79 Fifth Avenue, New York, NY 10003-3076, (800) 424-9836.

GRANTS DATABASE, Knight-Ridder Information, Inc., 2440 El Camino Real, Mountain View, CA 94040, (800)334-2564.

PROSPECTOR'S CHOICE; GRANTS ON DISK, both from Taft Group, 835 Penobscot Building, 645 Griswold Street, Detroit, MI 48226-4094, (800) 877-TAFT.

SOURCES OF FOUNDATIONS, Orca Knowledge Systems, PO Box 280, San Anselmo, CA 94979, (800) 868-ORCA.

FAITH-BASED FUNDRAISING

RELIGIOUS FUNDING RESOURCE GUIDE, ResourceWomen, updated 1999. 520 pages. $75.00. Available from Chardon Press, 3781 Broadway, Oakland CA 94611, (888) 458-8588.

> A compendium of guidelines and application forms for 38 grant and loan programs, plus a handy table explaining the hierarchy of each major denomination and suggestions for how to approach and address clergy.

CHURCH PHILANTHROPY FOR NATIVE AMERICANS AND OTHER MINORITIES: A GUIDE TO MULTICULTURAL FUNDING FROM RELIGIOUS SOURCES, Phyllis A. Meiners and Greg A. Sanford, 1995. 280 pages. $118.95. CRC Publishing Company — EagleRock Books, PO Box 22583, Kansas City, MO, 64113-2583, (800) 268-2059.

> This guide profiles 67 sources of grants and 34 loan programs specifically for communities of color. It also includes application procedures and sample grants, and offers ideas on how best to approach the funders.

FOUNDATION AND CORPORATE DIRECTORIES (GENERAL)

The following directories are large, expensive books that grassroots organizations should consider using (for free) at the library. Most of the Foundation Center Cooperating Collections also include *specialized directories of funders organized by their areas of interest:* arts and culture, health, conservation, gay and lesbian, social services, youth, and so forth.

CORPORATE GIVING DIRECTORY, Kathleen Dame, ed., 1996. 1,875 pages. $395. Taft Group, 835 Penobscot Building, 645 Griswold Street, Detroit, MI 48226-4094, (800) 877-TAFT.

> Profiles one thousand corporate foundations and corporate giving programs granting at least $250,000 per year. Includes biographical information on corporate officers and decision-makers.

THE FOUNDATION 1000, Francine Jones, ed., 1995. 2,945 pages. $285. The Foundation Center, 79 Fifth Avenue, New York, NY 10003-3076, (800) 424-9836.

> Extremely comprehensive information on the one thousand wealthiest foundations in the U.S. Lists a cross-section of grant recipients for each foundation.

FOUNDATION DIRECTORY, Margaret Mary Feczko, ed., 1996. 2,068 pages. $210 hardcover, $185 softcover. The Foundation Center, 79 Fifth Avenue, New York, NY 10003-3076, (800) 424-9836.

> Describes 7,500 U.S. Foundations with assets of at least $2 million or total annual grants of at least $200,000. These foundations award over 90% of all foundation giving.

FOUNDATION DIRECTORY PART 2, Margaret Mary Feczko, ed., 1996. 1,127 pages. $180. The Foundation Center, 79 Fifth Avenue, New York, NY 10003-3076, (800) 424-9836.

> Describes 4,900 U.S. foundations with assets from $1 million to $2 million, or total annual grants of at least $50,000 to $200,000.

FOUNDATION GRANTS INDEX, Linda G. Tobiasen, ed., 1996. 2,266 pages. $160. The Foundation Center, 79 Fifth Avenue, New York, NY 10003-3076, (800) 424-9836.

> Lists grants of $10,000 or more from more than one thousand of the largest foundations. Grants are indexed by subject area, geographic area, and organization — you can research which foundations fund groups like your own.

FOUNDATION REPORTER, Mollie Mudd, ed., 1996. 1,965 pages. $390. Taft Group, 835 Penobscot Building, 645 Griswold Street, Detroit, MI 48226-4094, (800) 877-TAFT.

Analyzes the top 1,000 private foundations in the U.S. Includes biographical data on foundation trustees, plus extensive lists of grant recipients.

GUIDE TO U.S. FOUNDATIONS, Their Trustees, Officers, and Donors, Elizabeth Rich, ed., 1996. 2 vols., 4,235 pages. $225. The Foundation Center, 79 Fifth Avenue, New York, NY 10003-3076, (800) 424-9836.

With 37,500 U.S. grantmaking foundations included, this directory covers the greatest range of funders, but in very limited detail. A good resource for compiling lists of foundation trustees in your area; also contains a useful bibliography of state and local foundation directories.

NATIONAL DIRECTORY OF CORPORATE GIVING, L. Victoria Hall, ed., 1995. 1,092 pages. $195. The Foundation Center, 79 Fifth Avenue, New York, NY 10003-3076, (800) 424-9836.

Contains brief listings of 2,600 corporate foundations and corporate direct giving programs, including sample grant recipients. Geographic index allows you to research which companies operate (and give) in your area.

GRANTS RESEARCH AND GRANTMAKER AFFINITY GROUPS

ENVIRONMENTAL GRANTMAKERS ASSOCIATION DIRECTORY 1996. 369 pages. $35. Environmental Data Research Institute, PO Box 22770, Rochester, NY 14692-2770, (800) 724-1857.

The Environmental Grantmakers Association (EGA) is a grantmaker affinity group focusing on conservation and the environment. This directory, which includes information about 189 EGA members, is drawn from a larger directory produced by the same publisher — *Environmental Grantmaking Foundations 1996* — which profiles 703 grantors and costs $90.

THE FOUNDATION CENTER'S USER-FRIENDLY GUIDE: A GRANTSEEKER'S GUIDE TO RESOURCES, Sarah Collins and Charlotte Dion, eds., 1996. 40 pages. $14.95. The Foundation Center, 79 Fifth Avenue, New York, NY 10003-3076, (800) 424-9836.

This brief book answers commonly asked questions about grants research in an upbeat, easy-to-understand style. A good resource for novice grantseekers.

FOUNDATION FUNDAMENTALS: A GUIDE FOR GRANTSEEKERS, Mitchell F. Naufts, ed., 1994. 222 pages. $24.95. The Foundation Center, 79 Fifth Avenue, New York, NY 10003-3076, (800) 424-9836.

One of the first and best guides to grants research. Includes sample worksheets and entries from various foundation directories, which you can use to orient yourself before beginning your research.

GRANTMAKERS DIRECTORY, Gilda Martinez et al., eds., 1996. 219 pages. $25. National Network of Grantmakers, 1717 Kettner Boulevard #105, San Diego, CA 92101, (619) 231-1348.

> The National Network of Grantmakers is a consortium of funders "committed to social, political, and economic justice" who promote "equitable distribution of wealth and power, cultural diversity, and mutual respect." This loose-leaf directory profiles 150 grantmaking institutions, including 30 that accept a common application form. Annual updates are available at a reduced price.

GRANT SEEKERS GUIDE, James McGrath Morris and Laura Adler, eds., 1996. 611 pages. $39.95. Moyer Bell, Kymbolde Way, Wakefield, RI 02879, (401) 789-0074.

> Primarily a directory of 250 progressive grantmakers, this book also includes helpful chapters on obtaining tax-exempt status, fundraising planning, proposal writing, and the pros and cons of becoming a United Way member organization.

PERIODICALS

THE CHRONICLE OF PHILANTHROPY, 1255 23rd Street, NW, Washington, DC 20037, (202) 466-1220. Subscription address: PO Box 1989, Marion OH 43305, (800) 347-6969. 24 issues per year, $67.50.

> The most thorough coverage of the nonprofit sector, including fundraising issues and strategies. Regular "New Grants" feature describes recent foundation and corporate grants; "Deadlines" lists current grant opportunities.

FOUNDATION NEWS AND COMMENTARY, Council on Foundations, 1828 L Street, NW, Washington, DC 20090-6043, (800) 544-0155. 6 issues per year, $35.

> This magazine is written primarily for foundation officers. Most articles focus on philanthropic trends and the profession of grantmaking.

GRANTSMANSHIP CENTER MAGAZINE, PO Box 17220, Los Angeles, CA 90017, (213) 482-9860. 4 issues per year, free to nonprofits at their business addresses.

> Half newsletter, half promotional brochure for Grantsmanship Center trainings and publications. A recent article compared and critiqued common grant application forms designed by regional and national associations of grantmakers.

GRASSROOTS FUNDRAISING JOURNAL, Chardon Press, 3781 Broadway, Oakland CA 94611, (888) 458-8588. 6 issues per year, $32.

> Brief, easy-to-read articles designed for social change activists and small nonprofits. Lots of useful nuts-and-bolts information on community-based fundraising.

NONPROFIT TIMES, 240 Cedar Knolls Road, Suite 318, Cedar Knolls, NJ 07927, (973) 734-1700. 12 issues per year, $59.

Includes features on nonprofit issues, plus regular columns on direct mail fundraising and managing a fundraising program. A new feature tracks Internet sites of interest to nonprofit organizations.

RESPONSIVE PHILANTHROPY, National Committee for Responsive Philanthropy, 2001 S Street, NW, Suite 620, Washington, DC 20009, (202) 387-9177. 4 issues per year, $25.

NCRP works to promote progressive philanthropy, including grantmaking for social change. Their newsletter analyzes federal legislation as it relates to philanthropy and also includes features on fundraising for social change.

PROGRAM-RELATED INVESTMENTS

PROGRAM-RELATED INVESTMENTS: A GUIDE TO FUNDERS AND TRENDS, Loren Renz and Cynthia W. Massarsky, 1995. 189 pages. $45. Foundation Center, 79 Fifth Avenue, New York NY 10036-3076, (800) 424-9836.

Includes a directory of funders who provide program-related investments, tips on how and when to approach them, and examples of more than 500 PRIs.

PROPOSAL WRITING

THE FOUNDATION CENTER'S GUIDE TO PROPOSAL WRITING, Jane C. Geever and Patricia McNeill, 1993. 191 pages. $29.95. Foundation Center, 79 Fifth Avenue, New York NY 10036-3076, (800) 424-9836.

While this book is designed for mainstream nonprofits, it contains lots of helpful information for grassroots groups, including a 20-page appendix with comments from foundation officers.

PROGRAM PLANNING & PROPOSAL WRITING, Norton J. Kiritz, 1980. 48 pages. $4. The Grantsmanship Center, PO Box 17220, Los Angeles, CA, 90017, (213) 482-9860.

A brief, inexpensive, and thorough guide with lots of helpful examples.

WINNING GRANTS STEP BY STEP, Mim Carlson, 1995. 115 pages. $25. Jossey-Bass, Inc., 350 Sansome Street, San Francisco, CA 94104, (800) 956-7739.

This workbook walks you through the process of developing and writing a grant proposal, asking provocative questions at every stage. My favorite question: "So what?"

Strategic Planning and Financial Management

Evaluation Guide: What is Good Grantmaking for Social Justice?, Carol Mollner, Ellen Furnari, and Terry Odendahl, eds., 1995. 21 pages. $15. National Network of Grantmakers, 1717 Kettner Boulevard #105, San Diego, CA 92101, (619) 231-1348.

This booklet, created by NNG's Philanthropic Reform Committee, asks, "How are funders accountable, and to whom?" Many of the questions it poses to grantmakers will be of interest to grantseekers working to define their constituency, develop their programs, and measure their impact.

Managing for Change: A Common Sense Guide to Evaluating Financial Management Health for Grassroots Organizations, Terry Miller, 1992. 137 pages. $22.50. PO Box 40485, Portland, OR 97240, (503) 235-5665. E-mail: 70611.165@compuserve.com.

This book, originally developed for the Partnership for Democracy, is a plain-English guide to planning, budgeting, record-keeping, reporting, and other nonprofit management issues. It is designed specifically for social change organizations.

Strategic Planning Workbook for Nonprofit Organizations, Bryan W. Barry, 1986. 72 pages. $25. Amherst A. Wilder Foundation, 919 Lafond Avenue, St. Paul, MN 55104, (800) 274-6024.

This easy-to-use guide contains a sample strategic plan, plus several exercises and worksheets you can photocopy and share with your board or planning committee.

Thinking Strategically: A Primer on Long-Range Strategic Planning for Grassroots Peace and Justice Organizations, Randall Kehler, Andrea Ayvazian and Ben Senturia, circa 1988. 40 pages. $10. Peace Development Fund, PO Box 1280, Amherst, MA 01004, (413) 256-8306.

Designed for the needs of social justice groups, this workbook includes a brief but helpful section on how to implement your strategic plan.

Winning Through Participation, Laura J. Spencer, 1989. 185 pages. $29.95. Institute of Cultural Affairs, 4220 North 25th Street, Phoenix, AZ 85016, (800) 742-4032 or (602) 955-4811.

Covers methods of group facilitation, including participatory strategic planning. Contains case studies of actual organizations. Also available in a Spanish-language edition.

Index of Foundations, Organizations and Personal Names

General Index

Resources for Social Change

THESE AND MANY MORE TITLES AVAILABLE FROM CHARDON PRESS...
publishing materials that help build a broad progressive movement for social justice

Special Reprint Editions of the Grassroots Fundraising Journal:

Keep up-to-date on new fundraising techniques and issues. Learn how to increase your income and diversify your sources of funding using proven, practical strategies, including special events, direct mail, major donor programs, membership campaigns and more. **6 issues/year; $32/year**

An introduction to the most common and successful fundraising strategies in 14 of the best articles from the *Grassroots Fundraising Journal.* Small organizations can put these strategies to use immediately. This reprint collection in Spanish only. **$12**

Donors who give major gifts each year are the backbone of a fundraising program. Learn how to ask for major gifts and upgrades, respond to put-offs, conduct major gift campaigns, and more in these 12 instructive articles. **$12**

These nine articles from the *Grassroots Fundraising Journal* will show you how to develop an effective—and fundraising—board of directors. Articles include Recruiting Better Board Members, 56 Ways Board Members Can Raise $500, and much more. **$10**

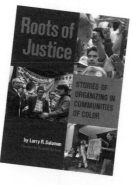

Kim Klein's classic how-to fundraising text teaches you everything you need to know to raise money successfully from individuals. Learn how to motivate your board of directors; analyze your constituency; plan and implement major gifts campaigns, endowments and planned giving programs; use direct mail techniques successfully; and more. **$25**

If you want to change the world, you'll want to read *Inspired Philanthropy.* Through clear text and substantive exercises, you'll learn how to create a giving plan that will make your charitable giving—large or small—catalytic. **$20**

Roots of Justice recaptures some of the nearly forgotten histories of communities of color. These are the stories of people who fought back against exploitation and injustice — and won. It shows how, through organizing, ordinary people have made extraordinary contributions to change society. **$15**

Explore the realities of the police, court and penal system and what you can do as a juror. Mara Taub, a prisoners' rights activist and teacher, interweaves her experiences on a criminal trial jury with instructive excerpts from legal cases, scholarly works, news stories, and opinion columns to reveal some of the inequities of America's justice system. **$17**

To order, call us at (888) 458-8588
(In the SF Bay Area, please call (510) 596-8160)
or visit our Web site at www.chardonpress.com

BULK DISCOUNTS AVAILABLE!
For more information about these and many other titles, contact us for a free catalog!

 **CHARDON PRESS**

3781 Broadway, Oakland, CA 94611 • FAX: (510) 596-8822 • E-MAIL: chardon@chardonpress.com

Grassroots Fundraising Journal

SUBSCRIPTIONS

Please allow 6 weeks for processing new subscriptions.

United States
- ☐ 1 year @ $32 _____
- ☐ 2 years @ $58 _____
- ☐ 3 years @ $84 _____

Canada & Overseas
- ☐ 1 year @ $39 _____
- ☐ 2 years @ $65 _____
- ☐ 3 years @ $91 _____

SUBTOTAL: $ _____

There are no tax or shipping charges for subscriptions.

SPECIAL REPRINT EDITIONS OF THE GRASSROOTS FUNDRAISING JOURNAL*

- ☐ **The Board of Directors** $10 _____
- ☐ **Getting Major Gifts** $12 _____
- ☐ **Cómo Recaudar Fondos en su Comunidad** $12 _____

* Please call for bulk discounts.

SUBTOTAL: $ _____

Books

☐ **Fundraising for Social Change** *by Kim Klein*
- ____ 1–4 copies @ $25 each ____
- ____ 5–9 copies @ $20 each ____
- ____ 10+ copies @ $15 each ____

☐ **Grassroots Grants** *by Andy Robinson*
- ____ 1–4 copies @ $25 each ____
- ____ 5–9 copies @ $20 each ____
- ____ 10+ copies @ $15 each ____

☐ **Roots of Justice** *by Larry Salomon*
- ____ copies @ $15 each ____

☐ **Reversing the Flow, 1998 Edition**
Taylor Root, ed.
- ____ copies ☐ Book **or** ☐ Disk @ $60 ____
- ____ copies Book **and** Disk @ $80 ____

☐ **Inspired Philanthropy**
by Tracy Gary & Melissa Kohner
- ____ copies @ $20 each ____

☐ **Juries: Conscience of the Community**
by Mara Taub
- ____ copies @ $17 each ____

☐ **Justice by the People**
by Terry Keleher/ARC
- ____ copies @ $10 each ____

☐ **Beyond the Politics of Place**
by Gary Delgado/ARC
- ____ copies @ $15 each ____

SUBTOTAL: $ _____

SHIPPING/HANDLING CHARGES

ORDER TOTALLING	SHIPPING FEE
$ 5.00 – 20.00	$ 2.00
$ 20.01 – 25.00	$ 4.00
$ 25.01 – 50.00	$ 6.00
$ 50.01 – 75.00	$ 8.00
$ 75.01 – 100.00	$10.00
$100.01 or more	10% of order

- ☐ 2nd day air +$5.00
- ☐ Overnight +$10.00

Overseas (including Canada & Mexico):
For each shipping & handling level above, multiply by 2 (Payment in U.S. dollars only).
Please allow 2–4 weeks for delivery.

Reprint Collections *Subtotal:* $_____ +

Books *Subtotal:* $_____ = $_____

In CA add 8.25% sales tax to above total: $_____

Shipping & Handling (see chart above): $_____

Grassroots Fundraising Journal SUBSCRIPTION *Subtotal:* $_____

TOTAL AMOUNT ENCLOSED: $_____

Name _____

Organization _____

Address _____

City / State / Zip _____

Change of Address: Enclose mailing label and write new address above.

CREDIT CARD ORDERS

☐ MasterCard ☐ VISA ☐ Discover ☐ Amex

Card #: _____

Expiration date: _____

Signature: _____

Please make checks payable to: **CHARDON PRESS**
3781 Broadway, Oakland CA 94611 • PHONE: (888) 458-8588 (toll-free) / (510) 596-8160 (Bay Area) • FAX: (510) 596-8822
E-MAIL: chardon@chardonpress.com • www.chardonpress.com